Praise for Jamie Graham Duprey's
The Yellow Sports Bra

* * *

"Jamie's great storytelling brought back very special memories of growing up in small-town Montana as a coach's son. All the familiar names and places put a smile on my face. Jamie does an unbelievable job helping us realize how many life lessons we learn from high school athletics, and how much pride and energy sports bring to these communities. Great job, Jamie! I really enjoyed and appreciate this memoir and know others will, too!"

—Tim Hauck, Philadelphia Eagles safeties coach

"In the great tradition of diaries translated to books, Jamie Graham Duprey's The Yellow Sports Bra is not only a vicarious thrill for those in love with small-town basketball and small-town life, but also a deep reminder of what these fast-disappearing cultures have to offer the world at large: a sense of community, faith, courage, interdependence, and strength in numbers. You will love it as I did."

—Philip Aaberg, Grammy- and Emmy-nominated composer

"Duprey's delightful memoir is a nostalgic look into small-town sports. Her honest, engaging, and often humorous voice takes the reader on a moving, exuberant, lighthearted adolescent journey. Anyone who recalls and cherishes 'small-town' life, athletics, love, and friendship should greatly enjoy this book!"

—Alan K. Simpson, former US senator (WY)

"The detailed play-by-play action sent me back in time to my days as Jamie's coach. The vivid descriptions of the basketball games brought back butterflies, nerves, frustration, intensity, laughter, and triumph. Jamie Duprey depicted a powerful story focused on her love of basketball, her team, and her community. This story will describe to young athletes the importance of work ethic, grit, and teamwork. The pride of small-town sports and small-town living resonates in this amazing story."

—Linda VanDyke, coach, entrepreneur, fitness instructor

"This book is such a great read. It brings back lots of great memories that I had forgotten about. Jamie tells a real story of the teamwork, identity, character-building, and life experiences shared by thousands of young athletes who have grown up in small-town America, like Chester."

—Casey FitzSimmons, rancher, former NFL player for the Detroit Lions

"This story will resonate with anyone who played a sport, especially those of us fortunate enough to grow up in a small community. I found myself smiling, nodding, and even cringing as I recalled similar experiences to those artfully described in the book. Thank you, Jamie Duprey, for highlighting the beauty and value of sports, friendships, and life lessons in the context of small-town Montana."

—Greta Koss, coach, former WNBA player

"Jamie Duprey paints an inspiring picture of small-town pride and commitment toward an ultimate goal of winning a state championship. Whether you grew up in a small town or not, Duprey's memoir will give you an understanding of what sports means to tight-knit communities and the positive effects they have on them. Her story reminds us that lifelong relationships along the journey are the ultimate prize!"

—Mick Durham, men's head basketball coach, MSU Billings

"Small-town basketball breeds small-town character. Especially in remote and cold places like the Montana 'Hi-Line,' there is no other sport that allows kids to bond as a team, mature as adolescents, compete on a high level, and move on as mature adult leaders. Jamie Duprey's heartwarming story of life, grief, and victory reminds us all of the treasure of youth sports."

—Sherry Winn, two-time US Olympian, NCAA coach of the year,
CEO/founder of The Winning Leadership Company

"Nothing beats small-town America. A fabulous collection of fun, inspiring, and action-packed stories, Jamie brings to life a dream that was kindled in her heart since the third grade. She truly shows that you can become your own champion and achieve your dreams on your own terms."

—Duane Martinz, professional speaker, sales trainer, life coach,
entrepreneur, and author of *Becoming Your Own Champion*

"I felt transported back to a time where emotions ran high, life seemed daunting and marvelous all at once, and the biggest concern was what to wear! I laughed, I cried, and I laughed some more. This story offers a glimpse into the quintessential small-town teenage experience. I knew Jamie was a remarkable person when I met her at four years old, and now she has proven to be a remarkable writer as well."

—Emily Repnak, former Chester Coyote, wife, mother, teacher

The
YELLOW
Sports Bra

A True Story of
Love, Faith, and Basketball

Jamie Graham Duprey

Aubade Publishing
Ashburn, VA

Edited by Joe Puckett

Cover design, illustration, and book layout by Cosette Puckett

Library of Congress Control Number: 2020931742

ISBN: 978-1-951547-03-5

Published by Aubade Publishing, Ashburn, VA

Printed in the United States of America

Dedication

To all my coaches and teammates, then and now.

To my three babies. My daughter, Jordan, my sons Justin and Jackson, remember that whatever you do, do it well. Control your attitude, work hard, be a good teammate, and be kind. Remember, it's all about the relationships. I love you more than you can understand.

To my parents, Jim and Karen Graham. Thank you for always loving me, being proud of me, and always showing up. Every person should be so lucky to have parents like you.

To my brother. Thanks for being such a good big brother. I am proud to be "Jeff Graham's Little Sister" (and I am so thankful you married the sister I never had).

And of course, to my husband, Jeremy. Your love gives me comfort and confidence, and you always believe I can do anything. Thank you for helping me to become the best possible version of myself and being the best daddy in the world. Where you go, I go.

Contents

Contents

Preseason

"For I know the plans I have for you," declares the Lord, "plans to prosper you and not to harm you. Plans to give you hope and a future."

— Jeremiah 29:11

Chapter 1

February 1992, third grade, Montana Boys' State Class C Basketball Tournament, Montana State University, Brick Breeden Fieldhouse, Bozeman, Montana

Dad parks the yellow school bus—with its black, bold-lettered brand "Chester Coyotes"—in the parking lot of the Montana State University Brick Breeden Fieldhouse. Our boys' varsity team, loaded down with heavy duffel bags and blue-and-gold uniforms hooked on hangers, follow Coach McLean as he strides off the bus then up the dome's steep back steps leading to the locker rooms. My brother Jeff and I wait with Mom and wish each player good luck as he passes our seat.

The bus lets out a final groan and sputter, Dad pockets the key, and we file out behind the team. Some families visit theme parks or go camping for vacation. We go to basketball tournaments.

As we enter the fieldhouse, there is a noticeable shift from the bitter February cold outside to the intense, combustible atmosphere inside. I love being here. Feeling this energy. Thousands of people in the crowd. Entire towns follow their teams during winter in Montana, with its frigid cold and unpredictable road conditions. Everyone sacrifices to be present and cheer on their players in these state tournament games.

The hairs on my arms prickle as our pep band, arguably the best in the state, plays "The Final Countdown." The music fills the fieldhouse and controls our crowd with some invisible force, as it rises in unison. The song then directs our boys to break their huddle and run onto the floor for warm-ups. I follow Mom to the Chester section, but I stumble a time or two because I can't take my eyes off the court: there's Reece Gliko, the star player for our opponent, the Highwood Mountaineers. He's cocky, and it drives my mom crazy.[1]

Mom is calm and sweet, always smiling and giggling—except when it comes to watching sports. Once, when I was upstairs with my friend Emily, she asked me why my mom and dad were yelling at each other. I told her my parents don't yell at each other and Dad wasn't even home. It turned out that Mom was just watching the Chicago Cubs playing on TV.

We squeeze through the crowd, climb up some stairs, find a few open seats, and stand for starting lineups. I can't stop bouncing around! All our players, managers, and coaches line up across one free throw line while the Highwood Mountaineers mirror them, the ritual for championship games. Mom touches my right hand because sometimes I forget which one goes over my heart. I watch the cheerleaders march out to the middle of the court. They have such pretty hair. I can't wait until I grow up and get to have a fluffy perm like that. And those sweet bangs.

I try really hard to keep my eyes on the American flag, but I glance up a few times at Mom singing along with the band to the national anthem. This song is nice and all, but it takes forever. I need to remember to ask mom who the "José" is that they are singing about. Okay, finally over. Time to go. I do my best to stay still while the cheerleaders march back off the court. There it is, the first clap. Now everyone in the whole place is clapping. All those claps make my spine feel all shocky.

Each player is announced, walks to center court, and shakes the hand of the enemy. The announcer calls out the coaches next, Coach Nelson, Coach Powell, and Coach Vanderpan for the Mountaineers; Coaches Mike McLean and Dad for the Coyotes. I scream at the top of my lungs when Dad's name is announced, looking all fancy in his shiny gray suit.

I can't wait until that's me out there someday.

---

[1] We may have found Gliko a bit cocky, but he could certainly back it up. Reece Gliko went on to hold Montana's record for most points scored in a high school career with 2,763. He was surpassed almost exactly a decade later by Kayla Lambert, who still holds the number one spot with an insane 3,453 points scored (Montana, 2019).

The boys head to their bench for another quick huddle. Let's get this show on the road, people! I cannot handle this suspense.

Opening tip.

Finally.

Mark easily tips it over to Cory who takes a quick left-handed dribble then jump stops, pulls the ball near his left cheek, elbows out, and surveys the scene. Cory makes a pass over to James (who wears my favorite number, 12) on the right wing who immediately tosses it to Mike as he cuts baseline. Mike catches it a little off-balance at the short corner and flips it right back to James. James reverses it to Hubbel on the left wing, down to Mike on the opposite short corner, then back to James. After a ball-screen from Mike, James takes the first shot of the game, from behind the arc. It falls short, but Mike crashes, grabs the offensive rebound, and gets the Coyotes on the scoreboard first, 2–0. Yes!

Gliko pulls the ball out of the net and inbounds it to McGowan. McGowan dribbles down the court, holds up his index finger with his left hand, and makes a one-handed pass to Knudson on the right wing. Dad says you should pass the ball with two hands. Knudson lobs it up to Bergstrom, who has Mark sealed at the low block. Cory! Where's the help defense?!

Wait. Somehow Knudson misses the wide-open bank shot, and Mark comes up with the rebound. He hits Cody on an outlet up the left sideline. Cody crosses half-court, then passes it down to Mike at the deep corner, then back to Mark who is now open at the elbow. I think that it's called the elbow. I still have a little bit to learn, I suppose, and Dad constantly reminds me to be a "student of the game." Mark takes a shot from what I am pretty sure is the elbow and, yes! 4–0. We are so going to win.

McGowan brings the ball up again, and it looks like he and Heggem are playing a little two-on-two over there on the left wing. Heggem screens for McGowan, who brings it back up to the top of the key and holds up one finger again. I guess they are going to give that play another try.

This time Gliko posts up on the low block, but luckily James remembers the whole help defense thing and tips it out to Mark. Steal! Nope. So close. Bergstrom gets control of the ball and gets it over to Gliko. Gliko takes one dribble baseline and pulls up for a

5

jumper. Miss. Wait, how did that short guy get the rebound? Mike, box out! Heggem makes a scoop pass to Bergstrom who drains a jump shot just below the free throw line. Well, I guess they had to score sometime.

Cody dribbles up with his left hand, passes it to James, and the ball is tipped by his defender when he attempts a jump shot. James tries to act innocent when he goes to pick up the ball again, but he is called for a travel.

Things go back and forth for a while. Man, this is stressful! Cory and Mark both pick up fouls, and Highwood is putting on constant pressure. Gliko swishes two free throws. It doesn't seem like it will be a great idea to foul him much more.

We are doing a good job of catching and facing the basket without taking random dribbles, but we have got to box out better. Cory already has three fouls, and we are barely halfway through the first quarter. Okay, Bergstrom fouls Mark, but we still don't score. Gliko steps out-of-bounds, but we still don't score.

Stop fouling!

Hubbel brings it up and gets it to Cody, who gets it to Mike, then down to Mark. Mark catches, pump fakes, and banks it in. Yes. Let's keep doing that. Get the ball to Mark more.

Now back on defense.

This time Bergstrom holds up two fingers. It looks like they are going to shake things up a bit. Hmm, this play looks like they are running the three-man-weave with dribbling. Mark deflects the attempt inside and immediately chucks it down to James for a fast break. And-one![2] James makes the free throw. Attaboy.

Highwood brings it up and McGowan attempts a sorta fancy sideways bounce pass to Gliko. Hubbel intercepts it. Oh, shoot, Gliko ties it up for a jump. Nope. Foul on Gliko! Yeah, baby. We don't score, though, and then we come back down so Hubbel can foul. Sigh. We are giving them quite a few free throw attempts already. I feel like we should stop doing that.

Whew. That was an intense first quarter. They are up, 17–20. Dang it. It's okay. It's only three points. We got this.

---

[2] And-one – When a player is fouled while shooting and also makes her shot, this is referred to as an "and-one," as the player gets the points as well as one free throw.

The Mountaineers inbound, then they get two attempts to score but brick both. Alright, back in our possession. We work it around, being patient with our motion offense. Pass, cut, screen away. Pass, cut, screen away. Get it inside to Mark. Bank and in.

Now Gliko drives all the way into the paint and, how did he make that shot?

They are doubling down on Mark now. Wait, Mike. I think they are doubling down on Mark because they would like you to shoot that three-pointer at the deep corner. However, I do not think Coach McLean and Dad would like you to shoot that three-pointer at the deep corner. Don't worry! Mark grabs the rebound and puts it up for an and-one! Ha! Double-team him if you want, but you still gotta box him out.

Another foul on us. The fouls are certainly lopsided at this point. One more and they will already be in double bonus.

James comes up with a steal after Mark tips a lob attempt, and James gets rocked in the face. It looks like he might be a little hurt. If I were him I would suck it up. Otherwise my dad will just tell him to rub some dirt on it, or ask him if he wants a tough pill.

After a bit more running up and down the court, Coach McLean calls a time-out. I can't hear anything he is saying, but he sure looks like he has some important things to say. Judging by the hand motions, I would say he is reminding them to hold on to that darn ball!

After the time-out we really spread out. We pass, pass, pass. Good. Hubbel misses a shot on the left baseline, but Mike seems to be in the right place at the right time and gets fouled. He makes his free throws. Nice! Then Gliko answers right back, scoring on a coast-to-coast jumper. We miss on our next possession, and then Gliko is fouled again. Argh!

Luke subs in for Mike. Also, our crowd is suddenly very quiet. I don't like this. Of course Gliko swishes both his free throws. Maybe we just need to get to halftime and get a little time to refocus. Ooh, maybe not! Heggem fouls James at the top of the key. Our boys stack up for the inbounds play, Mark receives the pass, but he misses.

Down on the other end Gliko gets it inside and scores. Again.

I was right earlier. We need halftime to come. We are down by ten. Double digits. That is not good.

Okay, our ball with about a minute left in the half. Mark gets it to Hubbel, who gets it to James. James dribbles up the left side, passes it to Cody, and Cody reverses it to Hubbel who cut across to the right wing. Just take care of the ball. Here's a whistle. Someone was apparently holding Luke. Luke steps up to the free throw line. Even though he looked a little nervous when he subbed in just a minute ago, he swishes both of them!

Twenty seconds to go. Play great defense and do not foul.

McGowan brings it slowly up the court. He swings it to Heggem, then they keep passing and weaving and screening and this is making my stomach feel tight. Gliko pulls up for a three . . . miss! Whew. Good. They just need a quick break and some motivating words in the locker room. We are only down by eight, 28–36. No problem. We got this.

Mom takes me to the concession stands to get some popcorn and Skittles. I am wearing my bright-yellow football jersey, the same thing basically every other child I see from our school is wearing. These are what we all wear to school on Fridays, and of course on special occasions like tonight. After waiting five hours in the women's bathroom line, we make it back to our seats when the clock ticks just under one minute.

Third quarter. Cody takes it out at half-court and passes it in to James. James keeps his dribble on the left wing and passes over to Cody, and over to Mike. Mike gets it back to Cody, screens, and Cody tries a bounce pass to Mark. Bergstrom reaches around and picks up his third foul. This time James takes it out, and he chucks it way up to Mark, who has Bergstrom sealed. Even though he bobbles it a bit, Mark pump fakes and puts it in!

On the other end Mark stuffs Bergstrom, we pass it up the court, James gets it to Mike, and Mike scores! Already back within four. Dad was right. Basketball can change so quickly. It's not over until it's over. You just have to keep at it and anything can happen. We can do this, guys!

Gliko hits two more free throws, but then Cory takes it inside with a spin move and scores. Good job, Cory. It's okay that you have three fouls. Sometimes you just have to play with three fouls. But now Mark fouls, and he has three as well. I guess each player gets five fouls, but this still makes me a little nervous. Back and forth, back and forth. Oh, this is a lot of pressure. Maybe I shouldn't watch for a while.

No, I can't not watch! We look a little tired. We look a little frustrated. They look really pumped up. They cannot miss. They go jumping into their huddle with a lot of excitement after Coach McLean calls a time-out. We have got to make some stops.

Fourth quarter.

Crap! I know I'm not supposed to say that word, but crap! Down 36–48 going into the fourth. How is this happening? We can't lose! We aren't supposed to lose. I look around me into our crowd and see only concerned, worried eyes. No one is cheering, just sitting, looking scared. I feel tears well up and my throat constricts. Why aren't they cheering? It's not over till it's over, right?! That's why there are four quarters, right?!

It is Highwood's ball. McGowan takes it out at half, and we match up man-to-man. Come on, boys. You can do this. Highwood is patient with it and puts up a shot. Grossman gets the offensive rebound and puts it back up. Miss. Heggem gets the rebound, dishes it to whoever this left-handed sub is that probably has close to ten points already, and he scores. No! Down by fourteen!

James dribbles all the way down and puts up a shot in the key. It's hard. We transition to defense and make a steal. Now James has an open layup and makes it!

Ooh, Gliko is not happy. He really did not think that was a foul. Heggem almost had a steal, then Gliko came on the other side and ended up getting a reaching call. Gliko rips out his mouthguard and slaps Heggem with a little-too-hard high five. While Gliko is still walking with his head down, Hubbel inbounds quickly and James gets it right down on the block to Mark who makes a beautiful catch—and-one! This fires our crowd up, that's for sure. Everyone is on their feet, and we stay there while Highwood calls a time-out.

Mark looks so calm out there and for some reason he has to wait forever to shoot his free throw.

It rattles in.

Within ten!

We can totally win this. I knew it. We're gonna win.

Heggem takes point, and Mike tips it to Mark for another steal. As always, Mark's eyes are already down the court, and he throws a baseball pass to James for another basket. We make another stop and Cory comes up with it. Cory takes it in and, miss. That's okay. Just keep up the great defense.

They hit one from the short corner. But we answer right back with a bucket from Mike on an assist from Cory. We switch a couple screens, Heggem drives, and Cory fouls. Finally they miss a free throw! We take our time and get it in to Mark. Back out, then in to Mark again. Over to Cory, and he is called for something. I do not understand exactly what that call was, but I can tell by the people around me that it is not good.

"It was an offensive foul." Mom stops groaning about what a terrible call it was and bends down to explain to me that people can foul sometimes when they have the ball, too.

So that means Cory is fouled out. Everyone stands and claps for him, but that doesn't seem to make him feel any better.

Meanwhile, Highwood is weaving and weaving again. James comes up with a steal after Hubbel tips it! James hits Mike who follows down the middle of the lane. Another and-one! Man, these and-ones are fun. I mostly love how they seem to cause everyone to fist pump like crazy. Even Dad stands up and pumps his right arm way down to the ground before standing back up to remind everyone where they need to be after Mike makes his free throw. Which he does.

There is a noticeable change with our boys now on defense. Feet are dancing, and there is something in their eyes that is new. An excited shiver wiggles its way through my body.

Now 48–52 with 3:36 to go.

Oh, no. Gliko is fouled and of course makes both his free throws. We get it back down to our end and work it around. Mark is way out there on the left wing. That's new. Hubbel passes it to Cody then on to Mark, who clearly wants it. He motions for the rest of his team to clear out and takes it to the hole. The ball bounces off the back end of the rim, but he gets his own rebound and makes his putback!

Down 50–54 with two and a half minutes left.

Heggem pushes it down, bounces it off to Bergstrom. Mark tips the shot and gets it out to James. Up on top to Cody. Cody makes an easy pass to Mike at the free throw line, and he bounces one in! The bench is jumping around all over the place, swinging towels above their heads. Their energy pulses up to us here in the stands. We are only down two!

Noo! We foul Gliko yet again. He makes them both, so we go back to where we just came from. The boys stay calm, though, and Mark confidently dribbles in and drains a short jump shot after a pass from James.

Whoa. That was a pretty cool behind the head pass from Gliko to Bergstrom. But he misses, so too bad, so sad.

Our ball again. Back to Mark on the wing. He drives in, pulls up, but misses.

Now Gliko gets the ball, and they spread things out. Ooh, Hubbel almost gets the pick, but Gliko scores, and this is just too crazy. I don't know what to do with myself!

Still 1:28 to go, our ball at the sideline, and the Mountaineers are up 54–58. Cody takes the ball out this time, and I really wish I knew what Coach McLean said during the huddle. Cody gets it to James. He dribbles over to the left wing, the favorite spot to start their offense. James makes a short pass to Hubbel, and Hubbel crosses over and takes it all the way to the hole for a layup!

Gliko to Heggem, back to Gliko who shoots. Miss!

Cody gets the rebound off a tip from Mark and immediately passes it up to James. James is fouled. Now Highwood calls a time-out. Down two with forty-three seconds to go. James takes three dribbles, takes a breath, and makes the first one. He makes the next one, and it is a tie game!

Gliko brings it up and forces a shot. It is way short and lands right at James. James gets it up to Mike at the top of the key, and then Mark joins him and receives a handoff. Mark holds the ball for a few seconds, glancing up and taking note that there are only fourteen seconds to go. He dribbles in, hits Mike, then Mike drives in and . . . in and out.

Overtime.

Oh, my gosh. I don't know if I can handle much more of this. We get the tip but Mike misses. Then Hubbel makes a wild swing toward Gliko and puts him at the line yet again. Probably the opposite of what we would like to have happen. Two more swishes.

Cody leaves the next shot short, but we get an offensive rebound. Mark misses short, too, but Mike gets another offensive rebound and scores!

Tied 60–60.

Gliko is long on a three, but gets the rebound and McGowan scores.

Mark makes a sweet spin move and answers right back.

Now Mike fouls. Surprise, Gliko is standing at the free throw line for what must be something like the eight hundredth time. I wiggle my fingers in the air like crazy, but it doesn't phase him.

We get a lucky call when it looks like Cody knocks it out-of-bounds, and then Mike dives down and scores on a wide-open bank on the out-of-bounds play. The clock ticks under a minute, it is 64–64, and Gliko brings it up the court. They look like they may stall, but Gliko shoots from just in front of the free throw line. He hasn't missed any actual free throws, but hallelujah he misses that shot, and the ball is tipped all over the place before going out-of-bounds. I can't tell who hit it out. The fans sitting under that basket—who are not even from Chester—seem very sure it should be Chester's ball as they madly motion for the refs to point their arms toward our basket.

Hubbel gets the ball over half-court and Coach McLean calls a time-out.

The cheerleaders have our crowd stomping and clapping after their floor cheer. The pep band picks up and we all shout, "Eat 'em up! Eat 'em up! Rah, rah, rah!"

Mark takes the ball out on the sideline this time, gets it to Hubbel, and he gets it right back to Mark. I am thinking the coaches would like Mark to take the last shot. I am thinking that is probably a pretty good idea. He passes it over to Hubbel, back to Mark, then to Cody at the top of the key. Cody pivots and fumbles the ball a bit. But he ball fakes and gets it into Mark. Mark turns, takes a dribble, and is fouled!

Highwood calls two time-outs in a row. I believe this is called "icing" the player.

Mark looks unshakable, though, and steps right up to the line, wanting that ball. It is tied, 64–64, with only six seconds to go. Apparently they fouled before the shot, so this is only a bonus, which means he has to make the first shot, or the ball is live. The ref checks all the players' positions and reminds them that it is a one-and-one. Mark takes three dribbles, lines it up, releases, and nothing but net!

YES!

One more. He nonchalantly looks away for a second, checking an opposing player.

He knows he is going to make it.

Swish.

Highwood pushes it up the floor, Gliko gets it on that left wing. Don't let him get a three off, especially on that left side! He dribbles and pump fakes. Three seconds. Two. He shoots.

It's short.

One.

We win! State champions![3] I knew we would win. We are the best! The boys from our bench charge the floor, followed by the managers, and my dad and Coach McLean head out to embrace their players.

This frenzy around me sweeps me up. People are going absolutely bonkers. Luke pulls Mike into a bearhug, James is jumping all over the place, Hubbel is holding up his finger in a "number one" sign, and Mark is received with a thousand hugs from the crowd. Cory even hugs his mom in public, and Cody goes in for a hug with . . . Dad?! Are those tears glistening in my dad's eyes? I guess this is a time when it's okay for even men in our town to show emotion. Hugging, crying, smiling. I feel the excitement, the energy oozing out of everyone around me.

This is what I want to do. Yep. I want to do this for our town, too.

---

[3] In fact, some of these players were now back-to-back state champions, as they beat the Roberts Rockets for the school's first title in the 1990–91 season. Roberts is an unincorporated town in Carbon County. Its population is just over three hundred and around sixty students are enrolled in high school https://en.wikipedia.org/wiki/Roberts,_Montana.

Chapter 2

December 1995, sixth grade, Chester, Montana

6:00 a.m.: Ugh. Pitch dark and twenty-three degrees below zero. Instinctively I silence the siren-like wail of my alarm clock and roll back over.

6:09 a.m: Mr. St. John will be at the gym. I don't get the impression he is completely convinced we will show up like we said we would. And Mr. H. told us we should focus on volleyball, because that would be the most realistic way for us to win a state championship. Volleyball? Pff. Why wouldn't we be able to win in basketball? What makes him, or anyone else for that matter, think we don't have what it takes? Because we're girls?

6:18 a.m: Okay, just get your butt out of bed, Jamie. I can hear Dad downstairs, making coffee.

6:30 a.m: Did I brush my teeth? My hair? Who cares. I just gotta remember my basketball shoes. And my dang sports bra. Maybe I shouldn't be so embarrassed about bras, but I am. When Colt tried to get my attention and went to grab my shirt the other day, he snapped my flipping bra. Mortifying.

6:35 a.m: After covering every inch of my skin, I brace myself for that first inhale of the finger-numbing cold. Only my eyes peek through the hot-pink scarf wrapped around my head three times. At least when it's this cold the biting wind doesn't always blow quite as hard. I begin my three-block trudge to school. We have never once driven to school, and no signs point to a chance of that streak being broken anytime soon. Dad assures us that walking everyday "builds character."

Whatever that means.

I stay on the street for the first block and a half, and then cut across the path that snakes behind the arts council building. I always think that building looks like a barn. A barn, or maybe a red church. As I cross the street to the school, I take a look east toward the sunrise. I heard someone joke to Dad once about the isolation of this place, that we are out in the middle of nowhere, that someone could watch his dog run away for days. That may be true, but I love these beautiful plains. If you stand out by the IGA[4] just where town ends and the road heads east toward Joplin, you can see all the way to the Sweetgrass Hills.[5] Heidi says the hills are over twenty miles away.

Finally I reach the heavy, freezing-cold blue door to the elementary. I manage to open the slippery metal handle without taking off my poofy pink mittens. My eyelashes and nose hairs are frozen. I can tell because if I squeeze my nostrils together and poke my lips up real tight against my nose, it takes a few seconds for my nostrils to flare back open; it kind of feels like I am peeling off a Band-Aid. I stomp the snow off my heavy pink boots on the black fuzzy rug, sit on the bottom step, and pull off my gloves and boots. I neatly pack my boots on one of the shelves lining the entrance, because I don't want to get a talking-to from the teacher on recess duty. Then I climb up the steps, slide in my socks across the hallway, and enter the "old gym" through the smooth wooden door.[6]

"Don't slouch." Without looking up from his paper Mr. St. John sips his coffee as he asserts his usual reminder on the importance of posture.

Right leg crossed over his left, he sits a few rows up in the blue wooden bleachers and dons his gray cowboy boots. A city boy if I've

---

[4] Independent Grocers Alliance grocery store.

[5] Chester is dubbed "Heart of the Hi-Line" and is the county seat in Liberty County. The beautiful Sweetgrass Hills are about twenty-six miles straight north of Chester, but it takes a good hour's drive on some nonpaved roads to get there. Located in north-central Montana along the Canadian border, the Sweetgrass Hills consist of three distinct buttes separated by vast sweeps of rolling grasslands https://www.bigskyfishing.com/scenic-drives/sweetgrass-hills.php.

[6] In Chester then, and still today, there are two gyms in the school building. The original school building included the "old gym" and was constructed in 1936. The "new gym" was built in 1974.

ever seen one, I wonder what makes him decide he can pull off cowboy boots. I guess he does look kind of okay.[7]

"I told you I would be here," I state for the record as I walk across the gym floor toward the locker room. (Let's be clear that I am only walking across the floor because I have socks on. I would *never* walk across the floor with street shoes on, nor would anyone else who knows anything about Chester Public Schools.)

I am sure he is pondering something philosophical, per usual. "Don't slouch," is the only response I receive.

The creaky wooden gym door squeals and Michele walks in, gym bag in hand. "Hey, Chelers!" I call.

"Hey, Jamers."

A few minutes later Mr. St. John, my dad, and Mr. VanDyke— Michele's dad—are watching Michele and me play one-on-one.[8] We aren't exactly sure what the onlookers are thinking, but we feel approval as they stand there, arms crossed, heads nodding slightly now and then.

As the weeks go on, more friends join us for these early morning open gyms. Emily and her brother John come, Amanda and Brian, three of Michele's four siblings, my older brother Jeff, and lots of other students who live in town. Pickup scrimmages happen these mornings, as well as Sunday nights. People from the "cities" tease that there isn't much else to do in small towns. Truth is, that's not too far from the truth at all, especially in the bitter, seemingly incessant dark and cold that is Montana Winter.[9]

Jeff and me after winning Elks Hoop Shoot, Shelby, 1995

---

[7] When I got older, I learned that Mr. Kevin St. John grew up in Opheim, MT, a town where no one would ever be questioned about wearing cowboy boots (Puckett, J., 2010).

[8] My dad, Jim Graham, was known then and always as "Coach Graham." I love when I am around when former students are talking to him, and they never call him by his name Jim, but always "Coach" or "Coach Graham."

[9] Small-town living may not appeal to some, but it offers a chance to be involved in everything, to learn all kinds of skills. When there are only around 25-35 students in every grade, kids have to be involved in multiple extracurriculars in order to field a football team or fill the risers for a choir concert. Having a full schedule is

When I was younger, if I didn't have friends around I just made them up. Tina was my friend in the mirror when my hair was curled under, and her brother Michael had an uncanny resemblance to Ralph Macchio, better known as the Karate Kid. (Tina let it slip that he had a crush on me.) When I would dribble down to the school playground on slow summer days, Michael Jordan, Scottie Pippen, B. J. Armstrong, Horace Grant, and other Bulls would fly in on a personal jet to dribble and shoot hoops with me.[10]

* * *

In the summer, my farm and ranch friends make treks into town for a few practices a week. These treks are anywhere from twenty to fifty-two miles, one way. Dad says this is a huge commitment for families. And he also says that is what it takes to go from being good to being great.

The twins who don't look like twins, Mari and Maci, often get rides from one of their two older siblings from their wheat farm twenty-three miles north of town. Heidi lives on her family's farm just a few more miles north of the twins. We all go to Heidi's farm every August for Heidi's birthday parties. We always check out all her animals, play tag in her yard around the swing set, and eat her Barbie doll birthday cakes, which are literally cakes with Barbie doll heads on the top. Delicious (the cake, not the doll heads). Chasi rides in with her dad Gary from their cattle ranch that is a half hour south of town, and Kaitlynn (Katy), has the longest journey, living fifty-two miles northwest on a cattle ranch, only a few miles south of the Canadian border.[11]

---

part of the lifestyle; it is not a negative thing. People have to be active and be involved in order for the town to thrive.

[10] The rural setting also bodes well for the imagination!

[11] I had the privilege of playing with numerous fabulous people over the years, but the girls I played most with were the ones in my class: Michele VanDyke, Mari and Maci Tempel (the twins), Heidi Cicon, Chasi Buffington, Emily Tranberg, and Katy Engstrom.

These summer practices are coached by my dad and Michele's mom, Linda VanDyke. They are prepping us to compete in Montana's Big Sky State Games, held each July in Billings. We are taught how to "strip it," to remove the ball with one hand when an opponent inevitably carries it across her body on a layup; "pick it," tip the ball from behind when the dribbler doesn't realize someone is right on her tail; and "squeeze" while boxing out on a free throw. We learn that it is best to press constantly, and how to talk so much it will drive an opposing team crazy while boosting our own confidence and intensity level. We learn all this while frequently being told that we are the "cock of the walk." We are told we are

Big Sky State Games, July 1996, Billings, MT

better than everyone else, and we believe it, no hesitation. (We also, of course, practice the hesitation dribble.)

We lose one or maybe two games (I generally choose to block out losses) during our junior high years, not one during the school seasons. Mr. Kulpas, or "Coach K," and Mr. Moore are lucky enough to be our coaches in junior high.[12] Coach K's ever-inspiring

---

[12]Mr. Moore is now an extremely successful speech and drama coach in Shepherd, MT, but I like to think he enjoyed getting to be part of an undefeated basketball season, even if it was junior high girls. Coach K taught and coached in Chester a total of twenty-six years. He often liked to act grumpy, but it was clear he loved

Seventh grade champions, 1996

taglines such as, "Unhitch the plow!" and "Get the lead out!" will always be remembered.[13]

Big Sky State Games champs, summer before freshman year, July 1998, Billings, MT

We roll over everyone we play, even scoring an unprecedented one hundred points against Browning in eighth grade. Kayla scores the one hundredth point at the free throw line. Her first attempt of the two-shot foul is dead on, but an airball. The second shot is a swish, causing a ridiculous amount of cheering not only from the crowd but from us, as we are told we aren't allowed to score that many points unless every member scores. Mystel, Marjorie, and finally Kayla are all in the scorebook. Two perfect junior high seasons. The future is looking bright.

---

joking with his students. My classmate Chris Decker and I tried and tried (and failed) to get him to say "Great google moogly" just once.

[13]Mr. Kulpas is still endearingly referred to by former students as "Coach K."

First Quarter

Let us run with perseverance the race marked out for us.

—Hebrews 12:1

1998 Chester Lady Coyotes

Chapter 3

August 1998, freshman year, first day of high school practice, Chester, Montana

6:00 a.m.: Am I gonna barf *already?* I'll just press snooze once so my stomach can settle.

6:09 a.m.: All our coaches around here, especially my dad, constantly claim that *if you're not fifteen minutes early, you're late.* What does that even mean?

6:18 a.m.: Okay, just get your butt out of bed, Jamie.

6:30 a.m.: Did I brush my teeth? My hair? Who cares. I just gotta remember my basketball shoes. And of course a sports bra.

6:35 a.m.: I hear Emily's tiny, white 1980-something Ford Escort hatchback screech to a stop outside my door. Jeff and I aren't allowed to drive to school, but there's no rule saying we can't hitch rides. I hear Emily open the squeaky front door. She, and any Chester youth, knows to only use the front sidewalk and not tread one toe on Mr. Graham's immaculate lawn. Mom, in her long, navy blue cotton bathrobe is giggling with Emily and sipping her Lipton tea. She drinks her morning tea from a mug that states, "How does it feel to be 29 . . . again?" I do not get why that is funny or clever. I hustle down the stairs from my bathroom, duffel bag in hand, and feel those Cocoa Puffs sloshing around in my stomach. I may soon regret that breakfast decision. After kissing Mom goodbye, we rush out to the car. I pull up the passenger seat and toss my bag in the backseat on top of hers.

"Hey, Emmers."

"Hey, Jame."

"You ready for this?" I ask.

Emily, often deadpan and naturally hilarious instantly responds, "I was born ready."

6:45 a.m.: I pause briefly as I step into the gymnasium from the locker room, close my eyes and take a deep breath of that freshly waxed gym floor scent. Lacquer? I have no idea if that's what it is, but I like that word. And I love that smell. The sneaker-squeaking from our "Air Swoopes" team shoes on that maybe-lacquered floor brings a contented smile to my face. Even if I do hurl from the timed mile or seven-minute drill this morning, this really is my favorite place.

7:00 a.m.: We obediently herd to half-court as we've been conditioned to for years following a shrill whistle blast. Coach VanDyke keeps her opening speech fairly short and sweet, considering how much she loves making speeches. She introduces our new assistant coach, Willie Schlepp: he is energetic, a bit sarcastic with just the right amount of humor and sass, and knows his basketball. He is fresh from a stint as a student-assistant at Northern Montana College just down the road in Havre.[14]

Our first high school practice blurs by. There is that intense, dry northern plains August heat in the non-air-conditioned gym mixed with running. Lots and lots of running. According to every inspirational sports movie out there, teams that want to win must be willing and able to outrun any opponent. It looks like we are going to test that hypothesis.

* * *

Two weeks and sixteen practices later we again gather at half-court, eyes and ears on Coach VanDyke. Our first game is tomorrow night versus the Class B Shelby Coyotes, forty miles west. We are the Class C Chester Coyotes (and it is pronounced "*Ky-oats*," **not** "*Ky-Oat-ease*," thank you very much).[15] There are numerous towns scattered

---

[14]Havre is about fifty-five miles east of Chester. It is the county seat of Hill County and Montana's eighth largest "city," with a population of 9,310 (City, 2019).

[15]Shelby, like Chester, was established with the construction of the Great Northern Railway (Shelby, 2019).

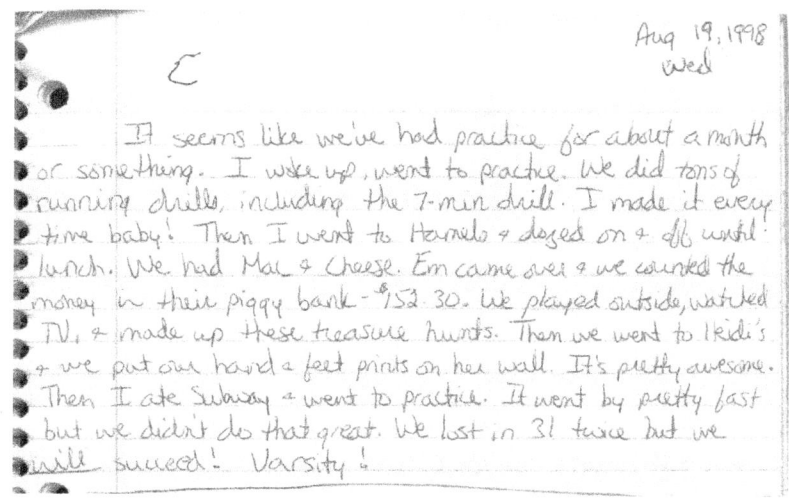

Aug 19, 1998
Wed

It seems like we've had practice for about a month or something. I woke up, went to practice. We did tons of running drills, including the 7-min drill. I made it every time baby! Then I went to Harriet's & dozed on & off until lunch. We had Mac & Cheese. Em came over & we counted the money in their piggy bank - $152.30. We played outside, watched TV, & made up these treasure hunts. Then we went to Heidi's & we put our hand & feet prints on her wall. It's pretty awesome. Then I ate Subway & went to practice. It went by pretty fast but we didn't do that great. We lost in 3! twice but we will succeed! Varsity!

My journal entry after practice on August 19, 1998

along our "Hi-Line" on Highway 2, and even though distances that separate towns are small, rivalries are huge.

Coach briefly touches upon our game plan—press like crazy then run and gun—and announces the starters: Carly, Coach VanDyke's oldest child at six feet tall, a returning all-state selection, and one of our two senior leaders; Annie, one of Carly's best friends and the best role player a coach could ask for, not to mention the feistiness and strength that comes from being the only girl among four brothers, and the other senior; Devan, a junior, Carly's other best friend and our best three-point shooter; Michele, Coach VanDyke's second child, a freshman and one of my besties, as well as the most athletic on the team, able to grab the rim at a lanky five feet nine. Then Coach announces my name. I blink, taken aback briefly, but continue to look forward and show no expression.

I don't feel a lot of emotion at this news. I do not think much about playing time, I just can't wait until we win State, and I will play wherever I'm told in order to make that happen. Wait. My brother told me I had four games to become a starter, if I wanted to match him. So this means "Jeff Graham's Little Sister" will start before he did. Hmm. Now that thought does stir a small satisfied smile.

Chapter 4

*September 4, 1998, freshman year, opening season game,
Chester Coyotes vs. Shelby Coyotes, Chester, Montana*

At the start of the JV game I realize I forgot my lucky yellow sports bra. Dang it! I hope this is the one and only time I forget something. I'll see if Dad will run home and get it for me.

Just before halftime I spot my dad walking past some parents in the stands, holding something above his head. Something yellow. They are all laughing. Awesome. That isn't embarrassing at all and helps calm the knots twisting inside my stomach.

In the locker room we have a sweet early '90s mixed tape blaring. Mixed tapes are vital as far as athletic competition prep. We have learned to be very careful about what we offer up on bus trips, however, after that unfortunate incident last track season. Dad was driving, and Brian passed him up a tape. Not more than three notes of some rap song screeched out before the tape was promptly ejected, first from the cassette, and then from the window. Lesson learned.

We sing along to "Brick," "Bitter Sweet Symphony," "I Want It That Way," "Tubthumping," and "Semi-Charmed Life." The beauty of mixed tapes lies in the name. It is an eclectic mix that at first glance doesn't seem like it may mesh or make sense. Yet somehow, it works. Just like a team.

Our managers Stacee and Kayla come in to give us the eight-minute warning. Coach soon enters and finds us facing the whiteboard near the coaches' office, ready for our pregame plan. For a group of twelve normally chatty teenage girls, the silence that settles is significant. This is the start of an important journey. We can feel it.

We watch intently as the matchups are written with a squeaky black dry-erase marker, followed by our plan defensively: make, in "cheetah" press; miss, in half-court man.[16] The reminders Coach gives are comforting and familiar; we've been preparing for this for years. We hold hands for the Lord's Prayer then file out of the locker room with a few claps and intense exhales. As the final JV buzzer sounds, we part naturally in the hallway and high five our teammates as they jog back to the showers, encouraged and motivated by the tone they have set with a decisive win.

As we filter into the gym entrance our drummer, Doug, looks to Carly for his cue. A moment later "The Final Countdown" begins, and the tune fills my body with exhilaration and adrenaline. We huddle at the corner where the Columbia-blue baseline and sideline meet. Carly and Annie take charge. We all share the words we have chosen for the season, words that mean something special to each of us.

"Intensity!"
"Discipline!"
"Determination!"
"Attitude!"

Me firing a three against Shelby

We break off with a chorused, "Ahhh, Coyotes!" and split off in two directions, join again at half-court, then proceed with our twenty-minute warm-up routine. The one-minute warning buzzer signals us to our bench. The moments that follow are a bit of a blur, as we stand in line through the national anthem, and then Steve announces starting lineups. Finally it is time for the opening jump, and the season begins.

When the thirty-two minutes elapse, the scoreboard reads 90–20. Jeez, we really pounded them. Should I feel bad about beating someone

---

[16] Cheetah – A full court 1-3-1 press where a quick guard sets up in the front as the "cheetah." The cheetah's job was to force the dribbler to one side or the other, where a wing was waiting to trap.

so badly? Well, if I should, I don't. Maybe I better keep that to myself. No one likes a cocky girl.

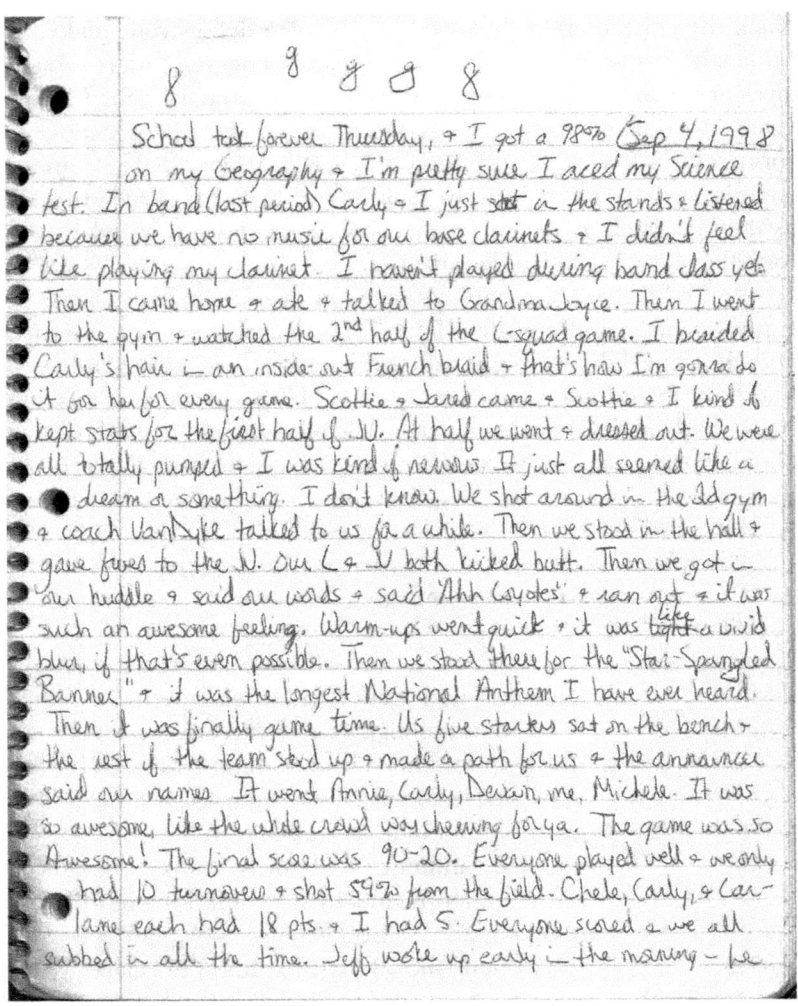

My journal entry after my first game as a freshman, September 4, 1998

* * *

The student body gathers at the Subway in Mike's IGA—the high school hangout—for the usual postgame sandwiches and more importantly, postgame socializing. The general babble exudes excitement. Dolan, a skeptical senior, walks up to me and looks me straight in the eye. He articulates a rare compliment, especially to a girl, and simply states, "Impressive."

I see Camon and Eric approach Carly and Annie. Eric cocks his head to the side, as if he's still working something out in his mind. He says, "That didn't seem like girls' basketball," and Camon nods in agreement.

What is that supposed to mean? They seem pretty pleased with themselves, so I assume it is a compliment.

I find a booth and attempt to sort out my feelings. As I listen to Mari and Heidi jabbering and joking across the table to Katy, I find I don't feel very different. I don't know what I expected, but I conclude that I am comforted by this. Comforted by the fact that things feel pretty "normal," especially after the crazy anticipation leading up to playing high school sports.

Chapter 5

*October 31, 1998, freshman year, final regular season game,
Chester Coyotes vs. Blue Sky Eagles, Chester, Montana*

I can't believe it is already our last home game. We didn't play great against Blue Sky last time, racking up twenty turnovers.[17] We cannot have games with twenty turnovers and expect to win many in tournaments.

We have a pretty intense rivalry, but one thing I do love is that Rudyard, only seventeen miles away, has the one bowling alley and movie theater within an hour. A night out for bowling and a movie is a big deal for us isolated up here on these windblown prairies.

It is senior night. I walk into the locker room and am struck by the lyrics resonating from a song playing on Annie's favorite tape:

When I see you smile
I can face the world
Oh you know I can do anything
When I see you smile
I see a ray of light
I see it shining right through the rain.[18]

---

[17]Blue Sky is a combination of two Hi-Line towns roughly ten miles apart, Rudyard and Hingham, who maybe have a combined population of 400. Both Rudyard and Hingham were also developed around shipping and grain storage for the BNSF Railway (History, 2018).

[18]"When I See you Smile" by Bad English

I have heard these lyrics a hundred times but for some reason tonight, they stop me in my tracks. My throat and chest tighten. I look over and see Carly, sitting on an uncomfortable wooden locker room bench, uniform on but shirt still untucked, tape tightly wrapped around both bare ankles. She stands, takes a determined step toward Annie and pulls her in. Carly's shoulders shudder and tears pour out. I notice a small tear track down the right side of Annie's cheek as she reciprocates Carly's hug and affection.

Carly VanDyke and Annie Diemert, our two inspirational senior leaders

For our locker room speech, Carly and Annie address us tonight. We ten underclassmen look up with anticipation and respect. Poised as usual, a natural encourager like her mom, Carly speaks first. "Tonight is the last night Annie and I will pull on our Coyote basketball uniforms in this building. It is the last night we will huddle with you all in this locker room, and it is the last night we will run out to 'The Final Countdown' on our home court. I want to thank you all for this incredible season so far. Even though this is our last home game, we will start a new season after tonight. So let's do what we always do, play hard, play together, and finish like we started."

Annie steps forward next. "Character is what we are made of. This team has a lot of character. This is the best team I have ever played on, and we play so well together."

Her next words are powerful, but none of us could ever know how ominous they are, how much we will reflect on them for years to come. "Always remember, if you don't have time to do it right, when will you have the time to do it again? No one knows what will happen next year, or even tomorrow. All we have is right now."

31

Annie, standing at five feet seven, donning a white T-shirt under her white home jersey and a short, chic haircut that only she can pull off, flashes us her infectious, gorgeous grin. We take her cue and huddle in.

Halfway through warm-ups the clock stops for special senior night introductions. I look on with pride, mixed with curiosity, as I watch Carly walk out with her arms linked to her parents, Kim and Linda, followed by Annie as she is escorted by her parents, Ed and Marcia. They all look emotional, puffy red eyes speak for themselves. I feel like I should *feel* more, especially when I see how many people in the crowd are tearing up. I am just feeling excited, though, not sad. Maybe I will understand all this when I am older.

When the game starts, our seniors keep their emotions at bay and lead us to a final home victory with an almost identical score to our home opener: we throttle the Eagles, 91–21. Carly leads with an insane 11 for 12 (92%) from the field, a season-high twenty-four points, four steals, and ten rebounds to boot. Annie continues to lead with her tenacity on defense as well as a game-high four assists. Now we enter what our math teacher Mr. Gordon, refers to as, "The best season of the year: tourney time."[19]

---

[19] Mr. Gordon goes on to be one of the winningest coaches in Montana history.

Chapter 6

November 12-14, 1998, freshman year, District 10-C Tournament, Shelby, Montana

Montana school sports teams have four classifications, based on enrollment:

Class AA = 825+
Class A = 825-340
Class B = 339-120
Class C = 119-1

There are right around fourteen Class AA schools, twenty-two in Class A, forty in Class B, and over one hundred teams in Class C.[20] These hundred-plus Class C schools, we share many commonalities. Isolated and rural, some teams travel up to three hours for regular season conference play, and it is not uncommon for teams to travel ten hours or more for state tournaments. Two weeks prior to this tournament, our boys' football team traveled 360 miles to win a playoff game in "Terry Terrier territory." (Whoever that radio announcer was, he really loved saying that.)

As for basketball, each team is part of a district, based on class and geography. The teams in a district are the same as a conference, but you can win one without winning the other, depending on season record and tournament performance. After Districts, the top two

---

[20] www.missoulapreps.com/montana-school-enrollment-numbers-and-reclassification

teams advance to the next eight-team tournament: Divisionals. Class C has four divisions, and from there, eight lucky teams move on to State. People love to get off the farm or ranch for a day or two, following their teams. Reaching the state tournament is an ultimate goal for many, including and especially us.

* * *

Our district tournaments have been held in Shelby since I can remember, and walking into the facility as a player this Friday night feels different. It feels important. We had a bye last night, the opening night of the tourney, due to winning the conference.

Tonight we play the Valier Panthers in the semifinal.[21] Like many rural Montana towns, people in Valier spend a lot time tending ranch and farmland, and a lot of time following high school basketball.

As we rush out for starting lineups, the dark-purple Panther uniforms clash with our Columbia blue and gold, and this ugly clashing seems an appropriate metaphor for this game.

Things start out rough on the opening possession. I turn it over and airball a baseline jumper all within the first minute. What the heck is wrong with me?! Near the end of the second quarter I attempt a left-handed behind-the-back pass to Carly on a two-on-one fast break. It's a little low and is fumbled out-of-bounds. Their tall forward laughs at me, and I want to punch her in the face. I gotta keep it together. Coach is officially torked and benches me. For the first time all year, we are losing at halftime.

When the coaches join us in the locker room for the halftime speech, a heavy hush ensues. Oh, no. Coach is gonna blow. I focus on trying to maintain eye contact, hoping she won't find a reason to lash out at me specifically. I can't seem to process anything coming out of her mouth. All I can see is that forehead vein popping, and all I can hear is a hissing noise from her teeth being clenched together so tight.

Listen, Jamie! What if she asks you a question? My stomach is churning like that chocolate river in *Willy Wonka*.

---

[21]Valier is located between Conrad and Shelby. Valier was built around Lake Frances, a man-made lake created for irrigation to feed the Hereford cattle brought in from Texas in the early twentieth century (History, n.d.)

Mmm, chocolate.

Focus! We have to get things under control. How can we get things under control?

* * *

I love those sports movies where the team comes out at halftime, after looking like there is absolutely no hope, then something clicks, all the players play like they never have before, and they inspire everyone watching with a sweet victory. I have imagined that happening to a team I was on a hundred times. Minutes into the third quarter I realize . . . it does not look likely that story is going to be ours tonight.

We continue to play tense and scared.

We trade buckets for the first couple minutes of the third quarter. Now trading buckets sounds just lovely, doesn't it? Like everyone is participating and getting equal turns and the world is all bubble gum and balloons. Well that is fine for preschool playtime, but not for this. Carly is short on a jumper from the block, and the Panthers board and outlet. They quickly reverse the ball, and then they have a wide-open layup lane. Dang it!

Wait.

Annie slides across the key. She takes a huge charge. Yes!

Instead of gaining more confidence and momentum, this causes a collective groan from their crowd, and a relieved exhale from ours. Devan inbounds to Annie who hits Carly at the block. Carly pivots toward the paint and sinks a soft jumper. A noticeable shift of posture occurs on our bench. Coach VanDyke looks at me out of the corner of her eye, arms crossed, and calmly asks, "Passing that behind the back was the best angle, wasn't it?"

"Yes," I reply.

Wait, should I have apologized for being flashy, especially when we were losing? But I wasn't trying to be flashy; it really was the best angle. Where is she going with this? . . .

She waves an arm toward the scorer's table, and I don't wait for her to change her mind. I bolt off the bench to check in.

We force a turnover and capitalize. They take it out again. Another steal. That's more like it. No more of this trading baskets

35

nonsense. I take a deep breath, pull my shoulders back and lift my chin slightly, collecting myself. We got this.

* * *

When I walk home from the bus late that night, I don't even mind that it's close to thirty below with the windchill. The light is on in the house, and Mom and Dad are waiting up for me. They both tell me how proud they are of me and give me kisses before heading up to bed. When I turn on the light in my bathroom, I am surprised by a light-yellow sticky note with my brother's handwriting:

> *Good job, stud!*
> *I told Casey* [22] *you were going to make that behind-the-back pass. Championship tomorrow night. You got this!*
> *Love,*
> *Jeff*

I reread this simple—yet special—note to myself several times. As a rule, Jeff doesn't generally have many positive things to say to me. In fact, he doesn't generally have many things to say to me at all. When he is not busy playing or practicing basketball, or maybe playing a season of Madden on his Nintendo, he is hanging out with his friends or especially with his girlfriend. Even though we live in the same house, we do not engage in much deep conversation.

In my gut I know my brother cares about me, I sometimes just wish he had different ways of showing it. Asking me who I like, and proceeding to telling me what an idiot said person is, may be his way of being protective, but it does not feel constructive. He has also confirmed my deep-seated suspicion that I am indeed not particularly pretty. (Luckily my dad tells me otherwise. Also, by acknowledging that I am not one to be described as a "beauty" takes away some

---

[22] Casey FitzSimmons was a senior when I was a freshman. His sister Heidi was one of our fabulous cheerleaders and in my brother's class. Casey went on to play college football at Carroll College in Helena (luckily, we're still friends, even though he chose Carroll), and then played for the Detroit Lions for eight seasons. We Chester folk are all still extremely proud of Casey, not only for all his accolades and accomplishments, but how well he represented our state and our town.

pressure and allows me to focus on developing an awesome personality.)

Maybe that is just what brothers say, but whether I want to admit it or not, I really do care what he thinks of me. So tonight, when I consider his gesture, I am surprised at how happy this little yellow square sticky note makes me. He does care about me, and basketball connects us.

* * *

Finally I get to line up out here on the court like this. Our entire team, coaches and managers included, are lined up on the west-end volleyball line, facing our opponents on the east-end line, for this Saturday night district championship game. The horseshoe-seating arena is packed to capacity at just over four thousand. I do a quick scan and figure 75% of the crowd is . . . not rooting for us. My stomach flips. We are playing the Heart Butte Warriors.

Heart Butte is a town on the Blackfeet Indian Reservation, and I don't quite understand this undefined chasm between "us" and "them."[23] We are warned when we play at reservation schools to "keep our heads down and get out of there without getting hurt" as well as to keep all our stuff locked up in the locker rooms. I have never had any personal trouble with members of the teams we play from Heart Butte, Rocky Boy, and Box Elder. In fact, I really like those girls. So I don't understand what all the fuss is about. The only "danger" I've experienced is when we had to wait awhile to board the bus in Heart Butte because there was a bear out on the playground. As with lots of things, I guess maybe I will understand this confusing tension when I get older?

As we stand facing center court, I feel like I am going to poop my pants. I already went four times in the locker room, for crying out loud. I try to take a steadying breath, but I cannot seem to stop my right knee from twitching. Act cool. Other people seem to handle this just fine. I've seen it a hundred times. There are only eight thousand eyes on me; I can handle this.

---

[23]The Blackfeet is the largest tribe in Montana, and Heart Butte is close to the Continental Divide and Glacier National Park (Heart Butte, 2019).

What if I trip when he announces my name? Where am I supposed to run again? Am I supposed to shake hands with the refs first and then the other player and then the other coach? Why do I need to shake the referees' hands at all? Jamie Marie, be nice. The refs are just doing their job.

Somehow I make it through starting lineups unscathed, dignity intact. Finally, on to something I actually feel comfortable doing.

The first quarter of the game is physical and intense. The Guardipee cousins are trees, and the lane clearly belongs to them. Our conditioning proves worth it, though, and we pull away in the second quarter. True to their name, the Warriors give us a run. In the end, we win by twenty and procure the 10-C district title. Our parents are excited and adorable as they pad onto the gym floor with their cute perms and Nikons. We pose with serious looks on our faces and arms flexed. On to Divisionals.

District and conference champs, freshman year, November 14, 1998. Carly VanDyke and Annie Diemert facing each other in front, holding the trophy

Mom, Dad, and me after winning Districts, November 14, 1998

Dad hugging Maci and me after Districts. "Tinky" Cushing,
Gail Matkin, and Gay Buffington are taking pictures and
smiling on, November 14, 1998

Chapter 7

November 19, 1998, freshman year, Northern C Divisional Tournament, Chester Coyotes vs. Centerville Miners, Lewistown, Montana

This is a big weekend for our town. We girls are going into the Northern C divisional tournament with an undefeated record, and our boys' football team is playing for the state championship at home Saturday afternoon. If all goes as planned, the diehards will be able to attend the football championship at one o'clock in the afternoon in Chester, cover the 155 miles to Lewistown, and make it in time to watch us in the Saturday divisional championship game at eight o'clock that night.[24] Numerous people have reminded us that this will all work out if and only if we win Thursday and Friday night. No pressure.

Thursday afternoon we find ourselves finishing starting lineups against the Centerville Miners. I don't know much about Centerville, but I know people there are tough.[25]

---

[24]Lewistown is a town of around six thousand people, and its school competes in Montana's Class A. It is located in the exact center of Montana. (http://www.enjoylewistown.com/).

[25]Centerville was first explored by immigrants in the 1880s and 1890s when coal was discovered in its gulches and coulees. Three towns—Stockett, Tracy, and Sand Coulee—sprang up, each with its own school. Later, however, these small towns were faced with the dilemma that seems to plague all small towns at one point or another: possible consolidation. When mines closed and many families moved on, the three schools did consolidate into Centerville (Centerville, 2019).

The Miners starters include the two Jessicas, strong, quick guards and the best shooters we've seen this year; a forward with the last name Lorang; and their towers, the Lyman sisters.

We start out tight. Our press is a bit out of sync, and our rim seems to have a lid on it. Workman is quicker than she looked in the film, and she has already buried a three on us. Not to mention her calves are ginormous, allowing her to fly for rebounds.[26] We also struggle defending Fanci Lyman. The Guardipee cousins were tall, but Lyman is even taller, and more agile. Plus her wingspan is deceiving, causing us to alter our shots inside the key. If only my Norwegian and Irish immigrant great-grandparents weren't so dang short. I never had a chance in the height department.

By halftime we are down 29–32. We jog into our locker room, and I feel a touch of uneasiness. This concerns me, because I always think we are going to win. I still expect to win, but I don't like this new, nagging feeling that makes me question myself. Where did that come from?

Coach VanDyke assures us that we are doing fine, but affirms what we suspect: "You guys have got to step it up! Rip it and turn that corner when you get it at the point. I know we haven't seen much zone this season, but we can handle it. You have to *know* you can handle it."

We nod our heads as she speaks. We have studied the film, and Coach Schlepp's scouting reports are thorough and spot-on. Now we just have to get to work. In unladylike fashion, we squeeze our sweaty, smelly bodies together, stack our slimy hands into a pile, grunt, "Win!" and hustle back out for the second half.

We huddle once more at our bench after getting a few shots up at halftime. Coach reminds us, "The third quarter is vital. We *have* to win the third quarter."

Noted.

We win the third quarter 17–13, putting us up one going into the fourth. I happen to glance into the crowd and see a Centerville player looking at a gruff-looking man in the crowd, dressed in a cowboy hat

---

[26]Four years later, I have the privilege of playing on Jessica Workman's team at Rocky Mountain College in Billings. One could not find a more genuine, kindhearted teammate and person.

and Carhart coat. She looks with worried eyes, and his crossed arms and shouts I can't quite make out don't communicate encouragement or comfort. I find myself wondering about this relationship. My dad never has anything negative to say to me. In fact, he constantly reminds me how wonderful I am and encourages me to stay positive, keep my chin up, be a leader, and always work hard. He especially wouldn't shout belligerently from the bleachers. That must feel mortifying. I don't even know what I would do if I didn't think my dad was proud of me.

I wouldn't even want to play.

I force myself to snap out of it and focus on what Coach is saying in the huddle. "Only eight more minutes. Keep your poise and composure. 'Cheetah' press after we score, full-court man on a miss. We have the momentum."

We keep that momentum until the final buzzer and win 60–50. Our goal is to keep teams under forty, and this is the first time a team has scored fifty points on us. I guess we are officially at a new level now.

Chapter 8

November 20, 1998, freshman year, Northern C Divisional Tournament, Chester Coyotes vs. Big Sandy Pioneers, Lewistown, Montana

Friday night. Just before the game Dad reminds me, "Step back. Take a breath. Take a look around and soak it all in. This is what it's all about."

The energy is electric. The sea of blue and gold in the crowd makes me smile. The cheerleaders are dancing to the pep band blaring "In-A-Gadda-Da-Vida" at three times its original tempo. And there's Richie, cheering and whipping around some sort of yellow flag, maybe? Wait a minute. That's not a flag. That's a . . . yep. It's a yellow bra. Leave it to Richie to show me love always mixed with that bit of embarrassment.

I peek over to the Big Sandy side. They are tall, graceful, disciplined, excellent outside shooters, and extremely well coached. Coach Lackner has been one of Montana's most successful track and basketball coaches since the seventies, and tonight he wears his jet-black hair in a long, sleek ponytail. I remember reading in the *Great Falls Tribune* that one year, not long ago, when his team won State, they averaged eighty-nine points per game for twenty-four games (Sunday, 2018). We are averaging right around eighty-two points per game. This could be a wild night.

The Pioneers' defense is the real deal, led in the frontcourt by the Darlingtons and Ritter, with Upham and Bitz and their impossibly long arms protecting the paint. The knee pads these girls

43

wear aren't just for show; someone is always diving for a loose ball. At halftime we lead by one, 30–29, and end regulation knotted at 53.

We line up at center court for a second time tonight, this time with four minutes on the clock. This game is the most intense I have ever played in. It is so insane, and so flipping awesome! Defense on both ends is unrelenting, constant pressure. At the end of the first overtime, it is still 53–53.

At half-court for yet a third jump ball, I can see that Coach VanDyke and Coach Lackner are shouting from their respective benches, but I cannot hear a word they are saying. Michele tips it to me, and I take a breath as I pull the ball safely to my left side, elbows out for protection, scanning the setup.

Dribble left, pull back, now right. Take care of the ball. Just take care of the ball. That is my job. I pass to Devan on the wing, and she lobs it into Carly. Carly pivots to the paint, but is cut off by Celeste Darlington. Carly looks to hit Michele on the opposite block, but Upham and Bitz are doubling down. Michele's twenty-seven points so far caused Coach Lackner to change his plan as far as which VanDyke sister to double-team. Carly kicks it back out to Devan, our best three-point shooter, but her shot falls short.

Back on D. The scouting report clearly stated my job is to stick to Ritter. Don't help, don't stray. Being the obliging, rule-following perfectionist that I am, I have noticed her mint gum has lost its scent. Ritter tries to drive inside, but Annie helps and forces her to pick up her dribble. A scoop pass to Bitz is intercepted by Michele, who outlets it to Devan, then up to me. I toss a high, quick lob to Carly, who trails, and she turns and hits Annie at the opposite deep corner. Annie makes a quick pump fake, rips it low, dribbles twice, and the ball kisses the backboard for two. The crowd goes bonkers.

"Attababy, Annie!" I shout as I give her a quick slap on her butt.
Up 55–53.

Our 1–3–1 full-court "cheetah" press slows the transition. They get the ball up the right side, though, and reverse it around to Bitz. That's not good. One of the purest shooters I have seen, Bitz has enough time to release a three and . . . swish. Down 55–56.[27]

---

[27]Katherine "Kat" Bitz became my college roommate and was a bridesmaid in my wedding (along with Michele, Kaitlynn, Heidi, Amanda, Chasi, Maci, my cousin

Under thirty seconds to go.

Once I cross half-court, Coach calls a time-out. "Alright, ladies. Twenty-eight seconds to go. We have to control the ball and take the last shot. Let's run Utah.[28] You know what to do. *Now just take care of the ball.*"

Hands in. Carly prompts, " *Win* on three. One, two, three—"

"Win!" we bawl in unison.

Okay, we have practiced our stall many times in practice. All I have to do is take care of the ball. That should be easy enough. It's what I do, after all. I have been dribbling since before I was strong enough to shoot a ball even near the hoop. All those practices I went to with Dad for years and years, dribbling on the sideline in my stocking feet for hours, have led up to this moment.

Maci, in for Devan, stacks up with me behind half-court. I receive the inbound from Annie and . . . dribble off my foot. I just dribbled the freaking ball off my freaking foot. Right out-of-bounds. Have I ever done that before? Um, I wonder what Coach is thinking. Perhaps "That was a wasted time-out now, wasn't it?" But the tone with a more Darth Vader-y quality.

Somehow, I still feel calm. Now I just have to make sure Ritter doesn't score. I gently press my forearm into her stomach and stare at her belly. Everyone knows that one can't really go in a direction unless one's belly turns that way, after all. The ball is inbounded to Darlington, who bounces it to Ritter after I am screened by Bitz. I hedge back and stay as low as I can, hands out but not breaking the plane, and pray that following all these defensive principles will pay off. Ritter jump stops in the key, pulls up for a highly contested twelve-foot jumper . . . and a whistle. Wait a minute. I am pretty positive I did not touch her. I turn and look at the ref with mounting anticipation. He holds up both hands and makes a "wheels on the bus" sorta motion.

Becca, and two college teammates: Shye Boggs and Jeri Matter). One couldn't ask for a kinder, more loyal friend, and I still attest that she was the purest shooter I ever got to play with.

[28] Utah – Stall play where we had two guards parallel each other at the top of the key, one player at the high post, and two players opposite each other at the deep corners. We ran this play at the end of a quarter when the ball was in our possession and there was under forty-five seconds to a minute left in the quarter.

Travel! Yes! Our ball, eight seconds to go. Just need to stay on the bull.

Michele takes the inbound, I call for the outlet, and glance at the clock while pushing the ball up the right sideline. Eight seconds to go. I chuck it ahead to Maci, who fakes and hits Annie coming off a picture-perfect screen set by Carly at the low block. Five seconds. Annie sets up to shoot a three. Wait, is Annie allowed to shoot threes? Three seconds. Annie releases with as much confidence as I have ever seen. Two seconds.

For a moment, the arena is silent.

Swish.

The buzzer is drowned out by my teammates and our crowd. Maci latches on to me, and I squeal and hug her tight. We collect ourselves long enough to politely walk through the "good game" line and high five each of the Pioneer players. Then our parents and other crowd members filter down from the bleachers, each one more excited than the next. I look over and see Annie being pummeled by her brother Dillon. That is so cool he came back to watch this. All her brothers flock around her, glowing with pride.

Alright, we have done our part. Now we pass the baton to the boys.

Chapter 9

November 21, 1998, freshman year, Northern C Divisional
Tournament, Chester Coyotes vs. Box Elder Bears,
Lewistown, Montana

We lie in a large conference room in our hotel Saturday afternoon. Pillows, duffel bags, and blankets are strewn across the floor, with meat and cheese platters, fruit, chocolate Rice Krispie bars, and numerous other goodies from bags that were packed for the bus so carefully by our sweet moms and other community members. A large boom box sits in the middle of the room, tuned to KSEN and the state championship football game: the Power Pirates hosted by the Chester Coyotes.

Many of our parents—sans my dad, who is one of the football assistant coaches and had to head back last night—are in the room with us, as well as various other Chesterites. We attempt to get as comfortable as possible in this room packed with people yet short on chairs. We snack and chat nervously during the pregame portion of the broadcast, as Mark Daniels and Jim Sargent reveal the starting lineups, backgrounds, and predictions for the afternoon contest:

Jim Sargent: *The Chester Coyotes started out strong this season, beating Sunburst, Valier, and Big Sandy, ending each game with the forty-five-point rule. Game four of the season found the Coyotes facing the also undefeated Power Pirates. Power routed the Coyotes in a 46–14 tilt.*

As mentioned before, the Pirates powered forward and remain undefeated.

Meanwhile, the Coyotes bounced back and pounded Hobson-Moore, and then Judith Gap. Then came what was likely the most important game up to that point. The Coyotes traveled to Centerville and squeaked out a 28–26 win. I do believe that game was played in quite a snowstorm, Mark, which sounds crazy, but we all know snow is not crazy at all anytime of the year out here under the Big Sky.

The Coyotes finished off the regular season with wins against Belt and Hays-Lodgepole before entering into the single elimination postseason. In the first-round playoff game, the Coyotes met up yet again with the tough Centerville Miners. The Coyotes won 34–14 and moved on to the quarterfinals where they played the undefeated western division Ennis Mustangs. Then last week in the semifinals they beat yet another undefeated team, the Scobey Spartans.

I have Coyote head coach Bill Schlepp here on the sidelines, as he looks on while his players warm up. Coach Schlepp, tell us how you are feeling about this afternoon's contest?

Coach Schlepp: *We got big heads after winning the first three games of the season. After Power put us in our place, we coaches saw a shift in our boys. They put their heads down and are determined not to let that happen again.*

Jim Sargent: *What did you tell the boys in the locker room this morning?*

Coach Schlepp: *I told them a key for us will be to keep Bomont Somerfeld out of the backfield. Power is big, and our offensive line has got to stay solid. I reminded them this is right where we want to be. If we want to be the best, we have got to beat the best.*

Jim Sargent: *Okay, good luck, Coach.*

Coach Schlepp: *Thanks. And thanks to KSEN for covering us.*

I eat another Rice Krispie bar. For some reason we call them Chicken Dinner Bars. To be honest, I do not care why or what we call them. All I know is they are delicious. Mark and Jim continue on with pregame chatter while I chew and attempt to picture the football game's scene. We hear the band play the national anthem, and finally, kickoff:

Jim Sargent: *And kicking off for the Pirates is going to be Somerfeld. Somerfeld kicks it out of the end zone, and the Coyotes will line up at the twenty. Scott Riggin snaps it to quarterback Jared Christenot. Christenot brings it out, first handoff of the game, gets it to Ryan Gagnon who gains a few yards for the Coyotes in their opening play of the game.*

These two teams saw each other earlier in the season, and the Power Pirates beat the Coyotes with a decisive win at 46 to 14. Let's see what happens here today.

The Coyotes will set up for their second down on this windy day here in Chester with just under twelve minutes to go here in first quarter of this state C eight-man football championship game.

Second down, Christenot fakes the handoff and is taken down hard on the keeper. The Power Pirates were ready for that one, and they have a huge defensive line.

Christenot's got it, third down and four in the backfield, and the wind's blowing right in his face here. He will give to Casey FitzSimmons, oh, but he is pummeled by the Pirates' line.

Our boys get off to a little bit of a slow start. We gain a first down, only to fumble on the next play where Josh Pfeifle recovers and takes it into the end zone. We luckily stop the two-point conversion attempt, but we fumble a few plays later! No!

Luke Toekes with a beautiful sack, allowing J. T. Stengrimson to pick up the fumble, and now Kyle Burgmaier receives the snap. Burgmaier takes a couple steps backwards, looks to throw and . . . he connects with Cody Loch on a beautiful thirty-yard touchdown pass! And this puts the Power Pirates up 12–0 here in the middle of the first quarter of this class C eight-man football state championship.

We groan as the Pirates connect on the conversion this time, which puts us down 0–14. Not an ideal way to start. We make it through the rest of the first quarter without letting them score anymore, but now we have got to put some points up. Sarge continues:

The Chester Coyotes are taking on the Power Pirates here in the second quarter of the state C championship. Power leading by

49

fourteen. Christenot, now has the wind at his back, second down and five. And he will pass for the first time. He airs it out to Riggin and . . . Riggin can't quite get to it.

It sounds like Camon and Logan are playing both offense and defense this game.[29] Good idea. We gotta keep our big boys in there against this giant team.

. . . we'll see what happens. Second down and four. The Chester line is a wall for Christenot and . . . touchdown Coyotes!

Wahoo! Everyone whoops and whistles. We continue to listen in anticipation, snacking all the way. Our boys march sixty-five yards down the field with seventeen straight plays. Sweet. Jared keeps it for the final three yards for another touchdown! Then just a few minutes after that, Ryan runs in another one. Now this is more like it.

. . . and as the final seconds tick off the clock, the Chester Coyotes are the 1998 state C eight-man football champions with a final of 36–20!

The room erupts and the scene must look something like the time at church when everyone stands up and says "Peace be with you" to everyone else, but with more hugging and jumping. This energy feels like a spark that catches and lights everyone in the room. I feel like I am about to burst. I cannot get enough of this feeling! I am so proud. Proud of my dad, my brother, proud to be a Coyote.

* * *

Inspired and pumped up from the boys' sweet victory, we head into the locker room with confidence. The pressure is lessened even more when Coach walks in and announces that Big Sandy just beat Grass Range in the consolation game. This means that even if we get second, there would be no challenge game, since we already beat Big

---

[29]Logan Lybeck and Camon Hunnewell historically only played defense, but Logan went in after the first series and Camon after the second to play both ways the remainder of the game.

Sandy. We play loose and disciplined against the Box Elder Bears, led by the Montes sisters and Kristie Pullin.[30]

These girls are legit, but we are firing on all cylinders tonight, and their shooting is off. We earn our school's first girls' basketball divisional title, 58–38. Here's that incredible feeling again. I think I'm addicted. . . .

Divisional championship game versus Box Elder, November 21, 1998. Me on the left defended by Dorrina Ojeda; Maci Tempel on the right defended by Sommer Rosette

The five fabulous freshman flexing after winning Divisionals, Nov 21, 1998
Maci Tempel, me, Chasi Buffington, Michele VanDyke, and Heidi Cicon

---

[30]LeAnn Montes goes on to play for the University of Montana Grizzlies, and Kristie Pullin plays, then coaches at Northern Montana College. Kristie goes on to room with Kaitlynn Engstrom in college, and she and I both get to stand up for Katy at her wedding.

Chapter 10

December 2, 1998, freshman year, on to State, Chester, Montana

Boarding the bus for the state tournament makes me feel like a big deal. There are banners and signs everywhere, as well as boxes filled with snacks and notes of well-wishes. Michele walks on right behind me and chides, "Now remember, Jamers, you have to share these snacks with everyone."

Carlane and Megan snicker as we shuffle back to claim our seats. I slide in beside Maci. "Can you believe we are heading to our first state tournament?" I ask incredulously.

"Been waiting for years for this," she responds with a wry smile.

As we turn left onto the highway at the Liberty County Medical Center and pass by the Methodist church, instead of hunkering down with our blankets and Walkmans as is the usual routine, our foreheads are pressed against the glass. "That one's my favorite!" announces Chasi excitedly, pointing to the "We're *Rootin'* For Ya, Coyotes!" sign propped up on some hay bales at the turnoff to the Deckers' pig farm.

I notice a *Great Falls Tribune* lying on the top of a box of fruit snacks stacked in the seat in front of me. Scanning the headlines I see,

Chester, Box Elder Hope to Extend Trend
By TRIBUNE STAFF

LIVINGSTON- Every Class C girls' basketball fan with a penchant for Montana sports history should know by now that the Northern Division has won the last five state championships, and six of the last seven. In three of the past seven years, a Northern Division school defeated another Northern Division school for the title.

Hmm. Good to know. The headline on the bottom right of that same page catches my eye next,

Small Town Cheers Its Mighty Coyotes
By AMY BETH HANSON

CHESTER-Farm prices are down and some businesses are closing in this Hi-Line town, but there is no gloom in Chester. The mighty Coyotes rule Class C high school sports right now, and the whole town is cheering.

The football team just won its first state Class C title, and the girls' basketball team is taking a 23-0 record into this weekend's state tournament in Livingston. It is the Chester girls' first trip to state since 1979.

"We're on a high," said 60-year-old Tinky Cushing, who renewed her interest in girls' basketball this year after taking a more than ten-year break.

"They treat me like I'm one of them. They don't treat me like I'm an old lady."

Cushing's neighbors are Coach Linda VanDyke and her daughters—Carly, a senior who averages 17 points and seven rebounds, and Michele, a freshman who averages 12 points and seven rebounds.

"These girls are like my own," said Cushing, who had just finished frosting some cookies for the team to take on the bus. "It's been kind of fun to get into sports again. It's fun to do something for someone else."

The school and its activities have always been supported by this north-central Montana farming community of about 1,000. But this year has been just plain fun.

"People that don't have any girls in the program or any kids in the school started coming to the games," said VanDyke. "Everyone says, 'They're just so much fun to watch.' "

"Just the atmosphere of the school has been great. Everybody's getting along," said Bill Schlepp, the football coach and principal.

Boosters have put up yard signs, athletes have signs on their school lockers, there are treats on the buses, and there was even an impromptu fire truck ride and parade for the football team after its 36-20 state championship victory over Power.

"We didn't even have that planned or anything," said Schlepp. "There must have been two miles of vehicles behind us."

But they didn't stick around town for long.

"There wasn't time to celebrate because the football coaches, players and pep band were on the road to Lewistown, to watch the girls play for the Northern C divisional championship," Schlepp said.

"We were one happy town," said Peggy Kimball, who went to Lewistown for the divisional semifinal on Friday, came back to Chester for the football championship Saturday afternoon, and was among the line of cars trekking back to Lewistown for the divisional championship Saturday night.

"I think to keep involved in the community and school you have to go to their sporting events and concerts," said Kimball, whose sons finished school a decade ago.

"Basketball provides a lot of entertainment for the people of Chester. In fact, I'd say (school sports) is their entertainment," said coach VanDyke. "It covers all ages. It ranges from senior citizens to preschoolers. Everybody in the family comes."

54

The success has those with gray hair acting like kids at games, and 4-year-olds belting out their rendition of the school fight song.

"I try not to be too loud," said Cushing, who admits to yelling, "Oh, Annie, I love you!" when Chester forward Annie Diemert made a crucial shot during a double-overtime victory over Big Sandy in the divisional semifinals.

"A friend told me, 'You're as much of a jabberbox as when your own kids played.' "

Harry Heimbigner, who's traveled to basketball games for nearly a quarter of a century, said high school sports are his source of entertainment.

"This is my thing, basketball," said Heimbigner, 62, who trades off driving with long-time friend Don Raunig, the owner of the Ford dealership.

"Don and I put on a lot of miles," Heimbigner said. "I guess we're the grandaddies of the team."

Heimbigner said he didn't quit following the school teams even after his children graduated and isn't one to miss a game.

"You gotta keep the interest up in small towns," he said. "If it wasn't for the school in Chester, Montana, it would blow away."

The players seem to know the impact they're having.

"I think they understand how involved the community is and how happy they are for them. I think they really sense that," said VanDyke. "When we went to Divisionals, we had 18 miles of signs along the road south of town."

Heimbigner plans to leave early this morning to catch the first-round game against Plevna at 12:30 p.m.

But half the students will be in school, and Cushing said she can't get away until Friday either. Those left in town likely will catch the first-round game on the radio.

"I'm sure there'll be teachers that will have it on," said Schlepp, who conceded that students

55

might not get much studying done Thursday
afternoon.
    Radios at local businesses will be tuned into
the game as well. If the girls win, many residents
will head south for Friday's semifinal.
    "If they play Saturday night, I think the town
will be empty," said Kimball.

I finish the article and look out the window. I read the last sign
posted at mile-marker 18, ushering us to State on Highway 223.
    Devan, who is generally quiet but has good timing when she does
speak, quips, "Man, we really make people happy, don't we?"
    "Of course we do." Annie adds.
    We all smile, and I watch the miles and miles of snow blanketing
the sleeping wheat fields. I don't remember a time when I have felt
so content.

* * *

Our practice at Carroll College in our state's capital city goes great,
and we head on to Livingston, the windiest place on the planet.[31] I
enjoy a delicious cheeseburger, my traditional on-the-road pregame
meal (Dad makes me scrambled eggs for home games) at Paradise
Inn. Our good-natured bus driver, Al, pulls us as close as he can to
the entrance of the Yellowstone Motor Inn so as to shield us as much
as possible from the sixty mph gales.
    Whatever thoughts are going through everyone's heads are not
spilling out a mile a minute, like they usually do. Instead, we are
uncharacteristically quiet as we are given our keys, room assignments,
and reminded of the rules defined and expected of us as student-
athletes in the Chester Student Handbook. Chester has a reputation
for being a class act, and we are reminded that we shouldn't need to
be reminded what that looks like.

---

[31]This is not hyperbole, if it had a population of more than 7,500 people, Chicago
would be ousted. It is not uncommon to see semis (eighteen-wheelers) tipped over
all around the Livingston exits.

Chapter 11

December 3, 1998, freshman year, State Class C Tournament, Chester Coyotes vs. Plevna Cougars, Livingston, Montana

After a fitful sleep and some delicious hotel buffet breakfast, we board the bus again, this time trudging through what must be almost two feet of fresh snow. Al carefully navigates through the parking lot, which isn't easy due to the wind swirling into what looks like small snow tornadoes, and attempts to stay on the paved tracks leading to Park County High School.

Carly takes us into our huddle as we wait for the clock. "Alright, ladies. This is what we've been waiting for. We are ready. Leave it all on the court."

When we run out, something feels a bit off. It doesn't feel like a state tournament. Or what I thought it would feel like to be competing in a state tournament. I try to follow Dad's advice and take a second to take a breath, look around, soak in the atmosphere. But it is twelve thirty on a Thursday, and this is proving to be difficult.

We are to face the Plevna Cougars. The only reason I know about Plevna, the tiny town in eastern Montana, is because the VanDykes moved to Chester from there. People from Plevna often compete in summer sporting events in North Dakota or South Dakota, as some of the bigger towns in those states are closer than those in Montana, like Billings. As we watched film on them last week, I thought about how thankful I was the VanDykes play for us now. As I look out at the Plevna crowd today, I imagine they are thinking just the opposite.

The three six-foot-two O'Connor cousins are an intimidating presence, to say the least, as we line up for the jump ball. Toni tips it to Stickney, who hits Lacey O'Connor for a quick two. That's not good. Okay, get it up the court. We're faster than they are. Or maybe not. Dang it! I was sure that lob was gonna make it. It feels like we can't get into our normal rhythm. Maybe it's because these girls are giant, and I'm just a tiny little person, for crying out loud.

End of first, down 12-16. Coach VanDyke has our attention. "Alright, slow start. Let's switch to our 'five' press and have our bigs pressuring the ball.[32] Obviously we are outsized, so we *have to box out*. Keep pushing it up the floor, but catch first and look. Ball fake, ball fake, ball fake. Let's go."

Annie takes over, "*Defense* on three. One, two, three—"

"Defense!" we chorus intensely.

The second quarter starts out better. We run "Duke" to Michele and start with an and-one.[33] The deafening cheers from our crowd surges through me, like I imagine the coffee does for Dad. We hit our stride and are tied with only seconds to go before halftime. This is more like it. Wait! Son of a B. Stickney lobs it to Toni O'Connor who capitalizes on a last second eight-footer. We run in for halftime down by two, 24-26.

* * *

Maybe their size intimidated us; maybe it was the pressure of being the first Chester girls' team on a state tournament court since the 70s.

---

[32]Five – A full court 1-2-1-1 press where the tallest girls were pressuring the ball on the inbounds. We went into this press when one of our taller players was shooting free throws. This made for taller players with longer arms making traps while shorter, quicker guards were in the back court preventing long passes.

[33]Duke ("D" or "4") – One of our "one-four high" set plays. A post player (the "4") takes the ball at the point. Other players set up at two wings and two elbows. One wing cuts across to the opposite deep corner. The post player—this was almost always Michele—enters the ball to the strong side elbow. The post player then rubs off the opposite post and cuts to the basket to receive an alley-oop and either tips the ball in or catches the ball and then lays it up. Arizona ("A" or "1") was another one of "one-four high" set plays. In this set, the point guard dribbles near the top of the key and passes to a high post. First option is a handoff from the post to the point guard who cuts shoulder to shoulder with the post who receives the ball. If the handoff isn't there, the second option is for the high post with the ball to turn and face the basket then look to shoot or pump fake then drive.

Or maybe it was that we only shot 66% (14 for 21) from the stripe, had a 35% (16 for 46) field goal percentage, and only 25% (1 for 4) from behind the arc. Yep. That sounds about right.

It is a blur as we file through the "good game" line. I glance once more at the red 47–53 glaring decisively down from the scoreboard. I walk into the locker room and see our seniors Carly and Annie in tears. Carly is especially beside herself. "Hey, Car," I offer. "It's okay."

Her fiery glare tells me that I am incorrect and it is indeed not okay. "That was it, Jamie. That was our shot. And now it's gone."

Note to self. Do not lose at State when I am a senior.

Chapter 12

*December 4–5, 1998, freshman year, State Class C
Tournament, Livingston, Montana*

It's a new day. As we head out of our hotel rooms this morning,
we are greeted by at least fifty Coyote fans, from Tinky to Harry
and Don to Bicycle Bob to all of our parents, and more.[34]
Chester people are the best.

Our awesome cheerleaders, coached by Coach Schlepp's wife,
Kellie, fire everyone up with some good ole "Wiggle Low" and "We
Are Proud of You." Carly, Annie, and Coach VanDyke offer a few
words of thanks and inspiration, and we take our first step to make
our goal of playing Saturday night and taking home some hardware.

---

[34]Like any good small town, Chester had a man who was forever riding his bike. I
take that back, it had two men always on bikes: Bicycle Bob and Bud. Bud was a
special-needs adult who always wore a cowboy hat and a faux sheriff badge. People
were very good to Bud, and it was always fun to see him riding by your road and
give him a wave. Bicycle Bob was tall and lanky with a full head of white hair and a
handful of teeth. He not only rode around our town, but he loaded his bike in the
back of his pickup and drove to most of our high school's out-of-town sporting
events. Often he would beat the bus there. Bob would park at the rival high school,
unload his bike, and he would get a good ride around that town before the doors
opened for the games. During basketball games, Bob liked to sit near the bench. I
recall having a few conversations with him while I was sitting out. Bob was a blue-
and-gold Coyote supporter, true and true, but he could not be described as an
optimist. On the contrary, even when it looked like things were really going our
way (i.e., we were romping someone by forty) he would express what he was sure
to be our inevitable undoing: "Well you can handle these guys, but Richey will get
ya." One just had to smile.

So this isn't exactly how we pictured it, so what. Like Coach said last night after the loss, "The real victory in defeat is bouncing back."

It's a new day.

* * *

Since Montana basketball tournaments are double elimination, now we either win or we go home. Coach Schlepp often warns of "One, two, barbecue," and even though I don't always exactly understand these things he says, I know I do not want to find out more about this phrase.

This morning we get to start the day with the Gardiner Bruins.[35] According to the newspapers, Gardiner played out of their minds at their divisional tournament last weekend, upsetting Drummond in the Western C Divisionals for a trip to State. Seven of the eight teams in this tournament have a combined total of only seven season losses. The Bruins currently have a record of 12-10, after getting romped by Richey in yesterday's opener. We would like to make that record 12-11.

Michele wins the tip, I chuck it to Carly who bolts down the left lane, and we make a statement immediately, starting 2-0 with only four seconds having ticked off the clock. We smother their guards with our "five" press and don't let up. By the end of the first quarter we lead 27-8. The rest of the game continues the same way, and we feel back on track with a 78-54 victory.

We gather in the locker room. Coach praises us. "That's more like it. That looked like the Chester Coyotes I know. Now we get a break the rest of the day, then we play two more games tomorrow. Win tomorrow morning, and we give ourselves an opportunity to end the season on a win. Only eight teams in the state get to end on a win. Let's make sure we are one of them."

We can still end on a win. Still meet our goal of placing at State. Let's do this.

---

[35]Gardiner is a picturesque town sandwiched between the Absaroka-Beartooth Wilderness and Gallatin National Forest, and is a main gateway to Yellowstone National Park (Gallatin, 2019).

Saturday morning finally comes, and here we are, lined up against the White Sulphur Springs Hornets. This is their school's first girls' basketball appearance at State, the last appearance being their boys' team in 1964. Legend has it that the hot springs in White Sulphur have powerful healing effects, that they soothe body aches and pains. Good thing for them, because they are going to need those springs when we've finished with them. Now that sounds a little sassy. Well too bad. I really do want to whoop them.

The game is intense. With the Gebhardt sisters at the one and two guard positions and six-foot-one Sulser in the paint, the Hornets match right up with us.[36] We of course press them, and they press us right back, which slows us up a bit. Okay, stay poised. Call something. "Connecticut!" I shout, as I cross half-court.[37]

Devan and Annie duck into the paint and pop back out to the wings while Michele and Carly establish themselves at the elbows. I hit Carly with a lob at the high post, wait until Annie crosses to the opposite short corner, jab-step right, then cut and rub shoulders with Carly. The handoff is not there, so I bust out, pushing Annie and Devan up. Carly faces, pump fakes, rips and dribbles once, straight to the hole. She pulls up at the block, shot fakes, and . . . nothing but net. Carly is the obvious go-to, shooting close to 60% (7 for 12) from the field and 100% (9 for 9) from the stripe.

Betsy and her sister Carrie break our press, hit their center Sulser at the block, as if to say, "We can do that, too, suckas."

The game continues this way, back and forth like a ping-pong match. At half we lead 25-24 and win the third quarter 13-9. The Hornets pull within two in the middle of the fourth, but we hang on and clinch the win with clutch free throw shooting. As I make two for two in the final minute of the game I give a silent shout-out to the Elks Club, and its National Hoop Shoot contest. We advance to the consolation game with a team field goal percentage of 46% (17 for 37) and 86% (18 for 21) from the line. Funny how when we meet

---

[36]I end up playing with Liz Sulser at Rocky Mountain College as well. She is as kind as she is tall.

[37]Connecticut ("C" or "3") – One of our "one-four high" set plays. Point guard passes to a wing and cuts through, looking for a "give-and-go." If the give-and-go isn't there, the second option is for the ball-side post to screen away for the other post. Wing looks to hit either the screener or the roller.

those measurable goals we set, we win. Now tonight we get another shot at Plevna in the consolation game.

* * *

Me driving against Plevna in the State C consolation game versus Plevna, Park County High School (Livingston), December 5, 1998

Saturday night. The locker room is deserted save for Carly and me. I sit on the cold aluminum bench and watch as she purposefully gathers up her bag and her blue-and-gold letterman jacket. Though I still feel elated from our third-place win against Plevna a half hour ago, I purse my lips tightly to suppress the smile underneath as I catch Carly's eye. I know she is happy. Or at least I think she is happy. We played great tonight, and we will take home our school's first piece of hardware from a girls' state basketball tournament. We ended our season on a win.

But she's been quiet, pensive (learned that word from Mrs. Rasmussen's Friday "Word Power" quizzes). "Great job tonight, Car. How you feeling?"

She doesn't answer right away. I study the expression on her face, her eyes, searching for clues about what she might be feeling. Carly has always been like an older sibling to me. This year, entering high school, I am thankful for the many opportunities I've had to be near her, observe her, and best of all, befriend her. We are the only two bass clarinetists in the band, and I love making her giggle while Mr. Hutchins is focusing on another instrument section.

After watching her play in high school for three years, I have been fully aware of what a privilege it is to be her teammate. She is a true leader, poised and intelligent, and carries with her an air of authority that demands respect. Though we are both "high school students," I often feel there is a significant distinction between her feelings and understandings of certain moments and my own. This is how I am feeling now. I remember her explaining to me, after our loss on Thursday, "That was it. That was our shot."[38]

Carly looks at me, and her expression softens into an affectionate, close-lipped smile. "I feel good, Jamie. I feel good."

I smile back at her as she pulls me in for our patented handshake, clasping right hands together, then pulling our fist first to my chest then to hers. We walk out of the locker room side by side. I have a spring in my step and feel frisson and contentment course through my body. I think what an awesome beginning this season has been to my high school career, how this 26–1 season with a third-place finish is a great start, with three more chances to win the championship. When I look over at Carly, though, I can't help but wonder how different this experience is for her and consider whether I will ever understand how she is feeling.

---

[38] Carly went on to play basketball at Carroll College in Helena, MT, where she was a three-year starter and graduated with a degree in Health Education. She then spent eight years at Carroll College as an assistant coach, coaching five All-Americans and fourteen All-Conference players. Following Carroll, she spent three years as the assistant coach at NCAA Division II Central Washington University in Ellensburg, Washington. In April 2014, she was hired as head women's basketball coach at Montana Tech in Butte, MT, where she just completed her sixth season as head coach.

Second Quarter

Yea, though I walk through the valley of the shadow of death, I will fear no evil: for thou art with me; thy rod and thy staff they comfort me.

—Psalm 23:4

1999 Chester Lady Coyotes

Chapter 13

August 1999, sophomore year, regular season, Chester, Montana

66 Should we buy one or two boxes?" Mari, or 'Mo' as she is most often referred, facetiously asks my opinion on how many graham crackers to purchase.

"You're always good for a laugh," I respond as I tuck a can of rainbow chip frosting under my arm, shifting the chocolate milk, and Mo balances both boxes with the Funyuns and Tombstone pizzas.

After I secure the Tang, we nod our mutual consensus and head to check out. "It's a good thing we gave up pop," Mari notes thoughtfully as she eyes our booty.

"Absolutely," I agree, grinning to myself.

I classify quite a few people in my "best friend" category, but no one seems to be on the same wavelength as me lately as much as Mari. We have so many similar interests, from our obsession with correct grammar to our opinions on the best movies and books (*Harry Potter*, obviously) to what we find attractive in boys. It sometimes feels like we share a mind.

"We need calories to replace the hundreds we just burned," Mo continues, verbalizing our justification as Margaret, who smiles knowingly, rings us up.

It has been a great summer vacation, essentially a replica of the past couple summers: babysit the Hamel boys (sleep in as long as possible when not babysitting), lift weights, shoot and record makes for the summer's ten thousand Shot Club challenge, play pickup games, watch movies at Heidi's or Michele's or the twins' house, repeat.

Every once in a while we float the Marias River or spend an afternoon jet skiing or water skiing at Lake Elwell, and our family trips to all the Graham relatives in Big Timber are my favorite. Then there are always those couple weeks when, as the August heat relentlessly beats down, we attempt to rid the Mattson family's wheat fields of wild oats, scouring then tramping through the rows of wheat, pulling, piling, then burning the unyielding weeds before harvest.

The Mattson family has farmland fifteenish miles north of Chester, toward the Sweetgrass Hills. Last summer I carpooled with various folks, anywhere from five to a dozen, depending on the day, out to the Mattson farm.

Many people do not seem to know what "picking oats" is, so it is worth describing. The purpose of this job is to clear the pesky wild oats (a.k.a. weeds) from the beautiful golden wheat fields. Here's the scene: two super-old pickups slowly carry the two oat-picking teams for the day. There is an oat foreman, we will call him, per team who is in charge of driving and just general directing.[39]

When the oat foremen decide which field will be the focus, the teams drive out bright and early. There is plenty of water, plenty of sunscreen, and always, always a giant boom box playing Hot 101.3 all day long. As is the way with radio stations, the popular songs play every hour, so there is no way of knowing how many times we hear "Follow Me" by Uncle Kracker or "I'm Like a Bird" by Nelly Furtado. Many times one member of a team realizes he or she has been singing certain lyrics to some random song completely wrong for years. "Oh!! It's *'One week since you looked at me,'* not *'One week since you drank some tea!'* "

We discuss many important life questions out in those fields, such as what is the most efficient and sanitary way to prepare the toilet paper before wiping. Things like that.

The best part of picking oats is the lunches, but they should be properly referred to as the "country dinners." These are the real reasons people agree to this brutal work. Mama Carol spends all morning preparing Thanksgiving-like feasts for the crews: always a

---

[39]Brothers Dave and Bob (we referred to him as 'Bobbio') were the foremen.

succulent meat course (roast, ham, etc.) with all the fixins' (corn, some form of potato, bread), and delicious desserts that contain Oreos and other crushed stuff. We wash the food down with multiple glasses of cold, refreshing lemonade. The meal is followed by an oh-so-lovely siesta. The TV plays The Game Show Channel, and we lie strewn about the couches, chairs, and floor of the living room as we hear people plead for "No whammies!"

Then, back out to the fields. While the pickup crawls up and down the field, all of us spotters are on the lookout for an oat. Hitting the side of the pickup with one's hand is the signal. The pickup stops, and the one who spotted the oat carefully tiptoes through the field to see if it was a single oat, a small patch that can be taken care of by said spotter, or if the whole crew needs to tiptoe out, spread out among the field, and pick up and down the rows. When the area is cleared, the crew takes various loads to the pickup. Later in the afternoon, the piles from the pickup are pushed off to the burn pile. And that is an oat-picking day, in a nutshell.

I smile at the memory of my unique summer job as I ride shotgun in Mari and Maci's new Del Sol, the car they get to share now that they are fifteen. When we get to their house, we carefully step over the tired bodies lazing across the living room floor, half-sleeping, half-watching *Dirty Dancing*.

"I need food," Michele moans as she opens her eyes long enough to notice our arrival.

"You always need food, Michele," Katy states, matter-of-factly.

"But seriously," Kaitlynn, who loves food just as much as the rest of us, continues earnestly, "You did bring food, didn't you?"

"Don't worry, you lazy sacks, we brought food," Mari announces to the living room packed with my favorite people, who just happen to be my teammates.

Chasi and Michele, legs entwined, are enveloped by the scratchy yet surprisingly comfortable gray couch, Heidi sits on the edge of the faded-orange easy chair as she braids Katy's hair, and on the floor a giant poofy white pillow supports Emily and Maci as they hum "Hungry Eyes."

Seventeen to twenty minutes later we enjoy our delicious Tombstone pizzas, Funyuns as a side, frosted graham crackers for dessert, chased by chocolate milk and Tang. We clean up our lunch mess and settle back down out in the living room. We wordlessly proceed to watch Patrick brace, launch, then hold Jennifer in the air. I hear quiet, serene sighs as we smile dreamily at the screen. Mari ejects the VHS and replaces it with *Austin Powers: International Man of Mystery*. "Turn the volume down a little," Maci implores, "I want to make sure I nap before tonight's practice."

Besides playing sports, hanging out at Subway, and driving around, watching movies is our other time-filler. Once we find one we like, we really test the "rewind" feature on our VCRs. Another of our favorite videos to watch is the one my mom recorded of the

Impromptu fashion show at the Tempels' house: Me, Michele VanDyke, Mari Tempel, and Maci Tempel, August, 1998

incredible dances we made up in junior high to songs like "Runaway," "Sugar Shack," and "Wannabe (I'll Tell You What I Want, What I Really Really Want")."

"We need to watch the 1992 championship game again one of these days," Chasi reminds us from the couch.

We all mumble our agreement, and Michele notes, "Yeah, we haven't watched it in a couple weeks."

I calculate the number of hours we have left before our second two-a-day practice. I have a love-hate relationship with preseason practices. I love that they mean basketball season has officially started, and I hate the rest. Only ten more to go. Then we officially kick off our sophomore season, the season where we will win our first state championship. As Austin Powers would say, "Yeah, baby."

Chapter 14

September–October 1999, sophomore year, regular season, Chester, Montana

This season hasn't been as smooth sailing as last year's season. When the season began, it felt a bit strange. It felt like we should simply pick up where we left off, but turns out we had to start completely over. Not just in basketball, but in all parts of school life. Losing last year's senior class seems to have changed everything. I suppose that's how it is in small towns. One group of kids can really make an impact.

After winning the state football championship, then us finishing third in basketball, the boys ended up second in state basketball to Kremlin-Gilford (and the Stuart brothers). Meanwhile, we couldn't quite hold off the Bridger Scouts in volleyball, losing to them in the championship game while they earned their insanely impressive fifth consecutive title (Bridger, 2019). Our wrestling team had two state champions in brothers Scottie and Brent Riggin, and a sixth-place team finish. Girls' tennis took Divisionals. Both boys' and girls' track teams swept Divisionals, with the boys placing third at the state meet. Not to mention the myriad of academic and music accolades accrued by our high school student body. I am not one to toot my own horn. Actually, I am. We are so awesome.

Anyway, my point is, this year has felt different. Last year was idyllic. Everything was new, we didn't know what to expect, and things just were so exciting and went so smoothly. Now it seems like there's all this other "stuff." Impending pressure and expectations exist that

I didn't feel last year. It feels like we have to win, like we are expected to win, when last year it just felt fun.

With Carly and Annie in college—Carly plays for the Carroll Saints, Annie for the Sheridan College Generals—Devan and Megan have stepped into those senior leadership roles. They are positive and hardworking, excellent leaders, but it is impossible to replace a Carly and an Annie. Our current record is 11-1. That's right. We lost a regular season game. To the Belt Huskies. One can argue that it was not a conference game so it doesn't technically count. However, if one did that, one would be deceiving oneself. They all count.

So tonight we are home against Brady.[40] With only five regular season games left, we have got to step it up a notch.

We shoot out of the gate at top speed, and lead 21-10 at end of the first quarter. We pull back to half-court defense when we get up ten, which is generally the unwritten rule. By the end of the third we are up 54-26. Alright, here we go. Things are feeling like they are back on track. Everyone is intense, cheering for each other on the bench, high fives all around. Okay, here comes Hitchcock. She's a legit athlete, so I gotta play her honest. Whoops, better keep my hands in the passing lanes. I'm thinking she's going to fake left and pass right so I will just cheat a bit over here . . . yep, I got this steal.

Son of a bleep!!!

That is gonna leave a mark. Did I hear a pop when that ball ricocheted off my finger? I'm sure it is just another jam, but dang! This mother hurts.

Coach subs for me and Dad comes down to take a peek. After checking things over he concludes, "Let's put her back in and see how she does with it."

I sub back in, upon request, and am surprised at how my left arm pulls back instinctively. I catch, dribble, and pass all with only my right hand. Trisha subs back in for me. Uh-oh.

---

[40]Brady has a population of around 140 and is located along Interstate 15. The town is likely named for the Brady brothers—Charles A. Brady was a physician and Thomas E. Brady was an attorney. Brady consolidated with Power and Dutton in 2001 (ABC Fox Montana).

* * *

This X-ray room is cold anyway, and the ridiculous amount of sweat I produce while playing is now dry and causes me to shiver. Or is that shiver caused by another feeling? Doctor Buker, who somehow seems never to be in a hurry, despite his demanding position, ambles into the room. He is followed by our new PA, Jeff Chelmo. Everyone says how lucky we are to have such a capable medical staff up here in the middle of nowhere. Dr. Buker has been a doctor in Chester for something like a hundred years and delivered many of my classmates. In fact, he delivered many of my classmates' parents. I really like Doctor Buker. "Well, it's broken." His words punch me in the gut.

Did I mention I never liked Doctor Buker?

It feels like the air has been siphoned out of the room. Yep, I'm gonna faint. Luckily I catch the exam table on my way down and avoid full blackout mode. Like the time in second grade when I landed directly on my chin in Mrs. Cicon's music room, right on the concrete, when I got too hot while singing "Frère Jacques." Or that time in third grade in Mrs. Hanson's room after receiving the TB shot from our county nurse. At least now I can tell when a fainting spell is coming on.

"Darn, sweetie," Mom says as she rubs my back.

"How long until I can play again?" I ask cautiously, not sure I want to hear the answer.

"It's a nice, clean break," Doctor Buker answers, whatever that means, "so you will have to wear a cast for three weeks, and then we can go from there."

Three weeks. That is the rest of the regular season. Okay, at least it is upper body, so I can still run and stay in shape. And we have already beat the five teams we have left to play. Yes, it will be fine. This is just a minor detour. Coach is always saying how the season is a journey. We are still on track to reach our destination. Even though I believe all this to be true, I feel a tiny tear trickle.

Chapter 15

November 1999, sophomore year, season snags, Chester, Montana

Boys are so maddening. That is not a strong enough word. They are so complicated, so ridiculous, yet somehow they hold this power that is impossible to pinpoint. I do not know what is going on between Brent and me lately, but it feels strange; it feels new. I don't even see him with Mari anymore. They never even talk. What is up with that? I will have to ask Chasi about it. Why does it feel different when he winks at me when I walk by? He has always winked at me when he walks by.

Brent and I have been good friends since he moved here three years ago. I was in seventh grade, he in eighth, and we sat together in the clarinet section. He always teased that I should dump whoever I was going out with at the time—Colt, then Jeremiah—but he was just teasing, right? I would always be the one who ended up talking to him forever on the phone when we had sleepovers and called each other's boyfriends, but that's just how it is in junior high, right? "Going out" with someone in junior high means you maybe sit by each other at sporting events, but you don't actually talk to each other, you just talk to your boyfriend or girlfriend's friends.

Today at lunch he asked me what I'm doing after tonight's game in Blue Sky. Why would he even ask that? Everybody goes to the IGA for Subway after the games. It's not like we have a mall or arcade or whatever those "big city" kids do for fun. So why did he ask me?

* * *

Man it sucks not playing. I am sure getting good at taking stats, though. Michele, two. Maci, assist. Chasi, steal. Heidi, offensive rebound. Heidi, two. I wonder if I could keep tallies with my left hand and this beautiful blue cast. Carlane, steal. Whoops. Nope. Better use my right hand. Dang it! Blue Sky has forty-one. We'll be running at practice Monday for letting them score over forty. We really need to box them out.

"We need to box them out!" Coach VanDyke shouts.

See? Maybe I could be a coach someday. I always know what she is going to say. But right now I just want to play. Being benched with this injury is making me insane. And sitting on the bench with this skirt on is a huge flipping pain. I have never known how to wear "girl" clothes. At least this is the last weekend I have to sit since Monday I get my cast off. Ladies, don't let them score again! Ah, well, there's the buzzer: 77–43. Conference champs. First season goal, check. Next, Districts.

* * *

As I take another bite of my delicious Subway Cold Cut Combo, I see Brent walk in the glass door of Mike's IGA. I try to pay attention to the story Emily is telling Katy and Heidi, but my eyes keep following his movements. He stops before he steps up to the glass to dictate his sandwich order. His eyes sweep across the restaurant area and land on me. I hold his gaze for a second, attempt a casual "Oh-how-funny-that-we-happened-to-be-looking-at-each-other-at-the-same-moment-because-I wasn't-staring-at-you" smile, and pretend to go back to focusing on my sub and my friends' conversation. When I look up a few seconds later, he looks my direction again. Is he looking at me? I check behind my shoulder. A commercial for Little Trees air fresheners plays on the TV hanging behind the corner booth. I know Brent really likes cars, but it does seem like he is trying to catch my eye.

Then I look a few booths ahead of me. There's Mari, sitting with Andrea, Chasi, and Michele. My eyes flit back and forth between the two of them, and neither seems to acknowledge the other's existence. Brian must be right. They must have broken up. I just wonder why

Mari didn't tell me about it? I should ask her. Or I could just ask Michele instead.

When I look back at Brent, he motions with his head for me to come over. Or is he suffering from a neck cramp? No, I think he wants me to go over there. "Hey, guys, I'm going to run up and grab another chocolate milk. Anyone need anything?"

"No thanks, darlin'," Kaitlynn sweetly responds.

I attempt to sidle out of the booth as suavely as possible, which proves tricky, due to the fact that I am still lugging around this gaudy blue cast and also, I am not suave (that's pronounced 'swä-vā, I do believe).

When I reach the red-and-blue Slush Puppie machine I am surprised at how high-pitched my, "Hey, Brenton! What's going on?" greeting comes out.

"Hey, Jamie. How's the hand?" he offers.

"Oh, you know. Still stinking and shrinking inside this lovely cast," I retort.

He makes that cute snuff noise out his nose, where he keeps his mouth closed yet smiles, but doesn't quite snort. I like making him smile. He runs his fingers through his dirty-blond hair, with just a touch of a curl at the ends, and narrows his blue eyes slightly. Man, he has nice eyes. "What are you doing till curfew? Do you want to ride around with us for a while?" he asks as he motions toward Jason and Sean.

"Sure," I respond, without stopping to think.

Wait, why did I say yes? And why did I say it so quickly? What will I tell my girls? Wait a minute. I'm not doing anything wrong. We are friends. Girls and boys drive around together all the time. This isn't any different. My girls could even come with us. "Just let me grab my coat."

When I head back over to the booth area, the congregation of CHS students seem to be simultaneously transitioning from the Eating Stage to the Driving Around Stage of the night. Heidi, Kaitlynn, and Emily are all putting on their coats. Em hands me mine. "What should we do now?" she asks.

"Well, I'm gonna go drive around for a while with Sean and Jason. And Brent," I add with a shrug, as if an afterthought.

"I don't really feel like driving around," Emily confesses. "Let's rent a movie."

Heidi and Kaitlynn nod indifferently, turn to go with Emily, and sing, "Have fun!"

"You guys, too. See you at church!"[41]

I wave as they head to the other side of the store, turn to see the crowd has thinned considerably, and see Brent hanging back. Is he waiting for me? I stride toward him, and he moves ahead to hold the door for me. How chivalrous. We walk side by side out of the store, and then he opens the back door of his red vehicle; Jason and Sean are already in the front. "Isn't this your jalopy?" I ask as I crawl in the back seat.

This time Brent snorts. "It's a Jeep, not a jalopy."

"I know. It just reminds me of the *Berenstain Bears'* vehicle. Plus, I like that word. And why is Sean driving?"

"Ah, you have so much to learn about cars," Brent says while shaking his head, but smiling, "and everyone loves to drive the Jeep."

He slides in beside me and closes the door. Our knees rub together. I feel a jolt of electricity surge through my leg. That's a new feeling. Did he mean for our knees to touch? Well, he certainly hasn't pulled his leg away.

We drive west on Highway 2, passing the Grand Bar on our left, Superior Feeds on the right. My mind wanders to the email Brent sent me last week. (This whole Hotmail fad is so cool; I am obsessed with it.) Everyone is emailing, now that we all have our own Chester Public Schools (CPS) accounts, so when Brent sent a quick one to me, I didn't think twice about it. Now that I think about it again, though, I remember that it did open with, "Hey, beautiful."

Beautiful. *Beautiful?* Me? I figured it was just a fun greeting, like how my Grandma Joyce always writes, "Hey, babe" to start her letters.

Maybe not, though. Could he really think that? People could describe me in lots of ways: outgoing, positive, hardworking, likes everyone, always ready to laugh, but beautiful is not an adjective that

---

[41]Heidi, Chasi, Kaitlynn, Michele, Maci, Mari, Amanda, and I led worship at church bimonthly our junior and senior years. We called ourselves the "Celestial Coyotes."

comes to my mind. (Except for Dad, of course, but he's biased.) I mean, it was only a few years ago when those girls were dying of laughter and pointing at me at the Great Falls Dodgers stadium because they thought a boy was going into the girls' bathroom. My paper-thin, cardboard-box brown hair that I didn't even know how to put into a ponytail until eighth grade isn't much to look at. It would not suffice to describe mine as a forehead, more like a fivehead. Not to mention, all my friends are way above average in the looks department. But maybe Brent sees something I don't?

Sean and Jason belt out "What's My Age Again," but my mind is muddled as I feel a finger brush against the back of my neck. I realize this is not by accident, and my neck tingles. The sensation seeps through my shoulders and out my toes. Should I look at him? No. What if I do and he leans in? What will Sean and Jason think? What *do* Sean and Jason think? Why does it always matter what everybody thinks? Okay, it is getting hot in here.

"Closing Time" just finishes on the mixed tape, as if our cue. "It's 11:43, boys," I announce, as I snap out of the trance Brent's touch somehow put me under.

"I know none of you wants to deal with the wrath of Mr. Graham," I continue, with a response of short, vigorous head nods of agreement.

Sean turns onto Main Street, hangs a right at Monroe, and provides me with curbside service, careful to park nice and legal in front of our drivers education teacher's front door. "Thanks for the ride," I call politely as I fumble with the door handle and attempt to scooch out.

My un-casted hand is shaky, and the handle isn't giving. "Here, I'll get your door." Brent leans over and reaches across my lap.

I breathe in his scent—Extra peppermint gum, Irish Spring soap, and Old Spice deodorant—as his arm grazes the tops of my legs. Why does his touch make me feel like that sound of a fly getting toasted by a bug zapper? With one last stomach flip, I step onto the sidewalk and offer a last smile and quiet, "Thanks. Night."

"Night," he replies softly, looking directly into my eyes.

I feel those intense light-blue eyes follow me as I concentrate on not tripping up the two front steps that lead to our house. I will myself to keep my eyes forward as I pull open the screen and twist the brass handle on the unwieldy front door. I lower my left shoulder, shove, and thankfully the door gives fairly easily. I sneak a look over my shoulder toward the fire engine-red Jeep. I watch the back lights fade away. Then I let out the breath I did not know I was holding, turn to go inside, and wonder what in the world is happening as the door snaps closed behind me.

* * *

"What do you mean it healed in the wrong place?" Mom asks the doctor while I try to stave off the sudden, overwhelming urge to vomit.

Doctor Buker calmly explains again, "Sometimes this happens. That ring finger knuckle has shifted down a few centimeters. See how it sits lower than the pinky knuckle? Also, the other end of the bone that broke is healed, but see how it bulges out slightly, near her wrist?"

"So what does this mean?" Mom presses, clearly concerned.

"Well"—his square-framed glasses raise in unison with his bushy gray eyebrows as he sucks in a breath through his open mouth—"it means she needs to see a hand specialist in Great Falls."

I open my eyes as his statement hits me in the gut. I really don't like how his words keep doing this. "And then what?" I ask in a panic.

"Will I be able to play in Districts this weekend?"

His forced half smile and thoughtful head tilt bring me no comfort. "There will be no basketball this weekend."

There's that wave of nausea again. Yep, I'm gonna faint.

* * *

Wednesday, the hand specialist says an option would be to rebreak my hand and set it again, so the knuckle would move back up to its original position. This news of course induces my gag reflex. Well that sounds like an awesome idea. This so-called "specialist" thinks it is a good idea to break my hand again? On purpose?

I look over pleadingly at Mom, and it looks like she is thinking the same thing. She asks, "Is there is another option?"

Turns out, even though the knuckle looks a little wonky, the break is healed. Rebreaking it would be purely cosmetic. Hmm, let me think. Would I like to have someone purposely break my hand and wear a cast for four more weeks so my knuckle can look "normal?" It's not like the left ring finger is a big deal. My future husband won't care what my hand looks like; he will love me for my kind heart and hilarious personality. So thank you, but no. I will take the wonky-looking hand.

* * *

The 10-C district tournaments this year are, how can I describe this, anticlimactic? Since we enter the conference as the number one seed, we are again granted a bye on Thursday. Then my girls crush the Brady Bulldogs 75–28 for the semifinals and close out the weekend with a 76–32 victory over the Sunburst Refiners. I of course again rock at taking stats, and do my best to sit ladylike in yet another skirt. Second season goal, check. Next, Divisionals. Where I can guarantee I will not be wearing a skirt.

District 10-C championship, November 6, 1999. My blue cast is hidden behind the trophy.

Heidi, me, and Maci, District champs

* * *

Last week the focus remained on my hand and the tournament. I meant to have a chat with Mari about what was going on with her and Brent, but things were so hectic I just didn't get a chance. Plus, Chasi and Katy assured me that Brent would have told me if they hadn't broken up, and that clearly he likes me now. That sounds airtight.

Now it is Sunday evening, and I am at Heidi's house. We make popcorn and start *Armageddon* on the basement TV. Heidi and Matt have been dating a couple months now and are cozy on one couch. I hand them a bowl of popcorn then stride across the room where Brent sits on the other couch. I hand Brent the other bowl, and he pats the spot next to him. Right next to him. I fold my right leg under myself as I sit and immediately notice how nice it feels to have our shoulders pressed together. Moments after Bruce Willis discovers the impossible truth that he is the world's only hope, Brent turns and asks me, "How is your hand feeling?"

I instinctively look down at my left hand, then turn it over for further examination. "Well, it still looks a lot smaller than my right one," I state what is obvious at first glance, "but they say it will be back to normal in a few more weeks."

Brent's eyes linger on my hand.

Stomach flip.

"Poor hand," he says with a pout, then takes it, puny and pathetic, gently into his.

We continue watching the movie in silence, save for Matt's sporadic commentary on things like Liv Tyler's lips and Ben Affleck's rugged good looks. Brent has to leave before he can find out if they succeed in digging the hole on the asteroid deep enough, and I walk him upstairs. What happens next keeps playing over and over again in my head, each time causing my tummy to tingle.

At the door I say brightly, "Have a good night, Brenton. Drive safe."

He finishes tying his shoe, stands back up straight, and turns to face me, a determined look on his face. Before I can think of anything else to say, his fingertips dance around the small of my back before clasping together. I follow his lead and wrap my arms around his neck. I pull on a golden curl that lies softly halfway down his neck, wondering if my touch causes the same response in him as his causes in me. "Crap, I do not know what I am doing," I think to myself.

Luckily, my internal voice that sometimes plagues me with doubt and concern is quickly quelled as his confident embrace pulls me in for our first kiss.

* * *

I am the worst friend in the world. What is wrong with me? I remember Mrs. Rasmussen saying something about teenagers having prefrontal cortexes that aren't fully developed which hinders our decision-making. Maybe she is on to something.

Now today at school, I find a note from Mari regarding our friendship:

1/10/99

Dear Jamie,

Our friendship shouldn't end over some stupid boy. I was mystified and ticked when I heard about you and Brent, but I've taken this time to think. We are not best friends (you and me), but we are good friends who shouldn't be affected by this. I'm just going to ignore the "Brent" part of you. I just want an apology, and I will try to forgive and forget.

Mari

I can't decide whether this note comforts me or not. She says she wants an apology. That, I can do. I swiftly pen her a sincere apology and ask if she wants to talk about things. I end by again telling her again how sorry I am, how stupid I have been, that I should have talked to her first, and that I would never intentionally hurt a friend. I push the folded note in her locker through a slat at the top and feel better already. We have been friends since preschool, after all. Our friendship will make it through this, right?

The next seven days blur by. I concentrate so much on the fact that I am practicing with the team again that it almost blocks out the fact that the only time Mari talks to me is when forced to. Almost.

Chapter 16

*November 18–20, 1999, sophomore year, Northern C
Divisional Tournament, Great Falls, Montana*

My hand feels okay, and the wrap keeps my finger feeling stable and reassures me. I feel like I am playing at about 90%. Tonight we open our divisional tourney play against Blue Sky, a great draw for us as we beat them decidedly in the first two matchups, first by forty-two and next by thirty-four. During starting lineups, I notice Megan cheers the most when my name is announced. That is pretty incredible character seeing as she was the one starting in my place the last seven games and has to turn the spot back over to me tonight.

Michele tips it right to Maci off the jump ball, then Maci pops it right over to Heidi on the right wing who makes a textbook fast-break bounce pass across the paint to me for a left-handed layup. Might as well see how this hand is going to hold up. I stutter to get position as I time Heidi's pass, go up off my right foot and . . . off the backboard and in. I still got it.

The tournament environment is electric, and those familiar feelings flood me as I trap on the wing in the frontcourt of our press with Maci. She grabs the tipped ball and hits Devan for an easy bucket. We immediately reset into our 1–3–1 press positions, and I know in that instant this game is ours.

Everything feels back to normal. Finally. The final score is Good Guys 79, Eagles 36. I lead scoring tonight with fifteen points and six steals. All eleven other players score, too. That is something we pride ourselves in, the fact that anyone could lead in scoring on any given

The shirt we held up and read before every game, hanging on a mirror in our hotel room. The shirt reads: "Amazing what can be accomplished when no one cares who gets the credit."

night. Each player is a threat and none of us care who scores. That's why, before every game, Coach holds up my favorite T-shirt that reads, *"Amazing what can be accomplished when no one cares who gets the credit."*

* * *

It's Friday night, and we are in the first semifinal contest against the Denton Trojans. Denton holds a special place in my heart because it is where we lived when I was born.[42] We moved to Chester only a few months after, but return annually for the famous (or is it infamous?) Denton summer softball tournament and keep in touch with several families who still live there. This includes the Edwards family who has three daughters: Sara, Kelley, and Katie. Kelley and Katie are in the starting lineups tonight and they, along with Buckentin, combine for a dangerous trio.[43]

The game starts out as usual, with Michele winning the tip and getting it over to Devan. Devan immediately passes up to Maci who whips it across the lane to me. I pump fake and go up, but Katie's giant hand catches my attempt. Stuffed. That's embarrassing. We transition into the defense Coach Schlepp designed for tonight, with Maci and me double-teaming Katie. Unlucky for us, however, Kelley is scrappy and relentless, and has a radar for offensive rebounds. When we huddle in after the first quarter, losing 13–24, it is clear we are going to have to try a new strategy.

---

[42] I was born forty-five miles away in Lewistown because Denton, as with many small towns, doesn't have a hospital to deliver babies.

[43] Katie goes on to be an all-star for the University of Montana Lady Grizzlies, and I get to play with Kelley at Rocky Mountain College. Even after all these years, and after meeting lots and lots of new people, I still maintain that Kelley Edwards (Rice) is the funniest person I have ever met.

The second quarter goes a little better. We have possession and run "sideline" on the first inbound.* Devan pass fakes to me, then hits Michele at the deep corner after cutting across Heidi on the block. Michele drops it in to Heidi who in turn drops in a smooth turnaround jumper. We transition to full-court man defense, with the intention of keeping Katie's scoring down to a minimum, but no longer with the goal of completely containing her—the first quarter revealed that plan to be too risky. This strategy seems to work, but we still enter the locker room at halftime down 22-35.

"Okay, we have been down at half before."

Not by this much, I can't help but think, but decide to keep that happy little nugget to myself. Besides, I counter my own negative thoughts creeping in, it's only thirteen points. Seven more baskets, and we are fine.

"This third quarter is crucial. We need to come out with intensity and focus. We will pounce on them immediately. Play confident, not tentative. I know we have focused a lot on how we will defend this game, but we also *have to score*. You are all capable of scoring. If you are open, take your shot. When you miss, keep your head up and make a stop defensively. Let's start in our three-quarter-court 1-3-1 trap. Watch for the signal to switch it back up. We just have to chip away. Just chip away."

We all nod our heads with total buy-in. "Alright, ladies. We got this!" Megan leads us to our huddle, and we run out, chins up, for the second half. Our half.

The 1-3-1 trap throws them off, and we start the third quarter with two quick steals, capitalizing on both. Down nine. We got this.

We win the third quarter 14-3, and go into the fourth only down 36-38. I just need to be careful because I have three fouls.

What did I just say?! I need to be careful! Dang it. Fourth foul and only thirteen seconds have ticked off the clock. I really do not

---

*Sideline - Sideline out of bounds play where two guards line up just behind half-court. Two other players line up on the low blocks. The player on the block opposite ball-side cuts across the key and uses the other player as a screen. Inbounder passes to cutter, who looks to pass in to player on the block who is now posting up after screening. We had a few variations of this play, including "Sideline Swing-It" where the inbounder cut in, then the ball would swing all the way around the arc, then the inbounder would receive the ball for a shot on the baseline.

think that was a reach. Alright, can't control the referee. Just play smart.

It is back and forth for six straight minutes. Maci calls "Baylor."[45] She hits Michele on the right elbow, and I make the backdoor cut.[46] The pass isn't there, so I cut through to the opposite wing, creating a clearout opportunity for Michele. Chele pump fakes, rips high, takes a dribble and, yes! Finally we tie it at forty-two. Not only that, Kelley fouled out on our last possession. Without her in the paint, we should dominate the boards.

Back on defense. Okay, stay low. Move your feet. Play her straight up. Ooh, I know she is going to cross over right . . . now.

Tweet!

Why did he blow that whistle? When I turn back to look I see the sign for a blocking foul. Then the ref holds up first one finger, then two. I look up at the scoreboard to be sure. Tears threaten as I see it: Player - 12, Fouls - 5. In a daze, I try to hold it together as I make my way to the bench. The whole Denton team jogs over to give me high fives. It looks like they are telling me good game, but I really know they are secretly thinking, "You're outta here, sister! Good riddance!"

All my teammates stand and pat my back as I find a spot on the pine. No use moping. We still have time left, and we can totally do this. I need to be just as poised and intense on the bench as in the game. Have to be willing to fill any role. That's the beauty of who we are, after all. We don't rely on one all-star. Everyone contributes. "Come on, guys! We got this!" I shout, and when I hear myself say it, I believe it.

Only 1:46 to go. It is back and forth. Katie scores again to put them up two, but then we answer back with a short-corner bucket by Maci off "swing-it." Katie pulls up from nineteen feet nine inches

---

[45]Baylor ("B" or "2") – One of our "one-four high" set plays. Point guard enters the ball to one of the players at the elbows. If the player on the right elbow receives the entry pass, the wing on that same side cuts for a backdoor. If the backdoor isn't there, the wing cuts to the opposite deep corner and high post looks to shoot or drive.

[46]Backdoor - A classic play in basketball where a player cuts away from the basket to get open, but when the defender gets a hand between the ball and the cutter, the cutter pivots and sprints toward the basket using the "back door" to the hoop.

and . . . swish. Then we turn it over on a too-long lob attempt. Becky hits Katie again and . . . layup and the foul. Seeing as Katie has a ridiculous free throw streak going, it is not ideal to foul her.[47] Now we are down six.

We run "sideline break" and get it into Carlane for an easy two. A minute later, Michele drives in for another bucket, but we just cannot hold on and end up having to foul. As I watch the seconds tick down to zero, I feel like I am watching the world in slow motion. Three, two, one.

Lose, 48–52.

* * *

There is still hope. Since it is not yet the state tournament, we can win our next two games, put ourselves into third place, and then there is a possibility for a Monday night challenge game. If we challenge and win, we still qualify for State as the number-two seed from our division. So all we have to do now is move forward and focus on the next two games. We most certainly are not going to lose two games in one weekend.

The only possible hitch in this plan is that in order to challenge, Denton has to win the tournament. Here are a couple things I don't love: losing, and rooting for a team that just beat us.

* * *

We come to play Saturday and whip both the Winifred Red Raiders and the Belt Lady Huskies by more than twenty. Okay, we've done our part. Now come on, Denton, you gotta beat Big Sandy.

My stomach is twisted like a pretzel as I find my family in the stands for the championship game. Grandma Joyce gives me a kiss and Aunt Kathy rubs my back. My family is always there. My aunts and uncles and grandparents drove from Big Timber and Bozeman to be here this weekend, but I feel like I have let them down. A tiny rational voice inside tells me they are proud of me no matter what, but I can't help but think how everyone expected us to be playing in this game.

---

[47]Katie Edwards' consecutive free throw streak would later end at sixty-two in a row.

At halftime I move to the top-tier bleachers and find my girls. Nobody speaks. Ritter is shooting the lights out and Katie Edwards, unlike last night, can't hit a thing. Denton trails in the first three quarters. This is the worst. I hate this helpless feeling, counting on someone else to determine our chance to advance. Denton pulls within one. Bitz hits a deep three, and I hear deep sighs all around me. As the final buzzer sounds, we trudge dejectedly back to our locker room.

The heavy locker room door swings closed decisively, like this season. Chasi, who often wears her emotions on her sleeves, cries openly. Maci, who is generally pretty composed, hugs Chas with tears streaking down her cheeks as well. This causes a chain reaction. We all just hug and cry, cry and hug. After a few minutes of this, we wordlessly join into a huddle. "Heads up, ladies," Carlane charges.

"Coyotes on three," Megan cues. "One, two, three—"

"Coyotes," we sniffle pathetically.

I guess we better go out and accept our subpar third-place divisional trophy.

As I walk out to the floor I catch Brent's eye in the crowd. I recall the phone conversation we had just after our night together at Heidi's. We agreed even though we like each other, it is best for us not to be together. It feels too complicated right now. Things just did not start out right.

I break eye contact and sneak a look over at Mari, walking onto the court beside Michele. It is pretty obvious my relationship with Mari will never be the same. I apologized, she accepted, but things have changed. The only times we talk is when obligated to, either in practice, a game, or during a class at school. I am such an idiot. I screwed everything up. Now I have lost a best friend, a boyfriend, messed up my hand, and blew another chance to win State. How can things get any worse?

Chapter 17

November 26, 1999, sophomore year, Chester, Montana

I roll over in bed to check the time on my clock radio. Quarter past nine. I will just sleep for a few more minutes. Or a few more hours. My window gives me a glimpse of the gloomy, dreary day outside. That is appropriate for how I feel this morning, and how I have felt every day this week. I still cannot believe our season is over. This is not the way it was supposed to be.

Careful not to exert too much energy, I lean and dangle the top half of my body over my bed to reach my basketball binder. I pull it up, open to the first page, and scan its contents. It is covered with quotes about winners: *"Face it, nobody owes you a living."*

"Excuses are for losers."

"If you aren't willing to work for your goals, don't expect others to."

The last one, *"Winners meet life's challenges head on. They give it all they've got, knowing there are no guarantees, and they never think it is too late or too early to start. Time has no favorites, and it will pass whether you act or not,"* I read several times.

After I take a second to process, I continue to flip through. I read through some sage advice from John Wooden, characteristics of a championship team, individual and team goals, stats for the season, and last land on the letter Coach added at the team meeting on Monday.

The Yellow Sports Bra

Jamie #12,

Traveling on the basketball super-highway with the Chester Coyotes has been a lot of fun. Congratulations on a 22–2 record, conference champs, district champs, a third-place finish at Divisionals, and for being selected first team all-conference and second team all-state. Wow! Fantastic job, Jamie Graham.

Through our travels we grew as a team. A team is successful because of teamwork and togetherness. Together we set goals and work hard to reach them. Together we practice and play hard. Together we sweat, we laugh, we cry. Together, we are the Chester Coyotes.

We were all disappointed, maybe devastated would be a better word, that we didn't reach our goal of divisional champs. We were hoping to travel further on the BB highway. We hit a detour, not a dead end. So it is time to regroup, refocus, set new goals, and just get after it.

Jamie, you are a very talented athlete. You bring a lot of energy and excitement to the gym and to the team. You are a joy to coach. You play hard on both ends of the court and contribute so much with your shooting ability and tenacious defense. You are an excellent ball-handler and did a nice job of being the floor general for the Coyotes. The behind the back passes were awesome! Do not let go of your commitment to excel, your determination, your work ethic, and your dreams.

Sincerely,
Coach VanDyke

Well Coach seems to be somehow staying positive. Her encouragement lifts my spirits slightly, but mostly I still feel depressed.

The piercing ring of the phone interrupts my pity party. It is likely not one of my friends at this hour. Too early. I let Dad answer. After his, "Hello," I don't hear him say anything for a long time. Maybe it's a telemarketer. No, he would have found a way to politely hang up by now. An unsettling, portentous sensation creeps into my stomach as I slide slowly out of bed, swinging my feet for a second before standing. For some reason I feel like I need to brace myself. I shuffle down the hall into my parents' room. Dad hangs up and turns slowly toward me. The look in his eye confirms this feeling of dread in my gut.

I mean to ask him what's wrong, but the words don't come.

"There's been an accident," he says, barely audible. "It's Annie."

My stomach drops. The room is swirling around me, and Dad's voice is garbled with words like, "driving too fast," "drinking," "dark," "no seat belt," "prayer chain," "unconscious."

Dad pulls me in. Tears stream down my cheeks uncontrollably. When he hugs me tight I always feel loved, safe, like everything is going to be okay. Why does this time feel like everything might not?

* * *

The next two days pass by in a blur. There are lots of phone calls, hugs, tears, lots of prayers and wondering. With so many people exchanging so much information, and the status of Annie's condition still unknown, emotions are high, and the town is reeling. When one family struggles, everyone struggles. There is conflict and tension among folks around here of course, just like anywhere, but when times are tough, people pull together.

As far as I know, Annie is still unresponsive with broken ribs, broken vertebrae, a messed-up shoulder, a lung either punctured or collapsed, and possible brain swelling. When I think about all of this, my breathing speeds up and all my thoughts swirl together. Finally I get in a full breath and calm down enough to reflect on today.

I spent most of the day with my girls. We cried a lot at first, but then reminded each other that she is in good care, and there is always hope. Then we shared Annie stories, reminiscing about her shenanigans in the locker room, her contagious giggle, how gorgeous she is, how she won us the game against Big Sandy at Divisionals. Chasi is having an especially hard time, as she and Annie have such a special bond. We hear over and over again that these first forty-eight hours are critical, so now all we can do is pray for recovery.

My thoughts are again interrupted by the telephone. It's after nine o'clock in the evening, so it must be important. Instinctively I reach for the receiver on my bedstead, only to pull back slightly. I am not sure I want to hear what the caller on the other end may have to say. Gathering myself with a deep breath I answer cautiously, "Hello?"

"Hi, Jamie." It's Brent.

We haven't talked for a week, and when I hear his voice I become acutely aware of this intense feeling that floods me, this feeling of wanting to be near him now.

He gets right to it. "I just talked to Carlane and Danielle, and they say Annie only has twenty-four hours to live."

Silence. I do not even know how to respond. After what feels like hours Brent softly asks, "Would you like me to come get you?"

After realizing he can't see my slow nod, I finally manage to squeak a small, "Yes."

Minutes later I hear the rumble of his blue 1981 Oldsmobile Cutlass outside our front door.[48] My parents are at the Hamels' house and Jeff is with Maci, who he is dating again, so I scribble quick on a sticky note, *Driving around. Be back by 11:45*, press it down at the designated Sticky Note Area on the kitchen counter and switch off the light. (Two rules in the Graham household are to (1) leave notes telling where you are and when you will be home, and (2) *always* turn off the lights.) I grab my hoodie from our old squishy brown faux-leather chair in the front room, switch off the light, and pull open the heavy faded-blue front door.

I have been on autopilot since hanging up the phone, but now the cold air slaps me in the face, abruptly forcing me back to reality. My lower lip trembles as I tread down the two front steps and up the sidewalk to Brent's car. He gives me a meaningful look when I sit down beside him, then wordlessly shifts into drive. We end up parked behind the bleachers at the football field, right on the south edge of town. He looks over at me with sad eyes and holds out his right arm. I slide across the sticky leather on the front seat, burrow into him, and sob.

---

[48]Brent, his dad Bruce, and his younger twin brothers Matthew and Mitchell are all obsessed with cars. Because of this obsession I now know phrases like, "suicide doors," "three-on-a-tree," and the apparent importance of knowing the make, model, and year of all vehicles. This is why I refer to the vehicle now as a 1981 Oldsmobile Cutlass, instead of "that old blue rickety car."

* * *

Sunday morning finds me puffy-eyed and exhausted. I stand in the shower and face the faucet, letting the water spray over my face. I hope the water will rinse away my tears, but it seems somehow to produce more. Eyes squeezed shut, my tears mix with the water, and my mind is mixed with a million thoughts. There is a tiny knock at my bathroom door and Mom calls, "Jame, Chasi just called. It sounds like Annie squeezed a hand this morning, so they are going to observe her a little longer. Chas says her mom will drive you two to the hospital after you teach Sunday school to see her."

I don't know exactly what to do with this news. I manage a garbled, "Okay!" through the running water.

* * *

A few hours later Chasi, her mom Gay, and I step off an elevator to the third floor of Great Falls Benefis Hospital. We have been chatting excitedly for all ninety miles from Chester to here. As soon as we enter the waiting room, though, the chatting stops. Annie's room is just to the left of the elevator, and I warily peek in. I see the white hospital bed in the middle of the unfriendly hospital room. There she is, but . . . is she there? Then I turn back and take in the scene. Family members and friends embrace, and we hear Gail explain to her teary daughter, Kayla, "There is nothing more they can do."

There is nothing more they can do? Wait, she squeezed a hand this morning. She responded. We came today filled with hope that she would wake up. What about all those prayers? I have been praying nonstop for God to save Annie ever since the call Friday morning. This doesn't make any sense. Colt, Annie's youngest brother and our classmate, is sitting in a hard wooden chair bent over in the corner, shoulders racking softly, head cradled in his hands. What now? What do I do?

I bite the inside of my cheek as a dizzy feeling overwhelms me. It seems like I am watching a TV drama on mute. This cannot be real life. Somehow I watch myself walk over to Colt, lay my hand gently on his shoulder, take him in for a tight hug and whisper, "I'm sorry, Colt. I am so, so sorry."

93

Annie Nell Diemert
January 22, 1981– November 29, 1999

This is the fifth funeral I have been to for a kid, and I still don't understand.[49] Eighteen is technically an adult I guess, but she was just in school with us, she was just playing sports and doing homework and going to prom and I still don't understand. I know this world is broken and sinful and God gives us free will, but doesn't God promise to love us and protect us and give us peace and joy?

Nothing makes any sense.

Today is the day we are supposed to be playing for the state championship. We are not supposed to be doing this. Anything but this.

Coach Hamel passes out programs as we enter the packed sanctuary. There is a row saved for us, her former teammates, as well as her classmates, and I feel eyes upon us as we fill the pew. Then comes her family, and finally the casket. I notice Lonestar's song "Smile" playing softly over the stereo system and close my eyes, remembering walking into the locker room on Annie's senior night—her smile. That familiar swell in my throat returns. During volleyball and track last year we always listened to her tape with "When I See You Smile" and "Smile." This song brings me comfort yet somehow simultaneously buries me in sorrow.

> *Give me a chance to bow out gracefully*
> *'Cause that's how I want you to remember me*
> *I'm gonna smile, 'cause I want to make you happy*
> *Laugh, so you can't see me cry*

---

[49] The other youth funerals our town endured in that 90s decade included second grader Courtney Frederickson, my classmate and friend Colt Frederickson's younger sister; fourth grader Brent Perdue (as well as both his parents, Jerry and Donna Perdue); Tony Johnson (Jeremiah Johnson's older brother); and Magen Wickum. Magen died of cancer and was a close friend of Annie's. The other three were all involved in car accidents.

I'm gonna let you go in style
And even if it kills me
I'm gonna smile.

God, why did this happen? Did you really need another angel? Is there really a reason for this? Because that doesn't make any sense to me. This doesn't make any sense.

* * *

I open my eyes, blink, and look around my bedroom. It's 8:05 p.m. Did I eat dinner? Why was I sleeping during dinner? Suddenly memories of the afternoon flood me, and I remember the funeral. It wasn't a nightmare, but it sure feels like one.

There is a tiny knock on my door and Mom comes in. She sits on the side of my bed and rubs my back, just like when I was little. "How do you feel, sweetheart?"

I don't answer right away. That is a very complicated question.

"Mom?" I ask. "I keep hearing people say God took Annie because he needs more angels, or that everything happens for a reason. Do you think that's true?"

Neither of us speaks for a minute.

"I don't know, sweetie."

I look expectantly at her, and she goes on. "God doesn't make bad things happen. Bad things happen because this world is broken. And in this broken world, some things are just hard."

She pauses, trying to find the words. "Some things just suck."

Despite the grief I feel, this causes a slight tug at the corners of my mouth since "suck" sounds like a cuss word coming from my sweet mom.

"I also believe there is always hope," she continues, "even in tragedy. Someday God will wipe away every tear. Meanwhile, it's okay to be angry, and it's okay to cry."

I think about this and marvel at how bonkers life is. Our neighbor Joe has stocked up on canned goods and other supplies in preparation for this whole Y2K thing and the supposed end of the world as we know it. Well if that is the case and the world is going to end, then I have a few questions for God. So bring it on.

Third Quarter

No discipline seems pleasant at the time, but painful. Later on, however, it produces a harvest of righteousness and peace for those who have been trained by it. Therefore, strengthen your feeble arms and weak knees. Make level paths for your feet.
—Hebrews 12:11-13

2000 Chester Lady Coyotes

Chapter 18

Jan–Sep 2000, junior year, reflections, Chester, Montana

I lie backward on my bed, knees on my pillow, feet in the air. I prop myself up on my elbows and read through journal entries and notes from these past months.

January 1, 2000: Yesterday was supposed to be a crazy day. There were all kinds of predictions about computer crashes and lots of stuff I don't get. Last night we were at Heidi's house watching movies, and Matt said that since it was 9:00 pm here, it was already tomorrow in other parts of the world. So it looks like the world will go on after all.

January 5, 2000: Yesterday wasn't too memorable. I can't think of anything significant that occurred. We had practice, but I don't recall it, I had dinner, but I don't recall what, and I went to LYO.[50] I remember what we did there! Hallelujah! We played a game called "Electricity," and my team always got killed. Jason, Maci, and I even tried to cheat, but we somehow still lost. We got to have ice cream, and it was delicious. I mixed caramel in my vanilla. Mmmmm. Thank you, Jesus, for ice cream and games!

Today I had piano lessons at 6:00 and play practice at 7:00. I called Brenton around 9:00, and he seems kinda down this week. He says he is hating school and not getting along with his parents and said, "I can't wait for college," and stuff like that. Not quite sure what to do with that. I hate that he gets so depressed sometimes but don't know how I can fix it.

---

[50]Lutheran Youth Organization—this was our weekly youth group at church.

January 8, 2000: Thursday we had our first conference volleyball game versus Blue Sky. It went 15-0, 15-2, 15-1.[51] Even though we never practice volleyball in the off-season, we somehow still manage to romp everyone in our conference. Which is fun. Volleyball really is so fun to play, and our coaches are so great.[52] Then I had play practice right after the game. I hate that I have all the same friends and go to all the same places as Mari, but we never talk. Our class had to work concessions tonight, so I worked the JV game with Mrs. Rasmussen, Emily, and Kayla. I ate too much flipping junk food and felt kinda crappy during our game. Note to self: don't eat junk food before exercising.

January 22, 2000: This morning I went to the junior high basketball games versus Valier and both teams won—yay! Then I went to the Lions Club ice skating party with Kayla and Amanda and had hot dogs and hot chocolate. Delicious. Our bus left for Shelby at 2:45, and we didn't get home until 11:00. Our match went to five games, and it was crazy and nerve-racking. The first game we won by quite a lot, then we played crappy and lost the second. The third we were down 3-14, and then we came back and won 16-14. It was sweet. Then the fourth game was 14-7, and we somehow lost 17-19. We played rally for the fifth game and won 15-10. It was quite tiring but really good for us. On the way home Mari read this joke book, and she and I actually talked and laughed for once so I was very happy.

January 30, 2000: Maci and I taught Sunday school this morning, so that was of course fun and hilarious as usual. Those little kids are so cute. I brought donuts and chocolate milk to celebrate Maci's (and Mari's, but she was not there to partake) 16th birthday (five days late, but it's never too late for donuts). The kids of course loved it, and Jessica asked if they had donuts when Jesus was on Earth. I told her that is a good question, but as far as I can figure, Jesus basically dined

---

[51]These were the days before rally scoring; in order to score, your team had to have the serve.

[52]Coach Don Van Dessel was head volleyball coach in Chester from 1988-2002. He coached the team that won Chester's only volleyball state championship in 1992. Steve Hamel was head volleyball coach in 1984-85 and assistant volleyball coach from 1990-1992, 1994-2002.

on bread and fish. Jessica said, all serious, "Well he missed out." I laughed so hard milk shot out my nose.

February 11, 2000: Kaitlynn Rae's 16th birthday today! I got her a cute framed picture of us and some scrumptious chocolates. Maci and I wore poodle skirts to school today, so that was fun. They happen to be our costumes for the play, but we decided to get some extra use out of them. I walked downtown to the B 'n W with Brian, Chance, and PJ. Chance bought me some Corn Nuts, so that was nice. Then we joined a bunch of our classmates at our usual lunch hour spot, on the cold concrete stairs between the gyms.

Em drove me home after school today, and her car went completely crazy, like it was possessed or something. All she did was turn on the key, and it started driving by itself. Nothing happened even when she slammed her foot on the brake. Luckily she thought to pull out the key, and we coasted to a stop. And also luckily we were not parked facing the sturdy brick school building where we usually park. Freaky!

Tonight Heidi, Emily, Amanda, Maci, and I rode with Mama Jude to the boys' basketball game in Rudyard.[53] Brent wore the green suit he is wearing for the play before his game, and he looked like a leprechaun. That will be weird if I start being attracted to leprechauns. The boys' game was rough. They were tied at the end of the third, but then they got rocked in the fourth. Jeff had eight three-pointers, though, and some of them were like 24–25 feet out, so that was sweet. Our grandparents are all here this weekend, so we get to go to church and then brunch with them tomorrow. That will be wonderful. They are all so cute.

February 14, 2000: I gave Brenton some candy and wrote him this poem for Valentine's Day:

> *Happy Valentine's Day, Brenton*
> *You're as lucky as can be*
> *You're funny, smart, and sweet*
> *Oh, wait! I messed up, that's me*

---

[53]"Mama Jude" is what we all called Mari and Maci's mom, Judy Tempel.

He gave me a cute little Pluto stuffed animal and Mickey and Minnie keychain, then a note that said he hoped I would like it because he knows how much I love Disney. So sweet!

February 25, 2000: Chasi Lee's Sweet Sixteen! What did I get her for a present? A giant bag of tortilla chips and a bucket of our favorite cheese dip, obviously. I went to the gym with Chelers after school for the C and JV matches. We sat by Adam, John, and Matt and could not stop laughing. Those three are like the funniest people I know. They would really like to know why we don't wear spandex like the Harlowton volleyball team. Brent was at the games, too, but for some reason he would not even look at me. I have seen him walking toward Mari's house at lunchtime lately. What is up with that? Sometimes things can seem just so happy and great between us, and then five seconds later everything feels confusing and dramatic and quite frankly, exhausting. He says he doesn't want to hurt me, so what does he think I am feeling when he ignores me? I know he never wanted to hurt Mari either, though, so maybe now he is torn? Pure craziness.

March 11, 2000: We got second in Divisionals tonight, to Harlowton. We beat them in the morning match to go into the finals, but we struggled returning their serves tonight. Those Jones twins are so athletic and so flippin' strong! I wish I were that ripped. Better keep lifting. Next weekend is State in Lewistown. Let's try something new this time at State and not lose. It's not basketball, but it would be nice to win a championship in some sport.

March 18, 2000: We are gonna have to pull our heads out our bottoms if we want to be champions one of these days. We almost had Richey but couldn't hold on. Then we flat-out choked in the loser-out against Circle. Where in the blank is Circle anyway?[54]

Now we have track to look forward to. Running on a red cinder track with spring winds whipping, trying to avoid snow piles. Awesome. Not to mention the smell of either the sewer or the pig

---

[54]Turns out, Circle is super close to Richey. It is a farming and ranching community in northeastern Montana. It is located near the Big Sky Back Country Byway where the two major rivers in Montana, the Yellowstone and Missouri, meet. (Montana, Circle, 2019). It also boasts a unique tourist attraction in the McCone County Museum, featuring hundreds of mounted birds and animals displayed as well as a pile of dinosaur replicas out front (Plates, 2015).

farm, depending on the way the wind is blowing. At least it will keep us in shape and get us stronger for basketball. Dad says he thinks I should try the hurdles. That might be fun.

March 27, 2000: My 16th birthday! I shot around before school this morning for a while. I love shooting when no one else is in the gym. I don't recall much of the content in any of my classes today. Matt made me a card in English, and Ryah, Sean, and Jason sang me "Happy Birthday" at lunch. So sweet. We got turkey and cheese stromboli for lunch, which is one of my favorites. I like to think that Debbie made it just for me. Kayla, Amanda, and I practiced our clarinet ensemble in band, and it sounds okay. In track I did workouts with Heidi, and it pretty much sucked. Running just to run is not nearly as fun as running during a game, that's for sure. Then a bunch of us lifted. I made sure to sing Michele "Dream On" in my beautiful voice that, I like to believe, sounds just like Steven Tyler. Wait, when I write that out it doesn't sound as awesome as it did in my head. Mom made me delicious chicken fajitas and my favorite rice for my birthday dinner. Then I got cards and cash from aunts and uncles and grandparents. Then I got a totally cool letter from Mom and Dad. Spoiled I tell ya. Happy birthday to me.

April 18, 2000: After youth group tonight I went to Kaitlynn's and she, Heidi, and I talked about how complicated life feels. It's a good thing I have the very best friends in the world. Kaitlynn just broke up with Jared, and I am sure she and Scottie will get together soon. Heidi and Matt are still together, but sometimes he acts like she's not even in the room when other people are around. And don't even get me started on Brent. I of course see him at track, but we barely even look at each other, let alone have a conversation. He drives me crazy. Why do we spend so much freaking time thinking and talking about moronic boys? I wish our minds would just ignore those immature humans and focus on more important things. Like world peace.

May 5, 2000: Our wonderful lunch ladies served us fajitas today. Very cross-cultural. Sometimes I go for extended periods of time without showering. It takes a lot of energy to shower, and I am just going to get all sweaty again the next day. Plus, isn't that what deodorant is for? Same with shaving my legs. It is such a pain. The hair just grows back so fast. And it's not like anyone is getting close enough to smell me or touch my legs anyway.

May 30, 2000: Well, track season is over, and so is my sophomore year. Good riddance. State track was . . . hmm . . . memorable. I ran the second leg of the 4x400 meters relay and bolted like a shot after Katy's handoff. Then as I rounded the 300 mark for the last straight-away something crazy happened. My legs just sort of stopped working. They said it had something to do with surging cortisol blah blah flippin' blah. It was the most embarrassing moment of my life. Quite a few moments, in fact, probably about 15 full mortifying seconds with a giant audience. Michele kept having to scooch up to the white line so she could grab the baton from me. She said later she thought I broke my leg since apparently it looked like I was dragging along a lead stub. My brother, Brian, and Scott were laughing so hard they almost passed out. They didn't even bother to ask me if I was okay. Poopheads. Then I ran the same 63-second split in the finals the next day, managing to not have muscle failure that time, so thank goodness for that. Summer at last.

June 21, 2000: We just got back from a basketball tournament in Cheney, WA. It was a long drive, but we got to eat lots of delicious food. We played six games and won five. We won't talk about the fluke loss. We won the first game by 40-something, then the next four by three points, two points, two points, and one point. Coach says it's good for us to play in tight games like that because it builds our mental toughness and now we know we can handle them. The only sucky thing was Mari hurt her knee and has to have surgery. Emily just had surgery on her ACL after she tore it pole-vaulting. Son of a B! Dumb knees!

July 5, 2000: So Brent and I are officially together. Again. But this time feels different. I hope I am not being an idiot and making a big mistake. We have been hanging out a lot the last few weeks. He said he is so sorry for messing up my relationship with Mari. I told him it is not his fault (but really it is a little bit his fault), and we can't dwell on the past. Plus, we live in a tiny town. There are only so many people available to go out with for crying out loud. We were watching *Crocodile Hunter* tonight, and I go, "I love that guy." Brent looked at me and goes, "You do?" And I looked right in his eyes and go, "Yes, I love him." We both sorta smiled, and then I looked at the clock and saw that it was 10:45. I had to be home at 11:00. He had to hold the dog, and I started walking to my car. He tied up Rudy and ran over to me all urgently, and he was only wearing socks. He grabbed both my hands and gave me a quick kiss and was practically bouncing up and down. He asked, "Guess what?" I asked what and he said, "I love you." I smiled and said, "I love you, too." Then he took off his senior key he just got and put the silver chain around my neck. He told me to look at the inscription on the back. The front is blue and gold, has a "C" on it, and it is shaped kind of like a shield. I rubbed the smooth silver with my thumb and flipped it over. It says, "Smile." I felt like I was in the movies. I think I do love him. I mean, my stomach feels all full of butterflies when I know I am going to see him. And as soon as I leave him I can't stop thinking about him and can't stop smiling and can't wait to see him and talk to him again. Now I am going to listen to some Bryan Adams until I fall asleep.

August 14, 2000: First day of practice! This is our year. I can feel it!

September 2, 2000: We beat Shelby 90-30 tonight for this year's opener, so that was fun. Michele had 21, I had 15, Carlane, Maci, and Heidi all had 12, and Kaitlynn and Chasi had 10 and 8. I went to Brent's after Subway, and we watched *Fools Rush In*. Brent didn't want me to leave, so I didn't get on the road until after 11:50. Since curfew is at midnight on Saturdays, I was feeling just a little nervous driving back to town. I may or may not have driven a tad bit over the speed limit . . . When I pulled in to our alley, I could see Dad's silhouette through the glass door that connects the garage to the house. He had his arms crossed, biceps bulging, and was assuming his power stance. That made my heart jump into my throat. I kept checking the clock. It was 11:59 when I walked from the car to the house. I opened the door, looked at him, and he goes, "I love ya, but I won't lie for ya." If we had a cuckoo clock it would have cuckooed about four seconds after he said that. I can't remember if I actually made a noise, but I think I nodded. Then he just turned around and walked upstairs to his bedroom. Whew. Note to self: get home a little earlier than four seconds to midnight.

September 7, 2000:

Hello team.

I've been thinking quite a while now, and I am starting to calm down and feel better. To put it bluntly, losing sucks. But it happens. Bad stuff happens all the time, and that's just how life is. After our loss in Belt tonight, just like we did there last year, tons of memories from last year started coming to me. How many tears there were after Divisionals, how bad we felt. But there's nothing anyone can do about things that have already happened. Something that I've learned is you can't change the past, but you can learn from it and work to make things better in the future. On the bus tonight, I know there were many conversations held. Everyone was analyzing the game, and we were just plain angry. "If I woulda just made those free throws," "If I woulda hit the post sooner," "If I woulda gotten better position and not fouled," were some of the thoughts that were flying around. Then we were thinking about how we are afraid this might change things, there may be tension now, is it not going to be as fun anymore? I heard someone remark, "I haven't dreaded practice all year, but I'm already dreading tomorrow."

None of us should feel that way, because basketball is something that I think we all love, and we shouldn't dread doing something we love. I have a feeling most of the rest of you all are up right now, incredibly tired but not able to fall asleep. Coach VanDyke is probably up folding towels or something. But no one should lose sleep over this. After our loss to Belt last year, things changed. We became more tentative, we worried about making the coaches mad, we were afraid to lose, and we weren't having fun. I know I've learned from that experience, and I think everyone else has, too. If we don't make a pass that seems a little risky because we're afraid, we might miss a Play of the Game. A saying we often hear is, "Basketball is a game of mistakes."

If we never made any mistakes there would be no challenge, and how fun would that be? I know every one of us wants to win and wants to have fun, and nothing can stop us except for us. Sure we feel some pressure, but it's good pressure. Pressure challenges us to do our best. I talked to my dad when I got home, and he reminded me that it is fun to be rated #1, and it's fun to be known as the top dog, but it's hard, too, and good teams can handle it. My brother left a note for me, too. He said he was sorry, losing sucks, but we have to shake it off. He said to relax, stay confident, and have fun. And that's exactly what we need to do. We are the only ones who can limit how far we go.

Jeff also wrote a favorite quote of his, "Don't let a win get to your head, or a loss to your heart."

Okay, now this letter is quite lengthy, and I need some sleep. So let's just keep working as hard as we have been, learn from our mistakes, play ball, and have fun. Remember how lucky we all are to be part of something this special. Never forget that. I love you all, now let's play some ball!

Love,
Jamie Graham #12

September 15, 2000: We beat Brady last night 117-12. I would not say this out loud to anyone but my teammates, but it was actually kind of difficult in the second half, because we weren't allowed to score until we had made at least six passes. They only had five players and worked their tails off. We just couldn't miss and only had four turnovers in the entire game. In the Tribune today an article in the opinion section said, "S-P-O-R-T-S-M-A-N-S-H-I-P," then asked if the Chester Coyotes knew how to spell it. Well we do now because you spelled it out for us you anonymous bleepity-bleep.

Chapter 19

November 16-18, 2000, junior year, Northern C Divisional Tournament, Havre, Montana

We clinched our third district championship last weekend, so that was fun. We pounded Sunburst 92–48 then beat Valier for the chipper 67–43. Even though we won both games by a lot, it bugs me that we let them score above forty. Coach reminds us constantly how important it is to meet our goals, every game. We have got to step up our defense this weekend if we want to meet our next goal of winning Divisionals. I still have a horrible taste in my mouth from last year. We have got to win.

Mari Tempel, Michele VanDyke, Heidi Cicon, Maci Tempel, Kayla Matkin, Jamie Graham, Kaitlynn Engstrom, Chasi Buffington, and Emily Tranberg after Districts, Shelby, MT, November 11, 2000

* * *

Wow. That girl who sang the national anthem is legit. Now it's go time.

"Alright, ladies." Coach gives us just a few more reminders before starting lineups. "We have been here before. There is nothing to be nervous about. Keep your shoulders up and stay poised. We will start out just like we always do and adjust if we need to. We have got to double down on Oliver but be able to recover when she kicks it out. Talk, talk, talk."

Carlane wraps it up. "Lady Coyotes on three. One, two, three—"

"Lady Coyotes!" Shouting that in unison with my teammates never gets old.

"I got twenty-four!" Maci shouts at the mid-court ring.

We follow suit and declare loudly who we are guarding. The Stanford Wolves have had a great season so far. Too bad for them they have to play us today. They are led by six-foot-one senior Jacklynn Oliver and like to get up and down the court. Stanford is just off Highway 200, right between Lewistown and Great Falls. We always drive there when we go to visit the grandparents in Big Timber, and I always wonder what all the fuss is about with that white wolf.[55]

The first quarter is back and forth. We miss two breakaway layups, which does not bode well for us and our 70% made layups goal. Then Michele picks up two quick fouls. She can jump higher than everyone else in this gym, so she is the exception for the non-existent-but-everyone-loves-to-demand-it-angrily-from-the-crowd "over the back" call. The refs wouldn't call those fouls on her if she were a boy. Carlane and Heidi are doing a good job defending Oliver, but double-teaming is always risky, and she has already had two opposite-block assists. After eight minutes we are only up 15–14.

The game continues to be tight, and we just can't seem to break open the lead any wider than two. Michele is given her third foul

---

[55] In the 1920s, the "White Killer" contributed to the death of many cattle, not to mention numerous deer and elk, resulting in ranchers losing thousands of dollars. The white wolf roamed the Highwood and Little Belt Mountains for somewhere between 10–15 years, with a six-feet-long carcass, razor sharp fangs, and a giant head.

halfway through the second quarter and has to sit until halftime. Why do they say you are "given" a foul? That makes it sound like a gift. When the refs "give" me a foul, there are often a lot of things I want to say to them, none resembling any sort of "thank you."

We come out in the third quarter up 28–26. People don't zone us very often, and it seems to be throwing a wrench in our rhythm. One of our goals is to score at least seventy points a game. We better step things up if we are going to make that tonight. This third quarter seems to be dragging by. Dang it! I can't believe I missed that layup! I don't even have to look to see Dad in the stands closing his eyes in an attempt to keep his cool. Nothing drives him more crazy than a girl sprinting balls to the wall down the court only to brick it off the backboard. Heidi trails and gets her hands on the board, but she doesn't have great position. They "give" her a foul. Dang it! "That's my fault, Heid," I apologize.

"It's okay. We got this," she assures me.

After three we are still hanging on to the lead, 39–36. It would just be really nice if we could blow this open a little bit. It's our ball at half to start the fourth. Maci tosses it in to Chasi who pass fakes right then swings it over to me. I rocker-step forward then rip it through and dribble to the left wing. Shot fake, rip, then bounce it to Maci coming off Carlane's then Heidi's screens on the blocks. Maci doesn't hesitate as she catches and puts in the baseline jumper at her favorite spot on the floor.

Back on defense we set up for our 1-3-1 three-quarter-court trap. I tip it on the first pass and Chasi picks up her fourth steal. Chas passes it right back to me, and I capitalize. After their point guard travels just before half-court, their coach is forced to take a time-out. Coach subs in Michele, Amanda, Savannah, and Kaitlynn, and leaves me in. We set up in our "cheetah" press and Kaitlynn picks off their attempted lob downcourt. After the steal I relax. We go on to win 58-49.

* * *

The last time we played Big Sandy everything was the same, except the gym. Here we are again, Friday night semifinal game putting our identical records of 21-1 on the line. The Pioneers no longer have

Ritter, but in their program there is always someone stepping in to fill a role.

Michele gets her hand on the tip, but it goes to Bitz who immediately hits Silvan downcourt for an easy bucket. Down 0-2 after only three seconds have ticked off the clock. That is less than ideal. Heidi rips the ball out of the net, makes sure she clears the paint when taking it out (the last time she forgot to clear the paint during practice there was a piercing whistle blast followed by Coach—with smoke coming out of her ears, in my memory—declaring, "Run until I tell you to stop!!") and bounces it in to me on Big Sandy's right elbow.

I turn and face, pass fake, and dribble with my left toward center court, eyes scanning for a forward pass opportunity. Usually I can find someone to chuck it up to, but all my teammates are tightly guarded, so I pull back and hold up my right fist. My girls eye the fist and immediately set up in their positions for our "power" offense. I hit Carlane on the left wing, fake a ball cut, then screen away for Maci. Meanwhile, Heidi screens across for Michele who makes a curl cut through the paint. Carlane shot fakes and tosses it in to Michele, who catches and takes it straight to the hole for two.

We set up in our "five" press and slow them up slightly. Darlington gathers at the top of the key and tosses it to Silvan on the left wing. Silvan lobs the ball in to Upham at the short corner who hits Bitz coming off a down screen with a crosscourt pass. Bitz catches in triple threat right at the arc, and I can tell by the look on her face she is going to shoot. That is not good. Snap. First three of the game.

Heidi pulls it down and inbounds again to me. This time they press, and I have to screen across for Maci and roll open. Once we inbound and get to half-court, Big Sandy spreads out in their daunting 3-2 zone. I call out, "'Triangle!'" and pull back as Carlane, Heidi, and Maci create the triangle and Michele settles in as the baseline runner.

Instead of making the easy pass to Heidi at the high post, I attempt to zip it quickly to Michele at the short corner. Michele's arms are extremely long, but so are Bitz's, and she intercepts the pass. Note to self: when playing one of the top-ranked teams in the state, it is probably best to make the easy pass first to ensure a good angle. Bitz finds Silvan at half, and she hurls it up the sideline to Darlington.

We sprint to get back, but Darlington hits Upham on the trail for an easy two. Crap.

The rest of the first quarter is back and forth, and we trail by one going into the second, 15–16. We play okay in the second, but I brick three threes and Big Sandy hits a couple. We hustle into the locker room at half down 25–31.

"We're okay," Coach assures us fairly calmly, considering what's riding on this game. "We need to get more touches inside and get to the free throw line. Watch for us to change it up defensively, and we will start out the second half in our 1–3–1 half-court trap. Hands must be up, and we *must* keep talking. As you all know, the third quarter is crucial. We must win the third quarter."

Coach Schlepp wraps it up. "Keep your heads up. We got this."

As usual, we completely buy in and go into the huddle feeling confident and encouraged.

The Pioneers have possession to start the third and score on a sideline play similar to ours. Coach Schlepp highlighted that play in our scouting report. It drives me crazy when I know what the other team is going to run but we don't manage to thwart their plan. Ah, well, we are only down eight. One play at a time. We just gotta score, and then make a stop. Chip away. I inbound it to Maci, and she is trapped immediately. I did not see that coming. Flip! We turn it over and watch as they capitalize on our error. This is not good.

I can't help but hear Coach emphasizing how crucial it is to win the third quarter when I look up at the scoreboard, do a little mental math, and realize we just got crushed in the third quarter by a margin of 11–25. Now we go into the fourth, down 36–56. Twenty points?! We have never been down by twenty points before, and we most certainly have not been down by twenty points to end a quarter. We are getting pummeled. One of our goals is to win every quarter. Apparently we are attempting the exact opposite tonight.

We manage to stay with them for most of the fourth, but we start in too deep of a hole. At the end of thirty-two minutes, we come out the big, fat losers, with an embarrassing final score of 46–68.

We keep our heads up long enough to get through the "good game" line and all the way back to the locker room. Chasi enters and lets out a frustrated cry that can only be described as a noise a disgruntled banshee might produce. All I can do is nod my head.

That sound perfectly captures how my insides feel. The benches are slowly covered by sweaty butts—butts belonging to eleven other extremely disappointed Coyote players.

I slowly peel off the thin black Velcro band around my left jersey strap. We wear our black bands for every game, for Annie. I flash back to the last time we sat in a locker room the last time we played Big Sandy. I close my eyes and wish, somehow, that I could erase tonight, maybe even erase the last year and a half, and go back to that moment.

* * *

We board the bus early Saturday morning, and Coach reads us a Mike Ditka quote, "*You really never lose until you stop trying.*"

I cannot exactly wrap my mind around this at the moment, because we most definitely lost last night, but I imagine she is pointing us to something deeper. Better pay attention.

"We have a choice to make today," she continues. "We can hang our heads and feel sorry for ourselves and wonder why something bad happened to us."

I am guessing that is not what she is hoping we choose. Let us hear option number two, please.

"Or we can accept that we had a rough night, put that behind us, and use what we learned from that loss to fuel us forward today."

I fight back the urge to raise my hand. That's gotta be it.

"Take this time to visualize what you will do today when you arrive at the gym," Coach continues. "Picture yourself preparing for the game, and picture yourself warming up. Then, where you are when the game starts. You all know your roles, and you are all capable of fulfilling those roles. We still have the opportunity to advance to State. Control what you can control, your attitude, your body language, and your effort. If we do that, we will come out winners no matter what."

* * *

Now that was a much better day. Saturday is just about over, and I settle into my bed after a lively, late-night bus ride home from Havre. Our conversations included rehashing the details our two games, the first one merely to stay alive, and the second one to earn a challenge. We put the boots to Belt and won 72-49. Then we whipped Winifred 68-35 for third place. But we don't want third place. Thankfully Big Sandy beat Box Elder in the championship game (it still feels so wrong to root for a team that just beat us), which means we get to challenge Box Elder Monday night. When Big Sandy beat Denton last year, that meant the end of our season. Now we are being given the opportunity to reach the state tournament and potentially play for the title. All we gotta do is take this second chance.

Chapter 20

November 20, 2000, junior year, Northern C Divisional Tournament challenge game, Chester Coyotes vs. Box Elder Bears, Havre, Montana

The Box Elder Bears burst out of their huddle sporting shiny navy-blue uniforms emblazoned with gold numbers.[56]
Some people might say we upset them for the divisional title two years ago. I prefer to say we spanked them. It gives me some comfort knowing that we beat the state champions that year, but I realize it doesn't matter that we beat them in Divisionals; they won the one that really counted.

Pullin, now a junior, is still a starting guard for the Bears and their obvious leader. Her teammates from 1998 have graduated, but just like Big Sandy, new players eagerly filled those vacated roles. Pullin has a partner in Tami Infante, and the pair combine for the majority of their team's points. Rosette is their solid post, and is presently lined up opposite Michele at half-court. I grab the tip and remember Coach VanDyke's reminder to us: "Be disciplined. We must control the tempo and not let them get any streaks going. When they hit a

---

[56]Box Elder is around ten miles north of Big Sandy on Highway 87 and is the tribal headquarters of the Rocky Boy Indian Reservation. The Indian Reservation was established in 1916, after requests from Chief Rocky Boy were made to figure out a solution to the issue of numerous landless Chippewa Cree in Montana. Box Elder became home to the Chippewa Cree Tribal Council, the Northern Winz casino and Stone Child College. "Stone Child" is a translation of Chief Rocky Boy's Chippewa Cree name. One can also access the Bear Paw Ski Bowl through Box Elder.

couple, pull back, refocus, and be patient. We must control the tempo."

I feel like it is probably important to control the tempo, so I resist the temptation to fire it to Chasi down the sideline and set us up in our motion offense. Patience. I dribble left, pull back, crossover right and make the easy pass to Maci on the wing. She tosses it to Carlane on the block, who checks over her shoulder then kicks it back out to Maci. Maci whips it to me, and I instinctively rip, turn the corner and hit Chasi on the left wing. She fakes high and bounces low to Michele. They double down and Michele flips a high lob to Carlane who looks like she is going to tip it in. She is certainly athletic enough for the tip-in but gathers first and sinks a textbook baseline jumper off the block.

We stay poised and patient and find ourselves closing out the first half up by eleven, 29–18. After our uncharacteristically short halftime discussion we take the court with five minutes still on the clock, so we take the time to get a few shots up. A loose ball bounces toward our pep band area, and I glance up and see a few boys from my class. My mind unexpectedly switches over from basketball to boys, namely, Brent. A picture of us cuddling on a couch, holding hands and watching a movie pops into my head. This is not the time, Jamie. Stay focused. But I really wish I could be with him right now. What is wrong with me? I have got to snap out of it.

The buzzer blares and brings me back to the court. Note to self: get this mind-wandering thing under control. I place my ball back on the rack and trot to our bench for the huddle. Coach says a few things and I try to focus, I really do.

The Bears inbound from the sideline and score surprisingly quickly. How did that happen? Okay, set up the offense. Whoops, lazy pass. Frustrated about my unforced turnover, I reach in and pick up a silly foul. This puts them at the sideline yet again, and after inbounding and finding Rosette at the elbow, she turns and swishes it from fifteen feet. We transition back to offense, and I put up a rushed three. Brick. After they score yet again on their next possession, Coach calls a time-out. She reminds us to "control the tempo."

Oh, yeah. I have got to remember that.

She also tells us, "Keep shooting, but identify that Michele is hot tonight. Take your shot when it's there, but keep looking to feed the post. We must have inside touches. *Be patient.* We are in the driver's seat. Please, let's stay there."

At the end of three, the Bears have closed the gap and are only down 37–33. The momentum shifted their way a few times that last quarter, and if it weren't for Michele, we would barely be shooting 30% from the field.[57] We just have to hang on. Eight minutes left, no shot clock, up by four. Keep our composure.

The Bears are all over us and force two turnovers early in the fourth. Don't panic. Play intense defense and talk.

"Deny! Deny!" I shout as I make sure I have a hand in the passing lane while defending my man on the wing. "Chele, you got helpside!"

It goes back and forth, but then Pullin drains a deep three to put them within one. They make a stop and Infante drives, shoots, and misses but is fouled on the shot. Two free throws. Dang it! She is short on her first free throw attempt but swishes the second. By the time the last seconds tick off the clock in regulation, the Bears have won the fourth quarter 11–15. Overtime.

Now we can't just pee down our legs and give this game away. It is 0–0. Don't overthink it. Just play. Maci comes away with the tip and stands tall with the ball squeezed safely to her hip, right elbow jutting out as she takes in the scene. She passes it parallel to me just past half-court. Anticipating the trap, I make a quick fake and dribble middle, hesitate, then plow into the key and dish it to Michele who banks in her twenty-third and twenty-fourth points. We pick up full-court man-to-man, respecting their ball-handling skills and keeping a disciplined arm's-length away. Some coaches claim pressing constantly makes for tired legs at the end of games. Our philosophy is pressing constantly puts constant pressure on the other team, making each movement and decision just a little more difficult. It seems like a no-brainer to me.

Pullin crosses over then flicks it to Infante. Then Pullin bolts and gets the rock right back. Classic give-and-go, one of the oldest plays in the book, and we just got burned by it.[58] That is fairly embarrassing.

Tie game.

---

[57] Our final shooting percentage for the game was 23 for 61, 38%.

[58] Give-and-go – A classic play where the person with the ball passes to a teammate, cuts to the hoop, and the teammate immediately passes it back.

They pressure us right back, and Maci and I play a quick game of catch before crossing the ten-second line. Coach signals for "Duke." Michele lopes from the low block to the top of the key and takes the handoff from me. I dive across to the deep corner, just below Maci on the left wing. Carlane and Heidi plant themselves at the elbows, Michele whips it to Maci, ducks in briefly near the free throw line, then rubs left shoulders with Heidi and times her steps down the lane. Maci puts a high alley-oop toward the rim. The toss is spot-on, and Michele leaps like the state high jump record holder that she is, and gently guides it in.[59] The gym erupts, pumping a shot of adrenaline through me.

The Bears call a time-out, and our bench receives us with high fives, butt slaps, and words of encouragement. Coach doesn't say much, just reminds us that, "We are up by two with barely a minute to go. Play solid defense, box out, and run our stall when we get the ball back."

Carlane thrusts her hand forward. "Win on three. One, two, three—"

We readily join our hands. "Win!"

The Bears inbound the ball successfully, despite our best attempt to deny by face-guarding and attempting a quick trap after the first pass. The crowd is on its feet, calling out messages that collide—half demanding that the Bears score and the other half pleading for a stop.

"Screen coming!" I cry to Maci, followed by a determined, "Switch!"

Maci takes Infante while I cover Pullin, who, undeterred by our attempt to thwart their plan, pulls up for a three. I let her land and box out, while keeping an eye on the Baden[60] barreling toward the hoop. It rolls around the rim and bounces into Michele's eager hands. She promptly chins it, looks up toward the scoreboard, and we all rush together when the final buzzer declares us the winners. If one can call second place the "winner." For now, we will take what we can get.

---

[59] Michele set the Montana State Class C high jump record in 2000 at an incredible five feet seven and a half inches. Twenty years later, the record still stands.
[60] Basketball brand name.

Chapter 21

November 30–December 2, 2000, junior year, State Class C Tournament, Butte, Montana

Finally, we are back. Oh, how I have missed you, state basketball tournament. Before toting my giant forest-green Adidas duffel down to the locker room, I stop to get a feel for the Butte High School gymnasium. Dad always reminds me to take the time to really think about where I am. He says it is important to take everything in and appreciate what a privilege it is to be where we are, to be grateful for these opportunities and experiences.

"Butte, America," as it is often called, is about eighty-five miles west of Bozeman, off Interstate 90.[61] I think it was almost the capital of Montana, but Helena ended up claiming that title. I feel like there is still a pretty big rivalry between the towns today (not gonna lie, I don't pay much attention to sports in Montana's "cities"). You just can't beat small-town sports.

I study the scene. There are bleachers equipped to hold many more fans than back home in Chester, which is a little intimidating. The floor, however, still has that same deliciously lacquered scent, the hoops are still ten-feet high, and the free throw lines are still

---

[61]Butte was the first major city in Montana and actually had the title of being the largest city west of the Mississippi between Chicago and San Francisco at one point. It started as a gold and silver mining camp late in the 1800s. Right around 1900, there was a copper boom, and the city boomed as well. Its copper mining attracted miners from all over the world, creating a diverse population in the city set against the Rockies. Butte has many residents with Irish roots, and many in Montana connect Butte with its wild Saint Patrick's Day celebration.

fifteen feet from the rim. I feel like Jimmy in *Hoosiers*. Now if Coach Schlepp would just come out here with a measuring tape and Coach Norman Dale's reassuring words of wisdom to quell my nerves, I would be all set.

* * *

Flexing in the locker room at State: Katy Engstrom, Michele VanDyke, Maci Tempel, Chasi Buffington, Heidi Cicon, me

We are up against the Harrison Wildcats. To be honest, I had never heard of Harrison before this week when we watched film and studied our scouting report after Tuesday's practice. It might sound ridiculous that I hadn't heard of it before, but with over one hundred Class C towns in this giant state, I discover new ones all the time. It helps when Mom quizzes Jeff on car trips on all the counties and county seats.[62]

Just like freshman year, we are opening the tournament with the first Thursday afternoon game. From my limited experience with Thursday afternoon games at the state tournament, my instinct is that they are sucky. I know this is not a fair judgment and plan to love Thursday afternoon games in about an hour and a half. Our band

---

[62]Harrison is located on Highway 287, about fifty miles between Butte and Bozeman. It is right in the middle of the Tobacco Root Mountains and one hundred miles from the west entrance of Yellowstone National Park. The K-12 population is under one hundred students.

totally nails the national anthem, as usual, and the announcer makes it through his spiel. Now it is showtime.

The first two quarters go as planned, and we lead 29–22 at half. After the first few minutes of the third quarter, though, a foreboding feeling of déjà vu floods me. Suhr banks in a three, and it takes all I have inside me not to lose my mind. What in the world is happening here? Powell is unrelenting on defense and just will not get out of my face.[63] I have got to keep it together. This would not be an ideal place to get a technical (but let's face it, sometimes the sass just sneaks out). I miss and miss and miss again. Then just like that, the third quarter closes with us tied at 38.

In the huddle I struggle to hear what Coach is saying. Why can't I shake these sneaky doubts somehow infiltrating my usually confident thoughts? Luckily Coach still has confidence in me. "Jamie, keep shooting. Obviously make the easy pass when it is there, but you have to know you are a good shooter and stop doubting yourself."

Seeing as I am o-fer on the night, I appreciate her confidence in me, but am not sure I feel the same way at the moment. We step back onto the court and huddle again before the ref signals for the inbound.

"Come on, you guys. We can do this. We have got to win this." I say these things out loud not only for my teammates to hear, but for myself.

We match up and talk frantically on defense. The game goes on neck and neck. I finally get into the scorebook when I draw a foul on a drive and sink both free throws. Okay, the momentum is ours again.

No sooner does the momentum feel like it has swung our way than Maci fouls out with a ticky-tack call right above the top of the key. Chasi connects on a trey a few possessions later, only to be answered by Suhr as she banks in another one from the arc. Flippin' banked threes! Does she practice those?!

---

[63]Letty Powell goes on to have a successful career playing for Montana Tech, where I respected her greatly as an opponent when we competed in Frontier Conference games. Billi Suhr has a great career at Western Montana University, and she and I later both have the privilege of standing up as bridesmaids for my sister-in-law Megan, Billi's Western teammate.

I am surprised to see Coach calling for us to run "red." That means we have to foul to try to get the ball back because we are running out of time. How can that be, running out of time? How did this go by so fast?

Desperately I reach for a pass intended for Powell, hoping to get the steal, but only succeed in slapping her wrist and putting her at the line. When she makes the first, I realize it probably was not the best strategy to go ahead and foul their best free throw shooter. She calmly swishes the next one as well and, as we are out of time-outs, I receive the inbound and push it up the court. I call for "1-4 low," make one move and go, pull up and . . . short.[64]

Before I can fully grasp what is happening, I see the refs blowing their whistles repeatedly and wildly waving their arms. Thank goodness they are doing that, as if I can't hear the blasted buzzer signaling the end of the game, signaling the end of our third chance to realize our dream, leaving us with only one more.

* * *

Saturday night. The locker room is deserted save for Michele and me. I sit on the cold aluminum bench and mentally flip through the last two days' highlights.

Friday morning we got a second shot at Big Sandy. Silvan was out all weekend, so they were down. Of course we hope she is okay, but we took advantage of that weakness and dominated, winning 53-37. That victory put us back in a winning mindset, and in a position to recoup the rest of the day.

This morning found us up against the extremely athletic, extremely physical Harlowton Engineers. The girls on the basketball team are also the members of their defending back-to-back-to-back state track champs. Three championships in a row? Man, would I love to know how that feels. It was nice to beat them (54-35) in

---

[64]1-4 – An offensive setup where the person with the ball sets up near the top of the key, then two players—usually post players—set up on the two elbows and the last two players set up on the wings. In a 1-4 low, wings and posts move down.

122

something after that humiliating attempt to sprint against them in the 4x400 meters relay trials last spring.[65]

Tonight we played against the Brockton Warriors in the consolation game, making our journey through the backdoor for a trophy identical to our path two years ago. Brockton has the highest scorer in the state in Kayla Lambert, and Maci held her to only three

points in the second half (she still had a total of twenty-four points, but that is substantially below her average).[66] We led the whole game and at least finished another season with a win (85–55), even if it wasn't the exact win we wanted.

As I wait for Michele to gather the last of her basketball accessories, I think back to when I sat in the locker room with her older sister two seasons ago. I was a giddy, innocent freshman,

Kaitlynn Engstrom and me after earning third place at State. I am wearing a basketball necklace and Brent's senior key.

trying to suppress my excitement because I could tell Carly wasn't sharing my carefree thoughts and emotions. I wasn't able to understand her perspective at the time. I remember feeling like it was the beginning, that our journey was only just starting, that we had so much time left to accomplish our goals.

Now, for the first time, I think I understand how Carly was feeling that night. I recall that statement she made, about that being *her last shot*. The magnitude and finality of that statement did not resonate with me then. Suddenly I get it.

The fact is that we now only have one high school basketball season remaining. The fact is that we may start out with one plan,

---

[65] The Harlowton Engineers were led by twins Amy and Ashley Jones, who are athletic physical specimens, not to mention gorgeous. The Harlo girls spent a weekend in Chester with us during volleyball season our senior year, during which time we were able to form friendships. We respected one another and enjoyed competing in all sports. I was lucky enough to end up teaching elementary school with Amy years later in Big Timber.

[66] Lambert scored sixty-six points in a single game on November 10, 2000. She holds the record of the only Montana player to score over sixty points in a game, and she did it four times. She finished her high school career as Montana's all-time leading scorer, men and women, with 3,453 points. It really was a privilege to play on the same court as Kayla.

only to find ourselves attempting to navigate through totally unexpected territory. The fact is that time is bizarre, and somehow we find ourselves someplace and wonder how we got here so fast.

This time I am the one with the pensive smile. Don't get me wrong, I am happy. We have ended our season on a win again, third place at State, with a record of 23-3. I am proud of myself, proud of us. However, somehow in the span of these last few minutes I feel different. Do I feel older? Wiser? Have I had this wrong all along? Is all of this about more than winning one tournament?

I blink and hold my eyes closed a few seconds, overwhelmed by the inundation of these surprisingly deep thoughts. I shake my head quickly to shoo the complicated thoughts away. Michele's voice pulls me back to the *now.* "Well, Jamers, we didn't win it all, but I am still proud of us."

We instinctively pull together and perform our personal handshake, then linger after with a tight hug and she reminds me, "Love you, Jamers."

"Love you, too, Chelers."

"I bet I can eat more pieces of pizza than you tonight," she challenges as we exit the locker room and start for the bus.

Now that is a contest I am confident I will win.

Chapter 22

March 2001, junior year, pre-prom, Chester, Montana

Brent's phone sure has been busy a lot lately. I can tell no one is on the internet because there isn't that little beep before it rings. Mitchell and Amanda broke up, and I am the only one Matthew talks to on the phone. So who is Brent talking to? And these are not short conversations. I mean, I am trying not to be too paranoid. There's nothing wrong with trying the line every so often, right? Like every ten minutes or so. Or three . . .

Should I ask him about it? We have had a bazillion talks these last few months about trust, and I was starting to think we can finally move on from those exhausting conversations. I don't want to bring something up that will upset him, especially if there is a simple explanation, which I am sure there is. So if there is a simple explanation, he shouldn't be upset if I ask, right? Maybe I'll give it a couple days. He will share it with me if it is important, right? I mean, that is the foundation for having a trusting relationship, after all.

* * *

I pull up to a computer in the journalism room and look at my list for prom. I will get to my newspaper articles later, but prom takes precedence today, as it is only two weeks away. Okay, I have to focus. As junior class president, I need to set up all the meetings and finalize decisions about the DJ and decorations, as well as the details regarding theme. This year we have decided on "Under the Sea," because you can't go wrong with Disney. We are going to alternate two *Little Mermaid* songs, "Under the Sea" and "Kiss the Girl," while all the couples walk out for the grand march. I also need to contact the DJ and photographer, keep track of ticket sales, and order the wine glasses with the logo our class voted on. I am still not quite sure about the thought process behind having alcoholic beverage holders as a parting gift at our public school teen dance function, but we are just going to go with it.

Mom and I took a shopping spree up in Canada a few weekends back (since the exchange rate is in our favor) to look for a prom dress. I found a shiny-but-not-too-shiny plain pastel-purple gown with two spaghetti straps that connect at a V over each shoulder. My preference, when not in a uniform or practice gear, is jeans and a T-shirt (usually from some three-on-three or State Games tournament), a hoodie, tennis shoes, and hair tied back in a messy bun. I will admit, though, that I do enjoy dressing up every once in a while and am excited about how this dress swishes delicately around my ankles when I walk. It is girly and fun, and sometimes it is fun to be girly. The swishing is fabulous but more importantly, the skirt falls at just the right length so as not to hinder my stellar dance moves. A smile sneaks across my face as I picture myself dancing with Brent.

I feel pretty prepared as I stuff my mound of prom papers back in my binder before the bell rings. My brother is at a nearby computer editing an article for our school newspaper, *The Yellow Pages*, and of course downloading songs from Napster while listening to one of his numerous uber-random playlists. I listen a second and realize Tiffany's "I Think We're Alone Now" is playing, and that we are, indeed, the only two left together here in this small computer area. For the most part, he has his routine, and I have mine, though I will admit it has been fun working on the newspaper with him. He finishes typing a sentence and laughs out loud.

"What's so funny?" I ask, a bit suspiciously.

Jeff and I have a similar sense of humor as far as hilarious movies including characters like Mike Myers and Adam Sandler, as well as *Saturday Night Live* skits with Will Ferrell. We also agree that *Saved by the Bell* is the best sitcom ever produced. We don't always see things through the same lens, however.

"I'm working on the 'Spit it Out' column and found my favorite one in this edition," he replies, still giggling like a little girl.

126

"Spit it Out" is the favorite of most of the student body at Chester High School, as it highlights some of the most hilarious and/or embarrassing things uttered by students and staff alike. Kids are constantly approaching Jeff or me with new quotes to record in our ever-ready Lois Lane-like notebooks.

"Was it something Heidi said? Or Kayla?" I make the obvious guesses.

"Nope. Diemert. In civics class he asked, 'If I throw a nickel out the window, is it a five-cent fine?'"

Despite a feeble attempt to hold it in, a giant Jamie Laugh escapes.

"I don't think they heard you up on the top floor," Jeff teases, as we are in the basement.

"Well we can't all have flawless skin, 20/20 eyesight, and an adorable, appropriately-pitched and volumed laugh like you, Jeffer," I fling back, pretending to glare but the smile sneaks through.

The bell rings, signaling us to go our separate ways.

"Have a good rest of your day, sister."

"You, too, brother."

* * *

Busy again. Fine, I am going to drive out there. I will rent a movie and pretend like that was my plan all along. It's Friday, and the weather is quite beautiful for a change, so Richie and Steve invited Mom and Dad and the Lakeys over to sit out by the firepit in their backyard. Mom said Brent's parents were going over there, too, which is perfect. Bruce and Mary are great, but if Brent and I need to discuss something serious tonight, we need to be alone.

Jeff is at Maci's, and an empty house makes things easy for me. I scribble my whereabouts on a yellow sticky, then head out through the back entryway to extract the white Taurus from the garage. I drive up the back gravel road to the IGA and park around the east side, hoping to sneak in and out without being seen. Don't get me wrong, I love all my friends, but tonight there is no time for chitchat; I need to see Brent. Without the usual profound deliberation it takes to choose a movie, I quickly snag one from the shelf and take it up to the checkout. It has Nicholas Cage in it, and Brent loves Nicholas Cage, so it will do.

I crank up my newest burnt CD, which thanks to Napster is all the rage, and belt out Bon Jovi's "It's My Life" then Cyndi Lauper's "Girls Just Wanna Have Fun." I sing every word at the top of my lungs during the six-mile drive south of town. Man, I sound good in the car. Especially when the volume is really cranked.

As I pull up in the driveway, the Clarks' crazy dog Rudy snarls a warning. Since I do not wish to be mauled, I am forced to wait for Brent to realize it is not a family member, as the barking does not cease. A couple minutes later, Brent appears in the window of the front door. He smiles when he realizes it is me. I take this as a good sign. Why did I get myself worked up into such a tizzy? I need to stop overthinking things and worrying so much. I am sure everything is just fine.

"Hey you!" Brent greets me enthusiastically from the deck as he ties up the dog.

Now that it is safe, I get out of the car. Brent smiles at me. "This is a nice surprise."

See how happy he is to see me? Nothing to worry about. I walk up the stairs, across the deck, and into the house. Brenton closes the door behind me and gives me a sweet hug and soft peck on the cheek. "What movie did you bring?" he asks, gesturing to my hand clasped around the rectangular slate-gray case.

"*Cccc-ity of Angels.*" I scan the spine with a sideways glance and try to make it seem like this is not the first time reading the title.

"Ooh! I love Nicholas Cage," he squeals.

"That is brand new information!" I facetiously reply with a smile.

"The twins are watching a movie, but we can watch this instead. They love Nicholas as well," he assures me. He grabs my hand and we descend to the basement.

I offer my usual greeting to Brent's identical brothers, who are two years younger than I am. "Hello, Matthew Klay and Mitchell James."

"Hi, Jamers," they greet back in unison.

"What have you guys been up to tonight?" I decide to fish. "Does somebody have a new girlfriend I should know about?"

"Unfortunately, no." Matthew sighs. "Why do you ask?"

"Oh, the phone was busy earlier." I shrug casually.

"Brent was on the phone," Matthew states matter-of-factly, "as usual."

Brent shoots his sibling a sharp look, but he recovers so quickly I decide maybe I just imagined it.

Attempting to appear nonchalant, I turn to Brent and ask, "Who were you talking to?"

Brent hesitates slightly then his eyes lock on to mine. "My recruiter."

Who? This answer makes no sense to me. I didn't think he was going to pursue sports in college. Still confused, but wanting to be chill, I keep digging. "For track?"

"Um, no." His response does not comfort me, and I am more confused than ever.

I frantically search my mind for something to connect this to, but I cannot come up with anything. There is no stopping my expressive eyebrows from furrowing. I got nothing, so I keep eye contact and stay silent.

Matthew and Mitchell mumble something about getting snacks and slide upstairs.

Brent opens his mouth, then closes it again, like he can't figure out what he is going to tell me.

"What?" I urge, this time not even trying to conceal my concern.

"My Army recruiter," he admits.

"Army?" I ask incredulously, mind swirling. "But you've never mentioned anything about the Army before."

"I found out about it at that job fair in Great Falls that our class went to a few months back," he explains.

"A *few months* back"—I cannot quell my irritation and anger, and my voice rises—"and you are just now telling me?"

"Please don't yell," Brent pleads calmly.

"I'm not yelling!" I yell.

Brent takes a breath in and out through his nose, tilts his head to the side all cute like he does, and gives me those puppy dog eyes. Well that head tilt and those doggie eyes aren't going to get him out of this one.

"I have been going to tell you—"

"Yet you didn't," I cut him off. "I had to find out by accident."

"Look, can we sit down and talk about this?" he asks, as if sitting down and maturely discussing the future was his plan for the night all along, and that it is not a big deal that he hasn't shared his life-altering news with me before now.

"Fine," I say calmly, "so when were you planning on filling me in on these future plans of yours?"

I can be mature, too.

He sits on the loveseat and pats the spot right next to him. I am not feeling very lovey at the moment, so I opt for the computer chair and roll up next to him. I cross my arms, open my eyes wide, and jut my chin out. Then I pull my chin back in and narrow my eyes, imploring him to speak first.

"The Army has a lot of great options for me, and you know I haven't been sure about what I want to do, college-wise."

I think, "Blah blah blah," but manage to say, "Okay . . ."

He goes on. "This way I can have a little more time to decide what I want to do after high school, and I can earn money, too."

Well that sounds reasonable, I guess. Lots of people choose a military option, I suppose. It just never occurred to me before. Besides, it's not like he has made his decision yet for sure. Now we are discussing the matter, like mature people in a mature relationship. Look at us. I uncross my arms. He reaches over and covers the top of my hand with his. My shoulders relax.

"Plus, boot camp is only a few months, and I will write to you all the time," he continues.

"Wait"—my anger bubbles back up—"you've already made your decision?"

Silence.

"So not only did you not share that you were thinking about this in the first place"—I'm really revved up now—"but you have already made your decision?!"

"Baby—"

"Don't '*Baby*' me!" I cut him off and stand up. "How many times have we talked about how important it is for us to be open and honest?!"

"I didn't want to hurt you." Brent stands and faces me.

He tries to hold my hands, but I pull back. "Too late!"

"Jamie, I'm sorry," he says, attempting an apology. "Just because I'm going into the Army doesn't mean we can't be together."

There is a tiny part of me that wants to believe that, but this is just too much.

"I gotta go," I say flatly.

"What do you mean?" he asks worriedly.

"Brent, good-bye," I state.

"Good-bye? But you just got here," he protests.

As I start up the stairs he follows and persists. "Can I call you tonight? Can I come to your house tomorrow? Do you want to meet at Subway for lunch?"

On the last step I turn around and face him. "No."

I don't give him a chance to respond. "Look, Brent, if you can't include me on your important life decisions, then I don't see how this is going to work. Since you are leaving me in a few months anyway, why prolong the inevitable?"

He opens his mouth, but nothing comes out. I continue to the door, but then realize he has to hold the dog for me. Instead of fetching the dog, though, he stands at the top of the stairs, as if that will keep me from going.

"I'm not leaving you," he promises. "This just feels like a good decision for me."

I close my eyes and breathe, trying to stay as composed as possible. "Look," I manage, and my voice only shakes slightly. I open my eyes and continue, "I am glad you feel like this is a good decision for you." And I mean it. "It just doesn't feel like a good decision for *us.*"

He stops speaking as this truth hits him in the gut.

"I need to go," I firmly repeat.

Our eyes lock. Mine well up, as his search for some sign that everything is going to be okay. That we can "fix" this or figure it out. As the first tear slips down my cheek, I look down and carefully pull his senior key from around my neck and off over my head.

"What?" he starts.

I tuck the key tightly into his palm and quietly beg, "Please let me go."

He stiffens at these words. I brush his shoulder as I walk past him, careful not to make eye contact. I feel his despondent stare as

131

he holds the collar, white-knuckled, and watches me leave. My throat fills with that gross giant lump thing that always surfaces right before my ugly-cry outbursts. It takes all I have to swallow it back down.

I manage to make it down the stairs without stumbling, step across the gravel, and close my car door determinedly. The engine turns, and the last note of "Girls Just Wanna Have Fun" fades over the speakers. I pull out of the drive and focus on the next song, so I am not tempted to look back. Bret Michaels sighs and breaks it to me that every rose has its thorn. I attempt to blink back tears, only to immediately realize my attempt is in vain. As tears spill out, I can't help but wonder if Bret and that deejay have, in fact, ever felt like *this*.

* * *

It has been a week since Army Drama Night. I worry that my eyes may be permanently puffy and bloodshot. I can't keep avoiding him, though, especially because I do need to figure out logistics for prom next weekend. We blew back from a track meet in Cut Bank about an hour ago. I helped Dad unload the bus then came down here to his keyboarding classroom.

I log on to Messenger and sure enough, Brent is logged on as well.

"Hi," I type.

The cursor blinks at me several times before an eloquent "Hi" crosses my screen.

"Congrats on your amazing pole vault today," I continue, struggling to create casual conversation after a week of agony with no communication.

"Thanks. Looked like you did well in the hurdles," he replies politely.

"Hey, what time should we make reservations for dinner Saturday?" I decide to cut the chitchat and get to it.

Blinking.

More blinking.

I check to see if his internet maybe kicked him off, but his icon still comes up as "Available."

"Hello?" I type.

His words appear on my screen and cause that all too familiar punched-in-the-stomach feeling. "I am going to prom with Kari."

Now it is his turn to stare at the blinks. My mind reels as I try to make sense of this information. A million questions churn in my brain, but I am not going to give him the satisfaction.

"Oh," I respond, in the most unemotional way I can think of.

"Well I hope you have a blast, you incredible jerk." I can only be expected to stay unemotional for so long.

I am tempted to log out but for some reason keep reading, hoping somehow to make sense of the fact that he is telling me one week before my junior prom I do not have a date.

Here it comes. "Jamie, I'm sorry. I thought you didn't want to be with me anymore, and Kari and I had talked about going to senior prom years ago, if we didn't have other dates."

"That makes sense," I furiously type back. "That makes sense that you went ahead and got yourself another prom date without talking to me about any of it. This is starting to become familiar, you making huge decisions that affect me without actually discussing them with me. How silly of me. I should have figured it out on my own."

"Matthew doesn't have a date. You can go with him," he offers. Fury surges through me.

I narrow my eyes and clench my teeth while typing my final response. "Thank you for that kind offer for a pity date with your little brother (who I love, by the way, and this has nothing to do with him), but I am quite capable of finding my own date, thank you very much."

I block Brent from seeing that I am still online and continue to breathe noisily through my teeth. It takes about four seconds for me to think of who would infuriate Brent most seeing me with at prom. I manhandle my mouse and start a new conversation thread.

"Hi, Mike!" I preface.

Mike goes to school in Sunburst. My friendship with him has always driven Brent crazy, probably because Mike talks a lot and he talks loudly. And rumor has it he has a crush on me. Since I am in charge of creating the list for the grand march for prom (where all prom attendees wait in the wings in two separate lines while each couple is announced), I will make sure Brent and Mike will be near the end of the list, standing right next to each other for as long as possible. Picturing Brent in line clenching his jaw and fists while Mike talks nonstop behind him slightly suppresses my rage.

I am thankful Mike cannot see my face as I feign happiness and excitement with the words I type. "It's a long, boring story, but I am without a date for our prom next weekend. I know this is extremely short notice, but is there any way you would be able to drive over here and be my date?"

My cursor doesn't blink this time as Mike's rapid response races eagerly across my screen. "What time should I pick you up?"

Forget you, Brent Clark.

Chapter 23

May 21, 2001, junior year, Jeff's Graduation, Chester, Montana

Amanda and I file through the heavy wooden doors into the high school auditorium and sit next to Mom. My aunts, uncles, and grandparents fill the rest of the seats, and I wave at my cute little cousins scattered on laps and squished between adults. Dad is sitting at his usual station on stage, since he is and has been the senior class advisor for years. Each row around us tells a similar story with family members and friends gathered to witness this significant milestone. I remember attending these services since I was in kindergarten, but suddenly this one feels totally different. After today, my brother will be officially finished with high school, moving on to . . . to whatever one moves on to when becoming an "adult." So weird!

It has been a great week. Usually our family travels to Big Timber to visit our extended family.[67] This week, though, everyone made the trek up here to North Country. Grandma Joyce reaches across and tickles my neck with her trademark ruby red fingernails. Grandpa Helmar waves his cute little wave and Grandma Barb smiles and greets, "Hi, sweetie."[68]

---

[67] Big Timber, nestled at the base of the Crazy Mountains between Bozeman and Billings on I-90, is my favorite Montana town of around 1,500 people.

[68] My Grandpa Jim, my dad's dad, died of a stroke in 1996, and the high school football field in Big Timber has since been dedicated to him, as well as the town's civic center. Seeing the "Graham Field" sign above the field's scoreboard and his picture in the entrance to the gym always fills me with joy and pride.

My grandparents have lived right across the street from each other, on Stock Street and Fifth, since my mom's family moved in from the ranch on Otter Creek near the Yellowstone River in 1973. Mom was a sophomore, and it wasn't long before she met her new neighbor Jim Graham, the "big man on campus." He was the popular jock, and she the sweet, innocent, never-until-moving-to-town-had-running-water salutatorian.

Our family posing with my grandparents, Helmar and Barbara Branae, at Jeff's graduation from Chester High School, May 21, 2001

Our grandparents are hardworking, well-respected residents of Big Timber. When we visit, we take turns staying at one house then the other; if we stay at the Graham house for Thanksgiving, we stay at the Branae house for Christmas. Only recently have I realized just how idyllic this is. I always make sure to coordinate what time the sweet rolls will be ready at Grandma Joyce's and what time the homemade cinnamon rolls will come out of the oven at Grandma Barb's.

When I was little, there was always crazy snow in Big Timber over Thanksgiving weekend. One of my favorite memories is waking up at the Grahams' house to two-or-so-feet of snow. No plows had come through yet. Everything was untouched. I bundled up, opened the back door, and rolled out, down the back stairs that had turned into a snow ramp, across the backyard, across the street, across the next backyard, and to the back steps of Grandpa and Grandma Branaes' house. Just in time for second breakfast!

I smile down at my family members and feel a slight catch in my throat. Our superintendent's booming voice pulls my attention to the stage.[69] I study my brother. He is sitting in the middle of his classmates, wearing a silver graduation gown and one of those pointy hats. I wonder from where those crazy hats originated and why people still wear them? As with most things, though, Jeff manages to make even a silly hat look good. People often say we look a lot alike. That means I would be good-looking, if I were a boy. Anywhere we go, people know Jeff. I secretly call him Mr. Montana, and people not-so-secretly call me Jeff Graham's Little Sister. It never fails that I will be somewhere, meeting new people, and inevitably someone will say, "I didn't know Jeff Graham had a sister."

I politely smile and wonder what the reaction would be if I spouted, "You don't know how lucky he is."

To be honest, I am quite proud to be dubbed Jeff Graham's Little Sister. I would say 96.5% of the time. He has signed to play college basketball at Northern Montana College in Havre. We had a signing party for him at our house a few weeks back, and I imagine it will be quite fantastic to have him close by enough to watch several of his home games, but far enough away that I get the house and our parents all to myself (insert Dr. Evil "muahaha" here).

Somehow, the graduation ceremony is already almost over, closing with Leann Rimes' song "Please Remember." I can't help it. Even though I have been specifically trying to avoid this as much as possible over the last six weeks, I look up on the stage and directly at Brent. He is looking right back at me. My instinct is to look quickly away. Instead, his meaningful gaze grips me.

It has been torture, trying to avoid him in the hallways and the lunchroom and at track practice and track meets and the store, and everywhere! There are only so many hallways and only one

---

[69]Brian Barrows. Superintendent in Chester my junior year.

lunchroom, and we are on the same track team and have the same teachers and the same friends and this town is just so flipping small! No matter where I go or what I do, our paths constantly cross and tangle.

I met this great guy named Eddie on our "Close Up" trip to Washington, DC a few weeks back.[70] We connected on our first day there. We talked and made jokes and laughed, and it felt so nice. It felt like such a relief, so fresh and new and hopeful. We have been talking on the phone a lot ever since. I even have one of those 98-digit 500-minute phone card codes memorized. He is such a great guy and there is no drama.

So why doesn't that seem to be enough? Why do things still feel so confusing? Why does it still feel like this when I look at Brent? Like my heart is going to explode for pounding so hard. Like I can't pull in a full breath. Like I have no control. Why can't I control this??

Brent's stare stays steady. What is he thinking? I search his eyes for some clue to how he is feeling. He continues to look directly at me, intense and unblinking. Leann urges us to remember when we were there for each other. Salty tears cause me to blink, breaking our connection.

* * *

The receiving line for the graduates extends through the elementary hallway and ends at the old gym, where there is cake and punch and all that jazz. I squeeze in between Kaitlynn and Amanda. We hug and congratulate Carlane, Joe, Curtis, Andrea, Ryah, Heidi, Kali, Sean, Hannah, Johanna, Zeb, and then brother Jeffrey. I think about the note he recently scrawled across a back page of my yearbook that said, "Remember when you used to be Jeff Graham's little sister? Well, you still are."

How touching. I giggle as he hooks his arm around my neck and gives me a classic "big brother" hug. Though I often jest about exasperation with my brother (sometimes I jest, sometimes it is legit exasperation), I really do love him. Perhaps someday someone will query, "Jamie Graham has a brother? Who knew?"

---

[70] Edward "Eddie" Hawley, Jr. I met him on a "Close Up" trip the end of my junior year. We dated for a few months.

I become acutely aware of how close I am getting to Brent when Zeb, Kaitlynn's older brother, pulls me in for a hug very similar to Jeffrey's. For a brief moment, I worry that Zeb is going to give me a noogie, but he resists. Zeb mumbles something about coming back to check on us next year, but suddenly I cannot focus. I have a moment of panic where I picture myself fleeing through the back exit only a few feet behind me. Why did I wear these dumb heels and a dress? I cannot run nearly fast enough in this get-up. When did it get so hot in here? Is that deodorant going to live up to its name?

Zeb releases me, and I find myself standing face to face with Brent, caught by that intense sea-blue gaze. Curse you, sea-blue gaze! I am frozen, not sure whether to extend my hand for a shake, lean in for a wimpy side hug, or fake a smile and quickly move to the next graduate. He tilts his head to the side and produces that pathetic pout that always melts me. My shoulders relax as I exhale the breath I didn't realize I was holding.

I can't help it. I lean into his chest. He wraps his arms around me. His familiar touch still sends shivers through me. I instinctively reach out and twist a blonde lock between my thumb and forefinger. My fingers graze the silver chain that rests around his neck, and I am struck by a pang of regret.

Before I can stop myself, I whisper, "I love you."

Did I really just say that?! Oh, man, time to run. But before I can pull off my heels and book it toward the door, he clasps his fingers around my lower back. I shiver again when I feel his mouth graze my ear.

"I love you, too," he breathes back, barely audible.

I sink into him for a moment. Just a moment, though, because the momentum of the impatient line insists I move on. Isn't it obvious we are having a moment, people?!

I pull back and straighten up. "Good-bye, Brenton."

"Good-bye, Jamie."

139

Fourth Quarter

Do you not know that in a race all the runners run, but only one gets the prize? Run in such a way as to get the prize.

—1 Corinthians 9:24

2001 Chester Lady Coyotes

Chapter 24

August 2001, senior year, my girls, Chester, Montana

How did this happen? Usually I tease my parents and aunts and uncles for saying things like "time sure flies," or "now what happened to those years?" but I have to admit, now I can kinda see where they are coming from.

I just got back from hanging out with all my girls at Chasi's house since today was our last two-a-day practice. Ever. We watched *Anastasia* and cut Michele's hair, then we cut Amanda's. I am a little surprised people still let us cut their hair, after that accidental ten-inches-instead-of-two debacle with Chasi's 'do in junior high. We thought it would be a good idea for Mari to cut one side and I the other, but we thought wrong. We ate some graham crackers with rainbow chip frosting and talked about how crazy it is that we are officially seniors.

My fifth birthday party: Marjorie Dafoe, Kaitlynn Engstrom, Heidi Cicon, me, Maci Tempel, Emily Tranberg, Mari Tempel, March 27, 1989

I pull out the photo albums and yearbooks stacked under my bed (one would think these may be covered with dust, but nothing is dusty in Karen Graham's house) and find a picture of my fifth birthday party. A flock of five-year-olds don Mickey Mouse party hats and pose in front of a Donald Duck cake,

143

made of course by Carlane's mom. I smile when I see that almost all of my current teammates are in the photo. Those were the days. Things were so much simpler back then, when the only drama was deciding who would sit on which color line during alphabet time. My mind wanders back. . . .

Preschool was taught at the Methodist church that sits on the corner of Monroe Avenue and Highway 223, just across from Liberty Medical Center. Mrs. Krook was our teacher, and preschool was the best. When we gathered to sing or learn a letter, we all sat on a piece of one of the colorful taped-down lines that made nice, neat rows. The sensory table was one of my favorite sites to visit, what with its wonderful items to paw like sand, rice, and popcorn kernels. There were also places to paint and a fab collection of dress-up items, complete with several pairs of high heels.

My favorite preschool memory includes my first interaction with Heidi. Heidi, who was still a head taller than everyone then, caught me at free time, politely introduced herself and asked, "Who's your best friend?"

I responded, "Clay."

She shook her bouncy blonde side ponytail from side to side and tried to speak more clearly. "No. Who is your best *friend?*"

This time, a bit more slowly with my head cocked slightly I responded again, enunciating a bit more, "Clay."

Now that ponytail was really waggling, and the exasperation could be heard in her voice. "No! Not '*What do you like to play with?!*' Who is your best *friend?!*"

Now it was my turn to be frustrated, so I rose my voice to clarify once and for all, "Clay Herron!!"

Heidi quickly calmed down, her hair quieted, she smiled and said, finally satisfied, "Oh! It's a person!" And though Clay, the older neighbor boy across the street, was indeed my best friend at that time, Heidi quickly moved up the bench.

That Clay story ranks right up there with the time in freshman history when we were looking through our test packet to see if any errors had been made. Heidi took her packet—folded to the section on oceans—up front. Smiling politely, as if poor old Mr. Kulpas was losing it, Heidi defended why Mr. K. should not have marked that one particular question wrong: "I wasn't talking about the Pacific Ocean. I was *being pacific.*"

I sure do love that tall, beautiful blonde. Nowhere could you find a kinder, harder-working person. She lets us tease her about her "blonde moments" because she knows it is out of love. I had a feeling she would be special to me for a long time after that first preschool interaction, and I was right (as usual).

When we moved to Chester from Denton when I was an infant, we became connected with the Schlepp family. Our families lived next door to each other in two of the school's teacherages. Mr. Schlepp, or "Billy-boy" as I like to call him (not at school, of course), has been the high school principal and football coach for years. Stacy job shares with my mama at the Hugh Brown Law Office. Stacy and Mom swapped when we were little. Stacy would work one week while Mom babysat Jeff and me along with her kids, Brian and Amanda, and then they would switch. Due to this arrangement, Brian and Amanda have always been like siblings to us.

Brian, Jeff, me, and Amanda leading a cheer at a pep assembly the weekend of the boys' state tournament in Bozeman, 1992

I loved being at Amanda's house because of the constant supply of delicious treats, the excellent choice of VHS movies recorded from HBO, especially *Rainbow Brite* and *Care Bears,* and all of Amanda's toys that I coveted. There was a seemingly endless supply of scrumptious Red Vines licorice, yummy caramel corn cooling on flattened out IGA paper bags, and puppy chow (I realized that puppy chow may be the best treat in the world after confirming that Bill was just teasing when he told me it was chow for actual puppies). We all watched *Fun House* at three thirty, and I would often stay for dinner as well as Disney's *Kids Incorporated,* as long as I confirmed (by smell) that

145

they were not having canned spinach that night. Amanda and I spent hours playing with her Popples, Rainbow Brite, Cootie—that glow-worm doll—and My Little Ponies. Amanda has always been there for me, even when we have our random little tiffs, because she is the little sister I never had.[71]

Amanda Schlepp's fifth birthday party, me squinting in the sunshine, at a table between our teacherage and the Schlepps' teacherage, September 12, 1989

In the summers, similar to many small towns I do suppose, a lot of time was spent riding bikes, playing baseball (I mostly remember drawing pictures in the infield sand with sticks), and swimming at the city pool for hours every day. There were a lot of regulars at the pool, but Emily was my most consistent poolmate.

Emily could, and still can, make any activity interesting. From making up and recording episodes of *Montel Williams* with Barbie dolls (original commercials included) to recruiting a large percentage of grade school students to prank call 1-800 numbers, if you think you are ever bored hanging out with Emily, you actually are not. And the pool was where Emily really shined. She could make up games that would keep us entertained for hours. When I get extra hungry,

---

[71] I now feel so incredibly lucky to also have three amazing sisters-in-law—my brother's wife Megan, who I mentioned before, and my husband's sweet sisters, Naomi and Alycia.

I still flash back to treading water in the deep end for two hours, just to see if we could do it, and how a Tombstone pizza and Chester Fried Chicken (I was devastated to find out that chicken did not really originate here) never sounded so good.

Emily still struggles with her knee. She tore her ACL practicing one last pole vault the morning we were to leave for state track. She has decided not to play basketball this year. This makes me so sad. She has always been my teammate. It is what it is, though. She will still pick me up for school in her good old Honda, and if I need to be cheered up or just need something to do Emily still is my go-to.

Winters in Chester, high up here some fifty-odd miles from Canada, are as one might expect: freaking cold. A perk of having temperatures below freezing for so long is that I could lace up my skates on our front steps and skate on down to the rink right on the roads. This eliminated those awful, insufferably cold moments of switching from boots to skates on the rink's bench; if one toe touched a bit of snow, it was all over. It was also convenient having the rink be only two blocks away (to be fair, everywhere in Chester is about two blocks away).

I did a lot of skating with Amanda and Emily, but my Olympic skating partner was Kaitlynn, whose town house is conveniently located directly across the street from the rink. Now even though Kaitlynn had fancy skates that didn't bend and cause those painful, frequent ankle twists, and I got my skates from the annual county skate trade at the school cafeteria, we still made a pretty dynamic duo. Year in and year out, with Kaitlynn at the helm, we took the Olympic gold medal for figure skating (our Olympics occurred yearly, so we didn't have to wait the entire four years). There were times when it was extremely suspenseful, but we always kept our poise and pulled through.

Katy and I also often pretended that we had boyfriends (usually my boyfriend was her boyfriend's younger brother). We would fake call them on the phone and pretend dance with them while listening to Trisha Yearwood's "She's in Love with the Boy."

Kaitlynn is just now recovering from back surgery. Turns out, she was squished between the Jones twins fighting for a rebound last year at State. After somehow making it through both volleyball and track, quite successfully I might add, she found out she had not one, but two herniated discs that entire time. Kaitlynn is one tough cookie (we also both love Oreo cookies), an optimist and hopeless romantic, like me, and always there for a heart-to-heart.

Chasi Lee has always been stunningly beautiful, with her golden hair, dark eyebrows, adorable tiny nose, and gorgeous smile. When people first meet Chas, though, sometimes they get the wrong impression—that she actually isn't the sweetest person on the planet. This is due to her RBF (resting b**** face), which is completely misleading and also not her fault. That is just how her face looks when she is concentrating.

Back in elementary school, Chasi often sat by me at lunch. I am one of the slowest eaters in America (though I am not sure why). This has gotten a bit better, but when I was younger, it was especially awful. Every day during lunch, I would still be eating when the high schoolers came to line up. This was a huge deal. You did not want to be in the lunchroom when the high schoolers were lining up. Even though the risk of still being at a table when the "big kids" entered was great, Chasi always waited for me. And even in second grade, when Miss Murphy poked my top lip, discovered the peach I had stuffed up there and tried to conceal, then made me sit back down and swallow the gross slimy thing, Chasi remained by my side. She is loyal, she is dang tough, and I am always thankful to have her on my side.

Michele moved to Chester the summer before fifth grade. Moving to Chester from Plevna was a big deal for the VanDykes, since the population of Chester (around one thousand) is about ten times that of Plevna. That first summer, Michele and I rode our bikes around town for miles and miles and miles. At first I feared for Michele's safety, as it seemed she could not hear vehicles coming from behind and would generally ride in the middle of the street. We don't have to worry about too much traffic in Chester, but apparently there is a lot more traffic than she was used to. She also claims that she would call me to see if I wanted to play, and if my mom said I was still eating dinner she wouldn't dare call back for at least another hour.

Michele is generally up for anything and went through a phase of dyeing her hair a variety of colors. My personal favorite was when it perfectly matched her family's fire-engine red suburban. People are drawn to Michele and her laid-back personality. I would describe her as the most popular girl in school, but not like those snotty popular girls in the movies. She is popular because she just has that "cool" vibe about her, yet she is still nice to everyone.

My favorite thing to do around Michele is to tease her. I like to think of myself as her goofy sidekick. Mostly I focus on her impossibly long toes and try to give high fives to her feet. I love her sense of humor and how she often reminds me that everything is going to be okay, like that time she talked me down after I read the back of a box of tampons for the first time and was convinced I was going to die of toxic shock syndrome.

Mari and Maci, or Twin One and Twin Two, didn't spend much time in town until junior high, when their parents bought their town house. (When they did come to town in the summers, though, it was a big deal to get to go to the swimming pool with them.) When they got the town house, it quickly became my favorite place to hang out, as well as most other teenagers around town. The best thing about it is there are always kids around to hang out with, and seldom adults. We have watched a lot of movies and eaten a lot of Kool-Aid dessert in that house.

Maci and I were best friends in first grade, and we even made up a ceremony of sorts to make the friendship "official." It included both of us holding on to the circular zip line thing that was near the slides on the playground. We looked at each other and smiled all the way across. I remember once when we had a spat of some sort, probably about Four Square, and we held on to the zip line again, but this time looked away, with angry faces. One thing I love about Maci is that even when she is upset about something, or when things between my brother and her are off-again, she doesn't stay upset long, and she is always willing to do what is best for the team.

Mari and I had some good times, especially in junior high, from constantly quoting Pauly Shore movies to playing in pep band to performing in the community production of *Annie* as orphans together. I hate that things happened the way they did with her and Brent and me. I wish I would have handled things better. It all just got so complicated, so confusing, and so out of control so fast.

I am thankful Mari and I are the editors of the newspaper this year. Maybe I can work on building up a new relationship with her through our shared love for writing, and it does help that we get to be in charge. She has also decided not to play basketball this year, because of her knee injury, and I think I am in denial that she and Emily won't be out there on the court with us. We have had some different teammates now since being in high school, but in our class it has always been the eight of us. I know things are constantly changing and that's just the way life is, but sometimes I just wish they didn't have to.

"Jame! Dinner!" Mom calls up from the kitchen. I snap back to the present.

Glancing at my clock radio I see it indeed is six o'clock on the dot. One thing all my friends know is six o'clock in the evening is a non-negotiable because cute Mama Karen will have dinner on the table. Jeff and I can negotiate with our parents about certain things, they are quite flexible and understanding for the most part, but not when it comes to dinnertime.

I hastily slam the photo album closed and shove the pile of books back under my bed. As I rush downstairs I hear the theme song for *Jeopardy*. I imagine that someday, years later when I am out on my own and being an adult somewhere, I will hear the *Jeopardy* theme song and salivate, just like that whole Pavlov thing that I learned about. Now where did I learn about that? Hmm. I think it was probably a clue on *Jeopardy*.

Chapter 25

August 2001, senior year, beginning of regular season, Chester, Montana

We proudly don the same home uniforms, look expectantly at the same whiteboard, and sit on the same uncomfortable benches in the same locker room. Yet everything is different. It is our senior season. It is boggling my mind how familiar things can feel, but somehow at the same time, completely new.

I take a look around at my teammates: Heidi, Michele, Chasi, Maci, Amanda, and Savannah. Kaitlynn is here, too, but she is wearing street clothes due to the fact that she recently had her spine sliced open to repair her herniated discs. I thought that kind of stuff only happened to old men, but leave it to poor Kaitlynn to suffer some random, terrible ailment. Not only that, but leave it to her to come out of it like the rock star that she is, with a goal of suiting up just like us by senior night.

Coach VanDyke enters, followed by Coach Schlepp, and she exudes confidence and excitement as she smiles out at us. Her enthusiasm is contagious. We all sit up a little straighter as we smile back.

"Well here we are, ladies," she begins. "For six of you, it is your senior year. You set high goals years ago, and this is our opportunity to achieve those goals. Remember, a goal not written down is not a goal at all, it is merely a wish. So what do you suppose we are going to do here before we play tonight?"

I was very hopeful—and maybe a bit cocky—posing for basketball pictures
at the start of my senior year.

Good old Heidi, who usually has the right answer in class (we are tied for our class's valedictorian spot), pulls through again: "We are going to set specific goals for this season."

"Correct," Coach confirms. "Each year we have a theme, if you will. For instance, last year we focused on the fact that each one of us is unique, and that we play many roles. We talked about how we are called many names, such as "daughter" or "sister," just like that Jessica Andrews song "Who I Am." We are important to many people. This year our theme is going to be that we are all pieces of a puzzle. And what do you do if a piece of the puzzle is missing?"

Amanda immediately pipes up with confidence, "You put the pieces back in the box and sell it at a garage sale!"

My giant laugh explodes out of me, and my teammates join. Both coaches are shaking their heads, laughing. It takes a minute for us all to compose ourselves. Coach attempts to get us back on track. "Well, the answer I was looking for was that the puzzle will not be complete."

"Ohhh." Amanda—or "Bulldog" as we often refer to her, due to her generally expressionless face—nods her head to show that now she understands. "That makes more sense."

"Yes, so know that each of you is an important piece to our puzzle. And when each piece knows where it needs to be—knows her role—everything will line up. The puzzle will be complete. So what are the goals we need to meet in order to complete our puzzle?"

"Make 70% of our free throws," Maci starts.

"Make 75% of our bunnies," Katy continues.

"Hold teams under forty points," Chasi chimes in.

"Win every quarter," Savannah offers.

"Average seventy points a game," I add.

"Less than thirteen turnovers," Michele states.

"It's 'fewer,' Michele," I correct.

Used to my sass and insistence on good grammar, Michele quickly and instinctively responds, "You can shut it, Jamie," without even blinking or looking my way.

"Okay, good," Coach says as she catches up and gets the turnover goal written. "Anything else?"

Heidi, who has been listening intently, furrows her brow and suggests, "Why don't we just score more points than the other team?"

There is momentary silence that is shattered by hysterical laughter.

When we all finally settle down, Coach caps the dry-erase marker and agrees. "You know what, Heidi, that might be our best goal yet. If we can score more points than every team we play, every game, we will reach our ultimate goal of winning State."

We nod, smiling, then clasp hands to pray. As I recite the Lord's Prayer with my teammates, I silently add, *Dear God, please be with us this season. Keep us healthy and hardworking, keep us humble, and remind us that we are a part of something bigger than ourselves. Thank you for this opportunity to be on this team. Amen.*

* * *

So far so good. Things feel familiar and focused so far this year. We are off to a good 4-0 start, beating Joplin-Inverness 100–21 in the opener, Shelby 65–38, Fort Benton 65–37, and Valier 84–34. We revisit our season goals daily before practice, and we have added that we would like to have an undefeated season. Why not?

Practices are short and sweet this year, rarely exceeding an hour and a half. One reason is because there are only seven of us practicing on varsity at the moment, with Kaitlynn on the DL, so we get lots of reps in every drill and move constantly. Coach doesn't have to explain much and prefers to let us lead as much as possible. Tuesday practices are even shorter, because we each pick two drills, then proceed to run that drill for five minutes, timed on the clock. It has been interesting to note that many of our "favorite" drills are flat-out tough. Chasi especially likes to make sure we get in plenty of defense, her favorite being the grueling defensive slide figure eights.

We have learned the importance of pushing each other at all times. Not only is this important, it is key. I have heard about players, especially girls, being petty or selfish. I have seen players specifically not passing to a teammate due to jealousy. Or someone not speaking to a teammate off the court after a particularly heated moment during a game or practice. Or parents complaining about their daughter's playing time, disagreeing with the coaches' decisions, and on and on. None of this makes any sense to me. Our coaches work hard to communicate their expectations for us. We are fully aware of our roles and know that without all the pieces, the puzzle just doesn't connect.

Our practices certainly are intense, but to say they are always serious and bereft of shenanigans would be extremely false. Most days we pick a certain way to wear our hair (side ponytails, ridiculously high buns, Pippi Longstocking pigtail braids) or our clothes (inside out, backwards, or my personal favorite, pulling our drawstrings over our heads so our shorts are as high as our moms wear their pants). We of course talk during every drill, usually with the proper basketball lingo like, "Ball! Help! Deny!" Then there may or may not be some sass and trash talk peppered in here and there as well, all in good fun of course.

Today my shorts are hiked up to my boobs, and I sprint straight-faced through our passing warm-up formation, screaming each teammate's name at the top of my lungs before passing her the ball.

"Heidi!" I screech. "Chasi! Amanda! Maci! Savannah! Michele!"

Luckily Michele manages to catch and return the ball to me without bobbling, which is impressive seeing as her eyes are all squinty and tears are streaming down the sides of her cheeks. It looks like she may need to make a quick trip to the loo.

We transition to the corner and Chasi and Savannah go head-to-head in the zigzag drill. Maci and I step out next, and her eyes hone in on my middle as I attempt to juke her out while keeping the ball protected. "You want some of this?" I bait.

Maci stays low, but the smallest trace of a smile flickers across her mouth. She keeps me in front when I dribble low between my left leg then wrap the ball behind my back on the next dribble. She is already standing in my way. One thing about going one-on-one with the same people for seven years is they start to anticipate your moves, forcing you to either get frustrated and make excuses, or work harder and constantly evolve.

After we switch offense to defense, and I *almost* cause Maci to turn it over, we grab quick drinks and assume our positions on the baseline. Hearing the word "baseline" used to produce a formidable feeling in my stomach. Finally identifying I was letting that feeling of dread dictate my thoughts, I have since chosen to respond to that word with, "Bring. It. On."

155

Turns out, I actually have the ability to choose what I focus my thoughts on, then how I react with my words and actions. (I do believe my parents, coaches, and teachers have been trying to tell me that for years, but for some reason—even though I generally know they are likely right about many things—I cannot always accept what they say right away.) This doesn't mean I don't react impulsively or say anything wrong or make bad choices, but I am working on it.

Coach Schlepp jogs over to press play on our mixed tape we made for conditioning. Bon Jovi starts us off as we begin our up and backs for the endurance run. Our goal is for the team to run it under 10:45, which means we get through about three songs. When "It's My Life" fades out, Chumbawamba's "Tubthumping" takes over. As the clock ticks down to 4:42, Freddie Mercury's soft "I've paid my dues" sneaks across the court. We all turn quickly toward the speakers. Coach Schlepp sprints across the floor and hits stop just when Freddie lingers on "time after time."

That was a close one.

Every time "We Are the Champions" threatens to play on our conditioning tape, Coach Schlepp immediately stops and fast forwards through the power ballad. Ever since only taking third at State our freshman year, it has been forbidden to listen to a song that we cannot yet claim. As the tape screeches forward, we kick it into the next gear. Though the gym is quiet for a few moments, save for a few squeaks when we pivot, the thoughts inside my head are loud and clear.

Chapter 26

September 11, 2001, senior year, Chester High School, Chester, Montana

It is Tuesday morning, and a few of my girls and I lie near the piano on the stage in the high school auditorium. I lie on my back and use Heidi's stomach as a pillow, smiling as my pillow rises and falls rapidly when Kaitlynn finishes a funny story. High schoolers like to complain about, well, most things, but if I am truly honest, I do enjoy my classes here at CHS. My schedule is pretty great this year, and I love starting the day with my girls and Miss Goodheart in choir. Even though the bell hasn't quite yet rung, we know it soon will and prepare to warm up our beautiful voices.

Just as we are really getting into our warm-ups, our principal Mr. Schlepp enters the auditorium and walks determinedly down the aisle. He beckons to Miss Goodheart. She instructs Heidi to take over.

"La la la la la la laaaaaa," we scale, while keeping an eye on the intense conversation happening between our two superiors.

The scales stop completely at a gasp from Miss G, and now we don't even pretend that we aren't attempting to eavesdrop. Mr. Schlepp signals to us, and we file out the heavy wooden doors in quiet confusion. They lead us across the lunchroom then left down a white tiled hallway into the high school library. We join a crowd of students and teachers alike, looking appalled and staring in awe at the television perched near the periodicals. I glance around the crowd, trying to figure out what could possibly be going on. Mrs. Gordon's left hand is covering her open mouth. Miss Behem doesn't seem to trust herself standing and gropes behind her to find a chair, eyes glued to the screen. I spot Dad off to the right side near the front of the crowd, arms crossed and supported by his signature power stance. He weaves wordlessly through the crowd toward me, leans in, wraps a powerful arm around my shoulders, and kisses my forehead.

My focus finally settles enough for me to see that the picture on the screen is of the two towers in New York at the World Trade Center, and lots and lots of smoke. The reporter (Vince Cellini, CNN Anchor, according to the label on the bottom of the screen) attempts to share what is known at this point:

> It's obviously something devastating that has happened. And again, there are unconfirmed reports that a plane has crashed into one of the towers there. We are efforting more information on the subject as it becomes available to you (CNN, 2003).

More reporters describe the scene. Soon the picture switches to the Pentagon. My heart races, and so does my mind, trying to make sense of this senselessness. Words like "terrorist attacks," "uncertainty," and "helpless" gnaw at my nerves. I hear Mr. Rooley and Dad murmur something about us remembering this moment like they remember JFK.

* * *

It has been a week since the attacks. As usual, I try to avoid watching or listening to the depressing news as much as possible, but the word "war" keeps creeping in, despite my efforts. I know I should be praying more for all of the people killed and all their family members, for our leaders to make good decisions, and for some way to rise up against evils like this. And I do pray for that. But mostly, I pray for Brent. I get especially worried at night. I wonder where he is. I wonder what this means for him.

For the most part, it has been a pretty normal week. Normal as in there haven't been any more terrifying terrorist attacks and maybe things will somehow be okay after all. Practice was short and sweet, and we enjoyed wonderful yoga to wrap things up today. Heidi, Mari, and I ate Subway and went to play practice from seven to nine o'clock. It has been fun practicing for the community production of *The Wizard of Oz*, even though it sometimes means I don't start my homework until close to ten o'clock. (Or I just procrastinate and whip it out in study hall the next morning.)

Just after I reach my room, Mom and Dad come in for the nightly ritual of kissing me goodnight and telling me how much they love me and how proud they are of me. Cute Jim and Karen. When they leave, I see Mom left a letter on my pillow. I immediately recognize the handwriting. I can't help my hands trembling as I sit on the edge of my bed and carefully tear open the corners.

Wednesday, September 12, 2001

Dear Jme,

As you can imagine, things are pretty crazy around here. Yesterday I was in the midst of my phase 2 field training exercise (FTX, the Army loves acronyms). My battle buddy, Private Cook, and I were lying in our hasty fighting positions (foxholes) in our complete NBC (nuclear, biological, and chemical) PPE (personal protective equipment) suits and gas masks. We had been lying there for about three hours because they were acclimating us to wearing these awful suits. Complete agony let me tell you. That's when I learned that I am claustrophobic when my hands are gloved and those gloves fill with sweat.

We were not told right away about the terrorist attacks yesterday, due to us being so far away from those sites, but when we were notified one of the drill sergeants gathered everyone and tried to find out who was from New York so they could get them to a phone. I thought it was some kind of (weird) joke on the brand-new soldiers at first.

I don't know what all of this chaos and fear will bring. I don't know where they will send me next. What I do know is that when I heard about the attacks, and everyone was stunned and freaked out and wanting to contact loved ones, you were the first person that came to my mind. I'm not telling you this to make you feel sorry for me, or to ask you to get back together with me. I just want you to know that I think this means that wherever I am and whatever I am doing, you will always be special to me.

159

Please write to me to let me know how you are. I hope your senior year is going great. It really is like they say and goes faster than you think. It's weird because I couldn't wait to get out of Chester. Now I sometimes have a hard time remembering why. I hope you are kicking butt in basketball.

I love you, Jamie (and think maybe I always will).

Love,
Brenton

My thoughts are all jumbled as I read his words. My eyes scan and rescan, homing in again and again on the parts about me being the first person that came to his mind and wondering what this chaos and fear will bring and that he thinks he may always love me. How can this be real? How can someone I know be in the Army when there are rumors of war? Real live war. We are talking war like you-better-kiss-me-and-hold-me-because-we-may-never-see-each-other-again-*Pearl-Harbor*-Ben-Affleck-Kate-Beckinsale kinda stuff here.

Brent and me posing before going to the winter formal "Snowball" December, 1999

My arm instinctively reaches for the burned CD Brenton gave me the night before he left for boot camp. My sweet six-disc CD player whirs to life as I press the power button. I set his CD in the empty number four slot, sandwiched between Deana Carter's *Did I Shave My Legs for This?* and Matchbox 20's *Yourself or Someone Like You.* Then I lie back on the thick, woolly blue-gray carpet and close my eyes. Tiny streams of tears form down each cheek and drip onto the carpet as I listen to the first measures of the first song, "I Was Born the Day You Kissed Me" by Rascal Flatts. The streams swell when Lonestar's

160

"Smile" follows. Now my thoughts of missing Brent swirl with memories of Annie. These are the last thoughts I remember until waking sometime a few hours later, still on the floor.

I roll over and feel around for the lamp switch on my bedstead. I pull out a pad of paper from under my bed and pen a response to Brent.

Wednesday, September 18, 2001

Dear Brenton,

I am so, so relieved to read this letter from you. My hands were shaking when I was opening the envelope, and I am not exactly sure why. Last week was just so crazy. I cannot imagine how scary it was for you. I have been trying to pray a lot, but I do not always know exactly what to pray for or how to pray, you know? Mostly I end up praying that you are safe and that you don't feel too scared.

It sounds lonely where you are. All those weird acronyms do not sound like fun. Especially the parts about wearing wild suits and gas masks and being in fields for hours on end. Please keep me updated about anything and everything you are doing, if you can, and if you feel like sharing. I can't imagine all the thoughts that go through your head during those various exercises.

My senior year really is going great, and thanks for asking. It's been a little weird without you here, without Jeff and the rest of your class, but for the most part the atmosphere is really great. I love having your brothers in high school with me. We hang out a lot with them and their friends, like Isaac and Mitchy, and they make me laugh all the time (I know that's hard to believe since it is so difficult to make me laugh). Basketball is awesome. We are just a little ways into the regular season and rolling so far. Everyone is super focused, and I really feel like we are finally going to take State this year. Actually, I am not sure what I will do if we don't, so we just better win!

It is hard to know what exactly to write to you. I miss you. I miss you all the time. I know we dated off and on and things were too often complicated, but you were one of my best friends since junior high. When I become close friends with someone, I don't exactly know how to not be friends. I have always felt like God gave me a gift of being able to love many people. I don't mean like have a bunch of

161

boyfriends or anything weird like that, but I just really love people. I see the best in most everyone. I hate the thought of losing friends. You know how hard it was for me when my relationship with Mari got so bad. (She and I have been hanging out a lot so far this year, and I am so thankful for this.)

Anyway, I am not sure what else to say. I just kept rereading the part in your letter where you said you think you may always love me. I imagine that was maybe hard for you to write, but I am glad you told me. And I know you didn't write it so I would feel sorry for you or anything like that. In fact, I think I understand exactly what you mean. And I want you to know that wherever I am and whatever I am doing, you will always be special to me, too.

I love you, Brenton (and think maybe I always will).

Love,
Jme

I fold the page in half, half again, then one more time over before tucking it into a crisp, white envelope. I meticulously copy the complicated military address, making sure the "APO" part is clearly legible. I say a quick prayer for Brenton's safety as I lick the starchy weird but not too weird tasting glue and slowly seal the letter, careful to pinch all the bumps tight so it is nice and smooth.

* * *

It has been a great month and a half. We finally beat Belt in Belt, 63-53, after losing there both last year and sophomore year. We did get behind once, in the fourth quarter, but it was only once and only for a very short time. Coach told us we did a good job keeping our composure. Then we pummeled Heart Butte at home, 96-40. I could not miss that night. It really did feel like I was "in the zone." I shot a 74% field goal percentage (14-19), going 3-3 from behind the arc and 4-4 from the free throw line for a personal best thirty-five points, and also had eight assists and six steals. The best thing about that game was that it wasn't a big deal that I scored the most points I have ever scored. Every person on our team scored. *We* won, together.

The next weekend we beat Kremlin-Gilford 76–40, but we had a ridiculous twenty-one turnovers, followed by nineteen turnovers the next night versus Blue Sky, where the final was 93–35. No one was thrilled about those stats, and all the next week in practice we concentrated on *taking care of the ball, for the love!* That seemed to work, because in our 88–30 victory against Sunburst we got it down to twelve turnovers, and we had only eleven with our 120–21 decision over Joplin-Inverness.

Chapter 27

September–October 2001, senior year, homecoming, etc., Chester, Montana

Heidi and me saying the pledge on Patriotic Day during Homecoming week

September 24, 2001: Today's Homecoming dress-up theme was "Patriotic Day." I wore shiny blue track tights under my white shorts, a bright red shirt, and a red beanie with "USA" printed on it. Heidi dressed like a flag, and we looked amazing. People kept looking at us and laughing. Jealous. Practice was very easy tonight. It consisted of us doing yoga, cardio-ab, and we talked to the junior high girls forever. Hopefully we inspired them. Amanda and I ate Subway and then went to play practice. We then went to Heidi's house, and we got a bunch of songs on a mixed tape. We eight varsity players are going to make up a dance for the Homecoming bonfire. The JV girls are making up a dance, too, and we will go head to head on Thursday night. It is going to be sweet.

September 25, 2001: Today was a good day. Lunch was delicious, hot dog wraparounds. Last week when I had to miss lunch on Monday for a doctor's appointment, Debbie made me my own special stromboli the next day. How sweet is that? Then I walked downtown with Marjorie, Kylene, Cory, Chance, and Wade. Practice tonight was awesome. It was really hard, but we were so intense and it was just good. Our team ate pizza and spaghetti at Tempels', and then we met in Heidi's basement and made up our dance for the bonfire. We have all kinds of sweet songs like "Ain't Too Proud to Beg," "Eye of the Tiger," "Right Kind of Wrong," "Can't Touch This," "Come on Over, Baby," "I've Got the Power," and we are ending with "The Devil Went Down to Georgia." Heidi watched the last scene of *Coyote Ugly* a bazillion times, memorized the last line dance and taught it to us. It is so awesome. We caught Matt, Colt D., Chris, Geoff O., Cory, Wade, and Jeff C. trying to spy on us through Heidi's basement windows, so we had to hang up some towels.

September 26, 2001: Chester Homecomings are cursed, turns out. Last year Heart Butte canceled because I can't remember why, and today JI canceled tomorrow's game due to lack of players for some reason. They at least rescheduled for next Wednesday. I wanted to play tomorrow, of course, but I am very happy the bonfire is still on. School was alright, and practice was, too, but it was about as tough as yesterday so my legs are dead. Tonight after dinner (chicken, mmm) Mari and I did our English iambic pentameter at the school, and then we worked on the newspaper. We were there forever, but it was good. We went upstairs and talked to Debbie, Heidi, Brian, and PJ, who were at play practice. Turns out Mari and I are very funny people when we are together. I am still addicted to peanut butter M&Ms and seasoned sunflower seeds.

September 27, 2001: Tomorrow is finally Friday, thank goodness. Today was quite easy as far as school goes, and our practice was a bit difficult, but only at the end. We practiced our dance one last time at Cicons' after dinner so we could videotape it. Mari and I went to the store, play practice, and then to the bonfire. The senior and junior boys on the football team lost in a tug-of-war to the underclassmen, but I will say they had a lot fewer people, and the coaches helped the freshmen and sophomores. Our basketball teams' dances were both awesome, but the boys booed us varsity girls.

I can't be sure why they booed us, but it might have had something to do with a remark I made on the microphone when it was time for our dance that maybe the juniors and seniors would actually win something tonight. Then Tina and the other cheerleaders led us in some funny games that included shaving cream and eggs and the crowd did lots of cheers after that. Everyone went to the store afterward, and I got home around 10:00.

September 28, 2001: Today was our last float decorating day, ever. A few times I would just stop and look around at my class and think about all that we have been through together. Most of my classmates I have known since I was five. Everyone worked together so well the whole day, and it was a blast. The boys built and painted a giant ship out of wood on the trailer. The theme was "Disney," so one sign said, "U Can't Beat Us, Even in Never Never Land," and we had a sign on the front that said, "Class of '02: Coyotes Will Tinker Your Bell." We dressed up the stuffed coyote as Peter Pan and wrapped him around this giant round pole in the middle of the ship. We hung a doll with sparkly wings in the front, and she was Tinker Bell, and we dressed a life-size mannequin in yellow football shorts and a purple sweatshirt (the Big Sandy player) and a helmet. Then we draped the mannequin across the plank. It was amazing.

We have come a long way since making our first float as seventh graders. I remember there was a lot of chicken wire and tissue paper on that seventh-grade float, but since we live in the windiest place in the world, no one could actually tell what we had made and tissue paper was flying all over the place.

There was a brief, nerve-racking moment at the end of the parade today where we thought our float got disqualified, like last year. Last year our float really was awesome, with the giant garbage can that we made look like a toilet. Then the boys put a generator inside and made it whirl around and squirt water out. Unfortunately, the combination of the generator near the water and the toilet paper caused sparks and then a fire. In our defense, it was a very small fire. Anyway, we were nervous we were somehow DQed again today because our float driver had to pull out of the parade. It turns out the mast of the ship almost hit a powerline, so the driver just had to take a different route. So after the parade they announced that our float won! Finally. I am taking this victory as a good sign for our basketball season.

I marched in the parade for pep band for the last time, and then I went home and took a nap. Then I went to Tempels' and did hair for Hannele and Katherine, who are both Homecoming queen candidates, before the football game. Preston was with us, too, so that was cool.[72] A bunch of us ate at the taco/potato feed at the church, I sat with Trista and Megann, so that was fun. Then I played pep band for the football game. It was kind of sprinkling and there were two beautiful rainbows. Jeff came home with three friends from college, and I introduced myself and Chasi and Heidi. We talked to them for a quarter, and Chasi and I decided college boys are the same as high school boys. They never change. What dreadful news. There were a lot of people at the store afterward. Mari gave me a ride home, I iced my ankle, ate peanuts and ice cream, and watched Disney. Tomorrow we are all going to help Coach time the Fun Run at the Fitness Center. Peace.

October 1, 2001: "Madam I'm Adam"—same backwards and forwards. Mrs. Gordon showed us that during government class today. It has nothing to do with government, but I will probably remember that before I will remember Roe v. Wade or Brown v. Board. Anyway, today was a good day. Not much homework in anything and lunch was delicious. It was tuna noodle casserole and homemade cinnamon rolls, and I sat with Chris, Curtis, Geoff Osterman, and Jeff Cicon. They were giving me "pep talks" that mostly included reminding me how we choked the last three years, so we better not choke this year. I pretended to be mad, but of course I couldn't help laughing. In practice we started with yoga, then we each picked our own drill, and finished with cardio-ab. Kaitlynn and I ate at Subway, which was lovely.

When I got to my room tonight there was a letter on my pillow. As usual, my stomach dropped and my legs got all Jello-y because I immediately knew who it was from. I sat down on my bed and carefully tore it open. He asked me how school and basketball are

---

[72]Katherine and Preston Woods lived thirty-plus miles north of town on a farm. They rode the bus almost every single morning and afternoon, so it was a big deal to have them in town that night.

going. He said he will still be in Missouri for a while and will find out his next assignment hopefully in the next month or so. Then he said it looks like he will be home for a couple weeks right around Christmas. I can't decide if three months sounds like it is close or far away. There were some parts that had been scribbled out. He explained that he had started like three different letters but kept crumpling them up and starting over. It sounds like he is settling into more of a "normal" routine now, for the most part. He has PT every morning, then different exercises and jobs to do each day. Then he goes back to his barracks at night, unless they are sleeping outside somewhere for a field exercise. He said every night when he gets back to his bunk he listens to "These Days" by Rascal Flatts. I listened to that song like fifteen times after I read his letter. He also ended the letter reminding me that he will still always love me. At the end he wrote a P.S. that said, *I have been thinking a lot about that night you gave me back my senior key. I was crushed that you gave it back to me, but I didn't know how to tell you, to make you understand. Jamie, even though there was a lot of confusion and hurt between us, I want you to be able to smile when you think of me, because you have always been able to make me smile, even when I thought nothing could.*

When I went to put the letter back in the envelope, I felt something hard in one of the corners. I don't know how I missed it the first time. I slid my fingers inside, gently felt around, and pulled out the silver chain holding his key.

* * *

The first weekend of October brought a great test. We had a barn burner (I heard a radio announcer say that once, and I love it) in Fort Benton.[73] We had a great first half and were up 34-22, but they pounced and crushed us in the third quarter by ten points. The fourth quarter was back and forth, but we kept it together. We won

---

[73]Fort Benton is a Class B school and an hour drive directly south of Chester. It is located right on the Missouri River, the Lewis and Clark National Historic Trail, and the Nez Perce National Historic Trail. It is dubbed the "Birthplace of Montana" and the fur trading post was established way, way back in 1846 (Fort Benton, 2013).

60–58 with some pressure free throws down the stretch.[74] It is a good sign that we are winning these close games instead of panicking. That feels encouraging. Then we beat Valier for the second time, 81–51, to cap off that weekend.

These last five games have felt great. We dominated Belt at home, 70–48, beat Heart Butte 84–50, Shelby 71–46, Sunburst 65–38, and Kremlin-Gilford 80–14. Coach Henderson from Rocky Mountain College came up for our game against Fort Benton, and I enjoyed my visit down there a couple weekends ago. He is such a nice guy, and I love that Billings is so close to Big Timber and all my family. It is too crazy to think much about college, though, when we still have so much more to do here now. Tomorrow night is senior night, which I just cannot even believe. I get so emotional when I think about it. I hope I can sort of keep it together.

---

[74]One of Fort Benton's best players that year was Kaylee Shaw, who had moved from Chester only a few years before, and her dad was the head coach before Coach VanDyke. We all wished she still could've been playing for the Coyotes. Another starting guard for the Longhorns was Kyle Cook, who also later played at Montana Tech with Harrison's Letty Powell. Fort Benton went on to place third at the state class B tournament that year.

Chapter 28

October 27, 2001, senior year, Senior Night, Chester, Montana

This morning I drove to Belt with Heidi and Maci, and we watched our poor boys lose their playoff game. So that was their last high school football game, and of course they were very sad. We came home, met up with a bunch of other girls in the high school parking lot, and tucked little notes of encouragement in their windshields. All this "last time" stuff is starting to make me a little sad.

When I get home I take a shower and shave my legs (which of course only happens for very special occasions) before eating my delicious scrambled cheese eggs Dad always makes me before home games. Mom keeps rubbing my back and asking me if I need anything. She is just the cutest thing. Dad walks over when I am eating and says, "You know this is gonna be tougher on me than it is on you tonight."

I beg to differ. When I finish my eggs, I walk into the front room and play a million songs on the piano. Dad comes in after a little while with my bag and my uniform and sits on the couch to listen. Maci and the Del Sol pull up a little while later. Dad hands me my uniform and kisses my forehead. He looks me in the eyes and says, "You know I am always proud of you."

So obviously I am bawling when I tuck into the passenger seat, and Maci only has to glance at me before starting to cry, too. So much for keeping it together tonight. She parks in the giant gravel parking lot on the south side of the gymnasium, and we tote our bags and home uniforms past the empty swimming pool and into the back entrance through the heavy Columbia-blue metal door. We hug and then enter the locker room. Heidi and Kaitlynn look up and of course immediately notice we have been crying. They do the only natural thing for a group of teenage girls in this situation and begin tearing up themselves.

For the next hour or so there is lots of hugging and crying mixed in with Heidi and I doing the usual hair-braiding and all of us doing the usual pregame dancing to the usual pregame mixed CD. During this oh-so-emotional time, Coach VanDyke pulls each of us into the coaches' office one at a time and shares the special letters she has written to each of us. So of course this helps to quell the crying and encourage composure.

Before we go through the game plan and matchups on the whiteboard, I stand in front of my girls and somehow manage to share the letter I stayed up forever writing last night:

October 26, 2001

To my team,

It is the night before the night that I will play my last basketball game in the Chester gym. While I'm reading this, it will be the last time I get to shoot around in the old gym before a game, the last time I will change into my basketball uniform in our locker room, the last time we will be in the corner of our locker room listening to Coach tell us the game plan. It will be the last time we will stand around the gym door waiting for the JV buzzer to blare, the last time we will get to yell our words in the corner of our gym, the last time I get those crazy butterflies in my stomach when our band starts playing "The Final Countdown," and we run out in our house for our fans. We will get to hear Steve announce the starting lineups and see Bicycle Bob keep his stats for the last time for us here. And it will be the last time our basketball team will line up to listen to the national anthem played here. All these things may sound so little and insignificant, things we have all taken for granted these last four years. But like Coach says, it is all the little things that count, and it's all the little things we will miss the most.

You guys are my family and have been forever. When we were in sixth grade, we played ball in the mornings, on Sunday afternoons,

171

anytime and anywhere we could. In the summer after our sixth-grade year, when we were almost big junior-highers, we had our first tournament at the Big Sky State Games. We were little girls who just wanted to play ball and have fun. And that we did. I still remember the first real pregame talk that my dad gave us in that classroom with the big screen in Havre. We were all so incredibly nervous and didn't have a clue that basketball would be such a huge part of our lives for so many years to come. My dad told us then for the first time, not the only time, that we were the "cock of the walk," and everyone would always be out to get us.

That still holds true to this very day. We went to Billings that year, and it began a six-year tradition. We didn't win every game (pretty close, though), and I couldn't tell you the score of any of those games, but I do remember the restaurants where we ate together, the opening ceremonies we attended, all our laughing and all our crazy shenanigans.

Our two years of junior high were pretty much awesome. We went undefeated both seasons, and I will never forget when Kayla made our 100th point against Browning. I'll never forget the practice when Coach K. was playing an air banjo and doing "circle cheers." And I don't think any of us will forget when Coach K. told Michele to get out of the paint, and she calmly spread her feet out like a ballet dancer on the thin lines that weren't painted. In junior high we were inseparable, on and off the court. I remember that formidable night when Heidi and Mari were waiting nervously for the rest of us to come to the tree house after that dance because we were flirting with breaking curfew. And we had eight "surprise" birthday parties in one year.

When we reached high school, everything was new and exciting. My freshman year is one I will never forget. That year we were split up a little for the first time, and we had to experience playing with different people. But there wasn't jealousy, there wasn't selfishness or pettiness. We were always friends before anything else. We got to experience how good it felt to win Divisionals and even Dolan Hull told us we were impressive and that he lost his voice at a girls' basketball game because he was screaming so loud for us. I remember when Michele and I crushed Maci and Mari at pool, thus beginning our infamous "We're number one" chant. Our roommates locked us out of our hotel room for hours that night. I remember the Rudolph that was made out of blue-and-gold balloons and Coach Schlepp paying his respects to it when we buried the remains of the reindeer in the snow outside the hotel in Livingston. And I remember when half our town was thrown into our hotel pool, and when we all felt sick on pop because we hadn't had any pop all season.

Our sophomore and junior years are of course packed with memories, too, but I don't want to turn this book into a novel. Basketball isn't just about the hundreds of seven-minute drills and endurance runs we have run, though it was quite clever when we all ripped off our jerseys and presented our "It's Fun to Run!" T-shirts to our coaches. It's not just about the wins and losses (the very few losses, mind you). It's about the long bus ride conversations, the serious ones and the extremely crazy and hilarious ones. It's about the times we have eaten together in restaurants and the many, many laughs we have had. Like when our bus driver Al threw that ice across the room to the garbage and tried to blame it on me. It's about the hotels we've stayed in and the memories we will have forever.

This is our senior year of high school basketball, the end of an incredible chapter of our lives. We have been through some tough times. We lost Mari and Emily from our team this year, but we gained our two adopted sisters, Bulldog and Sav. We had to manage without our Kaitlynn for a while, but tonight we finally have her back. We are so far undefeated, and there is no more next year. This year for me so far has already been a year of reflection. I have thought a lot about all the things I have been through with you guys, and I've realized that we have helped to shape each other into the people we are today. We have been so unbelievably lucky to be part of this amazing group of people. The way we are, the bond we all have, is extremely rare, and that bond makes us unique. It makes us special.

I will never forget how my Kaitlynn refused to give up and helped me to see how important every single second of life really is. I will never forget how Heidi always needs to know exactly where to be in every single defensive situation, and how she may not have as much talent as Michele, but that doesn't stop her from working her butt off all the time and never one time complaining about the fact that she has to work harder. I will never forget how Michele and I "fight" all

173

the time, but it is only because we love each other. (And for the record, we are now best friends, and we will always be number one.) I will never forget the fire I have seen so many times in Chasi Lee's eyes when playing defense. If Chasi has fire in her eyes, on or off the court, look out, because she wants to do something, and we all know dang well she is going to do it. I will never forget how Maci has to ask the same question 500 times, and how we all just shake our heads and laugh. And I am glad she is indeed Little Maci, because though she may be little, she is fierce.

Amanda and Savannah, even though you two haven't been with us for six years, that doesn't make you any less special. Schlepp has been my sister my entire life, and Sav is the most genuine person I have ever met. They are the pieces of the puzzle that make our team complete, and the "Put it in the box and sell it at a garage sale" is a Schlepp quote that still puts a smile on my face.

I will never forget all of Coach Schlepp's quick remarks, his sweet "trick shots," and how he makes everything just a little bit better, a little bit funnier. And of course the clever names he thinks each year for us during the starting lineups, like "Juggernaut Juniors" and "Sensational Seniors." And last but not least, I will never forget Coach VanDyke. She has pushed me to be the best basketball player and person I can be. She loves her job, she loves us, and that is what makes her such a great coach. I have the utmost respect for her and always will.

I am telling myself that I am going to try and read this letter to you guys without crying, but I am thinking that will be highly doubtful. Especially since I am crying now, as I write. So now I will wrap this up. I love all of you, and I thank you for making my life so enjoyable. Thank you for always being there, no matter what, thank you for being my family. Things will never be like this ever again, but I hope I will never forget how things are at this very moment. This final season is not over yet, so I say we keep doing what we always do and finish with no regrets. Now let's play some ball.

Your teammate always,
Jamie Graham #12

Locker room senior night, October 27, 2001: me, Heidi Cicon, Kaitlynn Engstrom

Locker room senior night, October 27, 2001: Kaitlynn Engstrom, me, Michele VanDyke, Chasi Buffington, Maci Tempel, Heidi Cicon

Senior night, October 27, 2001: Kayla Matkin, Heidi Cicon, me, Kaitlynn Engstrom, Chasi Buffington, Michele VanDyke, Maci Tempel, Tina Johns, Coach Linda VanDyke (shirt reads Pretty in pink, wicked in uniform)

We run out to "Final Countdown," and as always, the music causes my heart to pump madly as I take a final lap around the perimeter of our home court. I catch my dad's eye in the stands and see my mom smiling away beside him. My parents have never missed a game. Without fail, Mom always has my uniforms and blue-and-gold-striped socks and yellow sports bra washed. On game days Dad always sneaks a Reese's or Butterfinger candy bar on the top ledge of my locker with a yellow sticky note reading something like, "Go get 'em tonight! Love, Dad," or "Play hard! P.S. Did you remember your lucky sports bra? Love, Dad," or "From your number one fan. Love, Dad."

I pass across to Chasi, get in line behind Amanda, then follow the queue in to the paint so we can each jump up and tip it off the backboard before Michele takes the final tip and lays it in. We immediately transition to two-pass layups before lining up at half for three-man-weave shooting. I love warm-ups. I love the process of mentally preparing for the game and getting each other pumped up. I love each unique handshake performed among all of us teammates, and I love slapping my girls' butts and don't care if anyone thinks it is something that should only be done by boys. If there is one thing I have learned from playing basketball in high school, or any activity for that matter, is that if boys can do it, then so can we, thank you very much.

* * *

The game is going okay, but I do feel a bit exhausted after crying so dang much. We are playing Blue Sky tonight, which is a bummer for them, and have a great first quarter ending at 22-6. Halftime puts us up 40-17, and by the end of the third it is 55-25. I hear a seemingly random cheer erupt from a section in the crowd near the concessions stand when we hit seventy points near the end of the game. This kind of outburst used to throw me, but I recently discovered it is due to the fact that over the years, fans have sought out ways to stay engaged with our games, and one of these strategies is to make friendly bets (or so they say) on the spread of each quarter and the final score. So this same group lets out a collective groan when the final ends up being 74-35. Sorry to disappoint.

And just like that, no more basketball games at Chester High.

Chapter 29

November 1–3, 2001, senior year, District 10-C Tournament, Shelby, Montana

Finally it is here. The best time of the year. Tourney time. Everyone at school is happy today, which equals a good day. During journalism we sell the last of our ads for the yearbook, so that is fantastic. Mr. Hoff has us dissect a cat during advanced biology, which is the grossest thing I have ever done, and in calculus I think I do fairly okay on another ridiculously difficult test. When our test is over Mr. Gordon is giddy with excitement, and all we do is talk about tournaments. Lunch is delicious ham and cheese deli, and in English we work on our *Scarlet Letter* presentations. Matt and Wade have a whole script worked out revolving around poor old Hester Prynne, so now all we need is to record the play using my Barbie dolls and my brother's WWF action figures (all the Barbies especially love George "The Animal" Steele), and we are all set.

Two thirty *finally* comes, and we pack up and load the bus to Shelby. We have an awesome practice from four to five o'clock followed by an oh-so-tasty dinner at Pizza Pro with lots of yummy pizza and lots and lots of laughing. We head back to the gym to watch the Dutton-Brady Diamondbacks[75] beat the Sunburst Refiners.[76]

---

[75]The towns of Dutton and Brady consolidated in 2005, but their sports teams had already merged. Dutton is an agricultural town of just over three hundred and located about forty miles northwest of Great Falls, and Brady is just eighteen miles north of Dutton (Dutton, 2005, Central: Brady, 2019).

[76]Sunburst is about thirty miles north of Shelby and is a port to Canada. The town is named due to the beautiful sunrises that emerge over the Sweetgrass Hills, which

We have our scouting notebooks out, and I figure I better write more than I have so far, "We are going to crush them," in case Coach Schlepp asks us to share specific observations on the bus ride home.

* * *

Turns out my scouting report was spot-on. We are off to a good 1-0 postseason start, rocking the Diamondbacks 84-23. We find ourselves up against Heart Butte yet again in the district championship game. I have a slight déjà vu during starting lineups and briefly wonder how we got from our freshman year to here so quickly. We finish the night holding our fourth consecutive district championship trophy. The scoreboard still displays the final score with red-lighted numbers, 77-45. Two down, six to go.

---

are the tallest freestanding hills in Montana, and the mascot was named because of the large population growth because of oil development in the 1920s. The Texas Company (eventually Texaco) built a refinery in the town during this time. My friend Mike, the one who went to prom with me my junior year, is from Sunburst, and he and I ended up enjoying a few proms together, both in Chester and in Sunburst.

Chapter 30

November 15–17, 2001, senior year, Northern C Divisional
Tournament, Havre, Montana

I really thought we were going to catch Coach Schlepp in the act today, but somehow he must have found out. How did he find out? Every day before practice, he comes into the gym before us and heaves up every single ball from the rack with his so-called patented 'three ball' shot. Then he goes to the coaches' office, and by the time we get to the floor, there are balls scattered all over the floor. When he and Coach VanDyke join us for the official start to practice, after we have done our dot drills and ABC ankle exercises, they instruct us to pick up all the balls and act so surprised that they have rolled all over the place.

Just a half hour ago today Heidi, Kayla, Marissa, Kristen, and I snuck over to the gym during eighth period (we already have our parts down for the next band concert anyway, so it was fine to miss just a few minutes of rehearsal to "go to the bathroom") and set up the video camera in the bird's nest above the westside bleachers. Kayla, the best manager ever who knows all the ins and outs of recording from that vantage point, made sure we had a fresh tape in and made sure the power button was switched to on. Then we went about our business as usual, but when we came in to get ready for practice, all the balls were packed tightly on the ball rack. Somehow he knew, the little sneak.

We are still discussing how our perfect plan was thwarted when our coaches stride all casual into the gym.

"Wow!" Wide-eyed, Coach Schlepp makes a point to really look around incredulously first at the ball rack, and then at the non-ball-littered floor. "It looks nice and tidy in here."

"Isn't that interesting?" notes Michele, her tone dripping with sarcasm.

"I wonder why that is," Heidi continues. "This is all such a mystery."

Coach Schlepp has his arms crossed and is shaking his head back and forth, as if truly stumped. "It really is," he agrees.

Smiling slyly, Coach VanDyke refocuses our attention. "Good afternoon, ladies. I trust school was good today, and you stayed completely focused on your studies?"

"Of course," I respond. "The fact that we are one day away from the first day of the divisional tournament has in no way affected our ability to concentrate and give our utmost attention to our schoolwork."

"Good." Coach looks down at her clipboard, still grinning knowingly. "Our quote of the day is, '*Victory never belongs to the individual. Victory belongs to the team.*' Let's remember that as we practice today. If we want to be the best, we have got to beat the best. Lady Coyotes on three. One, two, three—"

"Lady Coyotes!" We shout, and assume our starting practice positions.

* * *

After an entire morning of really truly trying my best to concentrate during my first three classes, the entire K-12 student body gathered in the auditorium for a fun yet brief pep assembly, and now we are *finally* boarding the bus. I take my seat near the back—we all have our own seats since our team is so small, but often move around to chat here and there—and unwrap my traditional bus pregame meal: a delicious Cold Cut Combo, of course. The Combo goes nicely with my sleeve of Ritz crackers, and I wash it down with some delicious chocolate Nesquik.

I slide up beside Amanda to braid her usual double French braids with a slightly fancy part toward the top, careful not to mess with the thick curled bangs. Then it is on to Maci, and I really have to maneuver myself just right in the uncomfortable, sticky gray vinyl

181

seat in order to twist and tie up all six cornrow braids in her very short hair, all connected at the end with her white Nike headband. Chasi is ready for me and flips onto her stomach while I weave one thick French braid backwards to the middle of her hair and secure it with a tight bun. I see Heidi finish a simple small braid wrapped around beautiful Savannah's long brown ponytail after taking care of the rest of the hairdos. (Except mine. I pull mine into a messy bun held in place by a cheetah-print scrunchie.)

We finish and take our seats just in time to give our full attention to the Backstreet Boys as we pull up the hill into Havre. As if on cue, everyone belts out, "I want it thaaaaa-at way!"

When we finish the song, Michele requests that I do the Molly Shannon Saturday Night Live "I Love It!" skit. I feign exasperation seconds before jumping into Michele's lap. I pull my chin to my chest and look intensely into her eyes. I kick my right leg up over the seat in front of her and tell her with a low growl and New York accent, "I *loooove* being your teammate, Michele. I love it. And I love how high you can jump, I just love it!"

I crawl over the back of her seat and into Chasi and Maci's seat. "And I love you two and how cute ya are." I boop Chasi on the nose. "I love sitting here"—I hold myself up on my arms, as if I am about to crab walk, and fling my foot in the air—"but I really love to stretch, and I love to kick!"

I lie across Chasi's lap, letting my head dangle down over the seat. I flip around and squat briefly in the aisle before crawling on Amanda and Savannah. I am getting really fired up now. I see Kaitlynn can hardly breathe, so I crawl onto her lap. Then I rub my cheek against hers, close my eyes, pull my right foot up in the air with my hand and shout, "I love it! I love it! I LOVE IT!"

My teammates are all shaking with glee. Chasi has tears streaming down her cheeks and is smiling so wide her eyes are squeezed shut. I sit up straight between Kaitlynn and Heidi, as if nothing unusual has happened. I watch my girls and pretend to look curious as to why they are laughing. I am sweating and breathing like I just finished a blood run, but a shot of joy zaps through me.

* * *

Al pulls into the Havre High parking lot, parks the yellow beast, and we unload. We file into the gymnasium, pretending like we are comfortable wearing these dresses and fancy shoes. The usher leads us to our locker room where we drop off our uniforms and bags. We then take the side stairs near our locker room up to the balcony section to scout the Box Elder Bears, who are opening the tournament against the Winifred Red Raiders.[77]

Winifred comes out strong, and it is a battle the entire first half. Pullin comes out on fire in the third, though, and the Bears pull away and never look back. This time when I look down at my scouting report I do not see, "We are going to crush them."

My guts twist a bit when I picture us playing Box Elder at Divisionals—again. The last time we had the privilege of playing here on Saturday night we were just so, I don't know, blindly confident? Innocent? Naive? Yeah, that sounds about right. I am still confident, but enough has happened that I am also aware of the reality that things sometimes do not turn out like I hope they do.

We silently head back down to the locker room to prepare for our first-round game against the Highwood Mountaineers.[78] Coach keeps reminding us about the importance of positive self-talk, visualizing ourselves performing at our best, and accessing the right mindset.

As I pull on each sock, first the left, then the right, I picture myself running out for warm-ups. I play each drill in my mind like scenes in a movie, and continue to prepare physically by fastening the two Velcro straps on the dark-blue brace that supports my right ankle. Then I push my left heel into my light-blue-and-white AND1 low-tops while picturing the opening tip-off. I fit my arms through my shiny Columbia-blue away jersey, and it settles over my clean-and-dry-for-now lucky yellow sports bra as I go through the first three

---

[77]Winifred is a town of right around two hundred people in central Montana, about forty-five miles north of Lewistown. It was founded with the growing Milwaukee Railroad in 1913 and is "a gateway to the Missouri River Breaks" (Winifred, n.d.).

[78]Highwood is about twenty-five miles east of Great Falls, right in the center of cattle-grazing land. Long ago, cowboys would ride from Highwood to Fort Benton for supplies to ship up the Missouri River. It is said the town was named for the high trees that grew on the volcanic Highwood Mountains (Highwood, 2019).

plays we plan to run in my mind. Remember to catch in triple threat, remember to ball fake, and remember to cut hard to the hole after passing away. Now I tighten the elastic band on my blue shorts with the thin white stripe and thick yellow stripe that falls just over the top of each knee. Whoops, gotta untie the elastic band one more time in order to make one of many inevitable visits to the bathroom stall.

I look in the mirror as I wash my hands and watch myself take a big breath, cheeks puffed out. "We got this," I say inside my mind. "We got this."

Kayla and Marissa come in to announce our eight-minute warning. We congregate on the two benches near the showers and face the whiteboard while the coaches enter.

"Here we are," Coach VanDyke starts. "Today we start the second of three steps in our final postseason journey. You all know your assignments. We walked through our game plan yesterday during practice. We will pounce right away with our press. Be ready to switch up our pressure and communicate constantly. Get in their face and don't let up. Everybody needs to know where Bahnmiller is at all times. Otherwise, just take care of business. If we play our game and control what we can control, we will win."

* * *

Michele tips it to Heidi, who doesn't love having the ball for long somewhere other than her paint, and quickly gets it over to Maci. Maci instinctively throws it crosscourt to me as I break, but the ball is tipped by two of their defenders, and bobbled out-of-bounds. That was not so smooth. Maci signals for our "Moses" out-of-bounds play, putting me on the opposite wing from her, Heidi and Chasi shoulder to shoulder at the elbow, then they spread out and make room for Michele to cut down the lane. Michele catches and puts it up just over the rim. Heidi rebounds but misses. It would be nice to get on the scoreboard here.

We pick them up full-court man-to-man and Chas dives on the floor after deflecting a pass from Bahnmiller. Highwood ties it up for a jump ball, and they take it out at our bench. We faceguard and keep the pressure on as they inbound. This time Heidi tips an attempt to hit their post, and I dive for yet another jump. (If one is going to become a spectator of girls' basketball, one must become used to numerous jump ball calls.)

The possession arrow now goes to us, I catch the ball and my breath, and take a minute to let my teammates set up before dribbling down the right side. It looks like they are going to try their luck with a 2–3 zone, hoping to force us to shoot outside. They may want to watch that high post, though, I think as I hit Michele wide-open on the left elbow. She turns and faces, takes a power dribble inside, and bounces one in to put us up 2–0. There we go.

We set our press a little deeper in the paint than usual. Sometimes you gotta be willing to take a little risk and see what happens, right? Give it a try and then adjust. At least that's what Dad says.

Our "cheetah" press has Maci in the point position, me ready to trap at the left wing, and Chasi ready at the right. Michele and her impossibly long arms flail at center court as she moves with the ball. Heidi is on a yo-yo string with and behind Michele, the safety so nothing long gets behind her. Bahnmiller gets the ball in, but her teammate's pass back is tipped by Maci. They stick with it, though, and reverse it over to Chasi's side; I imagine my intimidating presence drove them to explore another avenue. The guard soon realizes option number two is no better and hastily throws it back to her partner in the paint. This is going exactly as planned. The ref blows the whistle for the ten-second call right as their coach desperately tries but fails to call for a time-out.

Maci takes it out again to try our "two" out-of-bounds play, and the ball somehow bounces right through my legs. What in the world? I will concentrate on not doing that again. Gotta reset. Back in "cheetah." They inbound again, but the result is the same. The ref announces a second ten-second call. Our opponents look so frustrated. I almost feel sorry for them.

That is not true. I don't feel sorry for them at all.

Chasi takes the ball at the point, and it looks like they are going to stick with the 2–3 zone. Chas makes an uncontested pass over to Maci who drains a smooth fifteen-footer. We stick with our press because, well, why wouldn't we, and Townsend stutters and the travel is called. Chas puts up a three, but it is short and rebounded by the Mountaineers. Maci nearly picks off the next pass, but this time they make it past half-court. I have the next pass but make the rookie mistake of immediately putting the ball on the floor before looking. Townsend picks it up, tosses it to Edwards, and she makes a great crossover move to put them on the board.

Chasi rebounds a miss by Maci and scores on an easy putback. Maci gets another quick steal, and I am fouled but don't make the layup. I hit both free throws then take the point on the press. Highwood works it around, and they score on another textbook crossover move, this time on the baseline. We outlet quickly, and I can tell we are tiring them out. This is when I can stop and be thankful for the millions of miles' worth of endurance runs and seven-minute drills we have done throughout the season. After another steal, Maci hits Chasi for a three on the wing. It must be so hard to know who to guard. They are packing it inside on Heidi and Michele, only to have Maci then Chasi pop threes.

Don't get too cocky, Jamie. Stay focused.

The first quarter ends only 21-8. At half the score is 37-17, end of third 50-31, and the final is 67-39.

Chasi was lights out tonight, shooting a ridiculous 75% (9 for 12) from the field (2-2 from behind the arc), to lead all scorers with twenty points. Maci ended with thirteen, Heidi with twelve, and the rest of us filled in from there. We met our goal with only twelve turnovers while causing a ton, shot 100% from the stripe as a team (6 for 6), and we got lots of opportunities to work on our zone offenses, "Old Dominion" and "power." Thursday night, check. Tomorrow night we get to play the Box Elder Bears for the semis. Let's just keep checking things off the list.

* * *

Since the tournament this weekend is only in Havre, we don't get to stay over at a hotel. It is Friday morning, and I barely slept last night because I could not get basketball out of my mind. Needless to say, this may not be the most productive school day in my life. I keep replaying yesterday's game against Highwood and how fun it was, and then thinking about the scouting report for Box Elder that the coaches went through with us on the bus ride home.

All my cute grandparents were having tea and zucchini bread with Mom when Emily picked me up for school this morning. Now

I am sitting in journalism, and I am actually being productive and making some progress with Marjorie on our layout for this month's paper. Marj chooses the music today, so we are of course listening to some good ole Garth Brooks.

The bell rings and sends us to advanced biology, where Mr. Hoff allows us to eat seasoned sunflower seeds while performing experiments showing the difference between the center of gravity in males and females. Lunch is scrumdiddlyumptious grilled cheese and tomato soup, and the lunch ladies even made me my very own special sandwiches with extra cheese. We muddle through another scene of *Julius Caesar* in English, spending a surprising amount of time getting everyone to understand it is not the "Ideas" of March. I check my email and brush up on my solitaire during study hall, and then we finish off a stressful school day with a friendly game of Scrabble during math. Mr. Gordon is so dang excited about tonight's game that I don't even think he realizes we are playing a word game during this numbers class.[79]

The final bell rings at last. Off to my locker to retrieve my yummy treat and note from Dad, up to the store for my usual Subway sandwich, into the gym for a walk-through of tonight's game, then onto the bus to the divisional semifinal game. One step at a time. Just gotta take things one step at a time.

* * *

This place is packed. I can hardly hear myself think. There is extra energy during warm-ups, and even though I shout "Let's do this!" to my teammates as loudly as I can, my voice is completely swallowed up by the crowd's constant roar. Now this is what I am talking about.

---

[79]Coach Dustin Gordon took over the program in Chester two years after we graduated high school and led a fabulous group of young girls to a third-place finish at State just a couple years later. He and his wife Joni, who was our hilarious government teacher, moved to Fairfield soon after, where they continue to thrive. Coach Gordon has led the Fairfield Eagles to State year after year, winning *seven* state titles while coming in second three times. He coached Jill Barta, one of the Treasure State's most decorated athletes of all time and drafted to the WNBA (Higgins, 2018). During Barta's four-year stint, the Eagles recorded 104 straight wins, then added sixteen straight the next year to set the most consecutive wins at an unbelievably high bar of 120 (Mansch, 2018). I love to reflect on how many incredible teachers, coaches, and just flat-out good people have been and still are a part of the Chester school and community.

We get through the usual pregame process before Michele directs the ball right to Heidi on the tip, then Heidi over to me on the right wing, to Michele on my left, back to me, to Chasi, skip pass across to Maci and, boom. Nothing but net. We surprise everyone and sprint back to pick up on defense at half-court. I have no recollection of starting a game out without pressing. Gotta keep people on their toes.

Coach Schlepp has us in a triangle-and-two, with Maci in Infante's shorts and Chasi in Pullin's. I take the top of the triangle with Heidi and Michele covering the bottom corners, hands up. Pullin brings it up while Rosette sets a down screen for Infante. Infante pops out to the wing, Chasi on her tail, and receives Pullin's pass. Infante passes it up to the top of the key to Lawrence, who heaves one up from about twenty-one feet out. It lands hard, but Rosette pulls down the rebound on the opposite wing. Back out to Infante, to Lawrence, then inside to Shambo. She forces one up in the middle of the key, but I get a hand on it and Michele picks it up. She takes it all the way to our key and hits Chas on the left short corner. Miss.

They work it around on the next possession and Pullin pulls up and cashes a ten-footer. We spread into a five-out offense and watch as the Bears set up in a wide 2–3 zone. We work it around and Michele misses at the right elbow. Maci dives and makes a hustle play, and we get it back underneath. She inbounds to me, I hit Michele at the short corner. She shoots it over Heidi cutting across the middle of the lane, and she drops one in just over the rim.

We stay in the triangle-and-two, and I sag back and let Lawrence hold it out at twenty-one feet. Coach Schlepp made it clear that we are taking the risk of letting the other three score but making sure Pullin and Infante are constantly pressured. We do this knowing we will still get scored on, understanding this is the way the defense works. Lawrence holds it and holds it, then heaves up yet another long bomb and banks it in. Oh, for the love.

On the transition, Maci outlets it up to me, but I underestimate Pullin's quickness, and she picks it before it can get to Michele. On the fast break I sprint back and swear I strip it, but a foul is called. She hits both free throws. I walk it up this time and called "Old Dominion," and Chas is short on a three.

The quarter goes back and forth like this. We remain in our specialty defense, and they remain in their 2–3. We get up and down the floor a ton, the crowd is wild, and we get called for a handful of fouls. Chasi gets an opportunity for a last second shot, but it clanks off the side. By the end of one quarter, we are down 15–16.

The second quarter continues with the same pattern as the first: we go up one; they answer back. Everyone is sprinting at every transition, and we get to shoot a handful of free throws when they foul into bonus. Unfortunately I do not box out like I should and receive (thanks, but no thanks) my third foul. Savannah subs for me with about a minute to go in the half. The forward we are still knowingly leaving open hits a little twelve-footer on the right wing, putting us down two, 33–35. Heidi takes it out and inbounds to Maci. She dribbles across half-court and tosses it back and forth with Chas, taking time off, planning patiently for the last shot. Instead of picking up, Box Elder stays in their zone. Maci makes a pass to wide-open Chasi on the right wing who casually takes two dribbles, sets, and knocks down a three right at the buzzer.

As we run out of the locker room to start the third, I notice a large section of the bottom-row stands is lined with males from our community, including my dad, Gary, Mr. VanDyke, Mr. Gordon, and neighbor Joe, to name a few. This is new. And I like it.

The third quarter is more of the same. We stick with our triangle-and-two to start, as Infante and Pullin only have about a dozen combined points. Even though that means the rest of their team will continue to receive a fair number of wide-open looks, our coaches assure us we should stick to the strategy. Pullin and Infante each hit impressive threes off the dribble in two out of three possessions. Heidi grabs an offensive rebound on the next possession, though, that results in Pullin being called for her fourth foul with 3:35 left in the third. This is huge. She is benched, and now we gotta capitalize.

After a missed attempt on their end, Chasi takes it coast-to-coast and ends up at the free throw line. During this free throw Coach calls me over and informs me we are going into full-court man. I loudly attempt to relay the message to my teammates, who are lined up on the hash marks, but it is hard for them to hear over the crowd. I continue to shout while signaling with both pointer fingers, like Shooter McGavin in *Happy Gilmore*. Chasi misses the first and swishes the next, and then we hungrily match up while Rosette takes the ball out.

Infante takes it all the way to the paint, puts up a five-footer, and misses. Chasi fouls on a rebound attempt. They take it out, and we faceguard like crazy. Five-second call. Excellent. The Bears are hanging in a wide 3–2 zone, and I remind myself to rocker step, ball fake, and be patient. Even with Pullin out, we are somehow still down 47–48 with 2:32 left in the quarter. We have got to score!

I say we have got to score, but instead Heidi gets stopped by a triple-team, and though Maci ties up a loose ball, the possession arrow points their way. Infante gets it at our free throw line, takes four dribbles by us as if we are all standing still, and lays it in. Down 47–50.

Stay poised.

Maci connects on a twelve-foot jumper, Savannah helps and takes a huge charge on Infante, Michele hits me on a fast break for a jumper almost mirror image to Maci's, and Chasi pops a three. We run "Utah" with eight seconds left. I hit Maci on the left wing, cut through the key and off Michele's screen, receive a pass back from Maci, shot fake, dribble right, pass left to Michele posting up. Three seconds. Chele quickly fakes left, spins right, and kisses it off the glass just as the buzzer sounds. The roar of the crowd propels us to our bench, there are hand and butt slaps all over the place, and I finally feel Momentum take a seat on our bench.

The score is 56–50 going into the fourth, and we, like Stella, have got our groove back. We control the tempo the remaining eight minutes and advance to the Saturday night divisional championship with a final score of 72–58.

* * *

All week in practice we prepared specifically for Box Elder and Big Sandy. Last night after our win, we watched the first half of the other semifinal game, Big Sandy versus Belt. Big Sandy came out tentative and Belt played like they had nothing to lose, which was probably what it felt like for them. Belt was up seven at half, and then we left for Pizza Hut, assuming Big Sandy would kick it into gear and win. Turns out, Belt held on to win by four. Things just keep getting better.

Today I woke up and ate breakfast, and then went back to sleep for a few more hours. I figure I leaked out a few gallons of sweat last night and burned something like eight thousand calories over the last couple days, so I am a little tired. Better take a shower. I took one last night and will after tonight's game; this may be a record-breaking weekend on the shower front. After my shower I enjoy the delicious eggs Dad makes me, and then Maci picks me up for our walk-through at four thirty.

We get to the gym around six o'clock, and the place is packed. Now we just need Box Elder to win, and then there is absolutely no pressure on us. Instead, Box Elder doesn't get off the bus, and Big Sandy puts the boots to them. The Pioneers now get to turn around and root for Belt, the team that tipped them over last night. Been there, done that. Sorry, Pioneers, not gonna happen.

* * *

Well, it isn't pretty. But we don't need pretty, we just need to win. We start down 1–5 after three minutes of play against the Belt Huskies. Instead of succumbing to that sneaky voice telling me we are going to choke, however, I choose to listen to that louder voice reminding me how prepared we are, physically and mentally. Even after trailing at the start, we win all four quarters and take home the gold divisional trophy, final score 54–39.

Now we are 5–0 in postseason play and have completed the second of three steps in this final journey. Not only that, we leave home two of the top-rated teams in the state in Box Elder and Big Sandy. A part of me feels bad neither of those teams will get to make an appearance at State, but most of me is relieved, not gonna lie. We have also become pretty good friends with the Belt girls over the years, especially during track season, and it will be fun to represent the Northern C Division with them.[80] On to State. One. Last. Time.

---

[80] Belt holds a special place in my heart because my brother, his wife, and two sweet nieces and two adorable nephews live there. Jeffrey has coached in Belt the last twelve years, amassing six state championships (MHSA declared Belt and Winifred-Roy 2020 "co-champions" due to coronavirus) and placing top four in the state five other years. He has also had great success in football and track, but girls' basketball is where he has found the most success. Close observation of my brother and his teams over the years has confirmed my hunch that the difference between girls' teams being great—instead of good—has a ton to do with, not only consistent skill development and community support, but having a coach who is incessantly positive and truly loves and believes in each player.

Chapter 31

November 28, 2001, senior year, final preparations, Chester High School, Chester, Montana

66 Alright, everybody, let's head to the gym. It's go time, baby!" Mr. Gordon lets our advanced calculus class out early so we can go to the pep assembly before boarding the bus to State.

Lockers slam as we deposit textbooks and notebooks because let's face it, there won't be any homework getting done this weekend. My locker neighbor, Colt Fred, hands me a piece of mint gum like he does every day. I tell him thank you, pop it in my mouth, and tuck the wrapper in my jeans pocket so I can make it into a star and give it to him later. My classmates and I chatter excitedly through the high school hallway, across the cafeteria, by the weight room and locker rooms, and into the new gym. I am stopped in my tracks as I look up and realize the entire east side of the gym is jam packed with people. Not only teachers and students, but so many people from our community. An applause eruption breaks out as my teammates and I enter the gymnasium.

Chills.

I glance over at Chas and can tell she is about to lose it. I search the stands to find some hilarious little kid to focus on so I don't cry. There's Michael, making crazy faces at his fellow second-grade classmates. That does the trick. Our team gathers near center court. The pep band plays "Washington and Lee Swing" and the cheerleaders lead everyone in singing,

We are the Chester Coyotes
Can't you see
We're out to challenge
You to victory
Our blue and gold will shine
With honor bright
Because we know our team
Is out to win and fight
And if you ever meet a tougher foe
Coach VanDyke would like to know
Because our girls will fight
With might and mane
To get that name
For old Chester Hi-ii-igh!

Principal Schlepp greets the crowd with his deep, authoritative voice. "Good morning, everyone. Thank you for coming out this morning to support these girls. This group has been working hard for years. We are proud of their success on the court, but even more proud of their success in school and in this community. They are a class act, and we could not ask for a better group to represent our school at the state C basketball tournament this weekend. We hope to see you all down in Belgrade, cheering on your Lady Coyotes."

Everybody cheers and claps. Our cheerleaders—Tina, Kacey, and Jamie—motion over to us, and Heidi steps out first to address our adoring fans. Maci speaks next, and our entire team takes a turn. Speech making is not my forte, which drives me crazy. Why is it so difficult for me to talk in front of a crowd?! I just get so nervous and emotional for some reason. Everyone here is so excited and encouraging, though, so that helps.

When it is my turn I try to keep my voice steady and manage to say, "Thank you all for coming out and supporting us. We can't wait to come home and hang a banner on the 'West Side.'"[81]

---

[81] For years we talked about how the "West Side" in the gym needed more banners. Banners for winning Districts and Divisionals hang on the "East Side" in the gym, but only state banners hang on the "West Side."

Cheers erupt again. It doesn't take much to get this gang on its feet. Coach Schlepp and Coach VanDyke make their speeches, and then my dad and Mrs. Sargent come out in front.[82] When Dad faces the crowd, I swear everyone sits up a little straighter, sure to give him their full attention. He starts in. "Alright. Now this weekend, these girls have the goal of bringing something back to this gym that we have never had before."

He turns and points behind him to the rafters holding six gold banners. Each banner claims a Chester state title: 1991 boys' basketball, 1992 boys' basketball, 1992 girls' volleyball, 1998 state football, and two wrestling banners from 1974 and 1975.

"Now," he continues, chin tucked in, eyes looking just over the top of his glasses, directed especially toward the student body, "we need *everybody's* help to bring this banner here. And when we bring it back, we will raise it up over there"—he again motions toward those few, lonely banners.

"So everybody get down"—he crouches down low on his hands and knees.

Mrs. Sargent assumes the same position, and the entire crowd follows suit. It sorta looks like these few hundred people are bowing to us. Excellent. Dad and Sue lightly tap their fingertips on the floor and whisper, "Ban-ner, ban-ner."

Slowly, slowly, everyone begins to rise. As the crowd rises, voices grow steadily louder. I have a random flash of the scene in *Animal House* when everyone starts singing, "Shout!"

"Ban-ner, ban-ner . . ."

A little bit louder now. A little bit louder now.

Finally, the gym explodes. "BANNER! BANNER!"

Whoa. The sheer volume of the cry forces my eyes closed and excitement, gratitude, and joy flood me all at once. I open my eyes and smile, first at my so cute dad, then at our ecstatic student body, teachers, parents, townsfolk, and last at my teammates. Our coaches proudly lead us to the bus, and our fans' energy escorts us out. I have perma smile as Miss Goodheart cues up the pep band and we exit to a rousing rendition of "We Got the Beat." Best sendoff ever.

---

[82]Mrs. Sargent is the wife of Jim Sargent, who often reffed our games and was our radio announcer at the state tourney our senior year. She also taught fourth grade in Chester.

Banner one: Chester Coyotes, 1974 State Class B-C Wrestling Champions

Banner two: Chester Coyotes, 1975 State Class B-C Wrestling Champions

Banner three: Chester Coyotes, 1991 State Class C Basketball Champions

Banner four: Chester Coyotes, 1992 State Class C Basketball Champions

Banner five: Chester Coyotes, 1992 State Class C Volleyball Champions

Banner six: Chester Coyotes, 1998 State Class C Football Champions

Chapter 32

November 29, 2001, senior year, State Class C Tournament, Belgrade, Montana

So we meet again, Thursday quarterfinal at State.

Pregame rituals occur all around me. Jerseys pulled over lucky sports bras, shorts cinched up, tied up, jerseys tucked in and folded over just so. Deodorant generously applied, shoes double-knotted, and bathroom stalls active. We prep and prime in our locker room at the Belgrade Special Events Center.[83] (Aptly named, this most certainly is a special event.)

I make sure just the right number of buttons are fastened on my bright-as-the-sun warm-up pants after I shimmy them up over my shorts. The number and position of each snap is vital. If I button too many, the dramatic flair is lost because I won't be able to whip them off in one fell swoop, which is, as everyone knows, the whole point of warm-up snap pants.

We had two weeks off between Divisionals and State, due to Thanksgiving, which was wonderful for many reasons. First, I got to spend a weekend with my family in Big Timber. Not only did we get to spend time with my Montana family, but Mom's family from Alaska and California and Washington all came to celebrate Grandpa Helmar's eighty-fifth birthday. He and Grandma Barb are so incredibly lucky. They will be those people who end up dying on the same day or something. Hopefully not while lying in a bed on a sinking ship, though. I wish I could have gotten to know my Grandpa

---

[83]Belgrade is about ten miles northwest of Bozeman.

Jim better, but sometimes I just know I am like him in certain ways. It is hard to explain, but sometimes I just feel it. Like when I ran laps around the track on Graham Field Thanksgiving morning. It was extra easy to give thanks that day.[84]

The other reason I love that we had two weeks before State was that it meant we got a few extra practices in our gym. Then we had our last practice. I can't describe how that practice felt. There were times I felt sad, I suppose, but I couldn't really be sad, because it was not over yet. Mostly I just loved getting up and down that court with my girls.

Now it is finally here. What we have been waiting for, planning for, preparing for. How many times have we set up the scene: state championship game, down one, five seconds left, at the free throw line. How we will run to each other and pick each other up at the final buzzer. Who will be the lifter and who will be the liftee. We have pictured the crowd, anticipated their excitement. I can't wait to give this gift to our town again.

Before I get too far ahead of myself, we have to take care of today. Historically this day has been a tricky one for us, so I figure we have a couple choices. One, we can believe that we are somehow cursed, can't get the job done when it really counts, and pee down our legs. Or two, we can believe what we know to be true, that we have the skills, ability, and desire to *finally* go all the way.

* * *

All I know about the town of Jordan, Montana is a lot of T. rex skulls have been discovered in that place.[85] As far as girls' basketball goes, according to the film and our scouting report, Tierani Brusett, Chantel Harbaugh, Tarra MacDonald, Callie Weeding, and Katie Whiteside are their starters, and they are all solid. Guard Cortani Brusett would be starting, but was benched earlier in the season by a sucky ACL injury. The Jordan Mustangs bring a 23–3 record into the

---

[84]I have always been fascinated by the fact that my mom's family and my dad's family are so different. My dad's family is all about sports, and my mom's family is not; they are just so sweet and calm and even-keeled. On more than one occasion my Grandma Barb, my mom's mom, would approach me after a devastating loss and calmly say, "Nice three-pointer."

[85](Garfield, 2019).

tournament after placing second at the southern divisional tournament, beating out Ryegate in a challenge game. Turns out most of these girls are tough rodeo chicks, and we are certainly not overlooking them.

Warm-ups feel good. I run into our huddle with my head high, an extra spring in my step.

"Okay, ladies," Coach says as she recaps our locker room discussion. "Start out like we always do. 'Cheetah-man,' then be ready to drop into our half-court trap or full-court man. We will control the tempo. Know who you are guarding and remind each other at all times. When our bigs are shooting free throws, transition to our 'five' press. Offensively, run 'Old Dominion' or 'power,' because they will likely zone us. Then we will adjust as needed. Communicate and remember, focus on our defense and the offense will come. We are ready to take this Thursday evening quarterfinal game head-on. I believe in you."

"Together on three," I finish. "One, two, three—"

"TOGETHER!" we assert.

Kaitlynn wraps her pinky around mine then smacks my bottom as I head out to the court. I take a lap around the center circle to connect with my girls one more time before the opening whistle. First Maci and I grasp right hands, my thumb goes over hers, hers over mine, then hands slide apart. "Let's do this, Maci Lea."

"I'm ready, J." Maci nods as our eyes lock.

I catch Heidi where the circle meets half-court on our left, we wiggle our fingers together, and I ask, "You ready, C?"

She licks her fingertips, wipes her shoes, and gives me an immediate, "You know it, Graham."

I step in the circle quick to tap elbows with Michele, my right, her left. "How ya feeling, Chelers?"

"Ready to win, Jamers," she replies as she warms up with a practice jump and I get a great view of the number 42 etched in gold letters on her shiny-white jersey.

Chasi is waiting for me on the circle just behind Michele. "Chasi Lee, let's take care of business," I propose.

Chas meets my outstretched hands with hers and accepts. "That's the plan."

I adjust my right ankle brace and wipe each shoe down, one at a time, then toe the black circle and assume my jump ball position.

Michele easily controls the tip over to Maci. The ball starts out in our hands, just like we like it. Maci dribbles confidently up to center court, I head to the right wing, Chasi to the left, and Heidi and Michele set up in a high-low, as Jordan sets up in their wide 2-3 zone. Maci swings it over to me, and I almost start the game with a turnover as Whiteside tips a lob attempt to Michele. Note to self: pass better.

We inbound but aren't able to capitalize on our "fist" inbounds play. Maci gets it in to Chasi, then down to Maci on the deep corner, back to Chasi, and to me for a wide-open three. That I miss. Shake it off. I can control my defense, and I can control my talking.

"I got ball! Ball, ball. Deny. Help!"

Heidi closes out on Whiteside and causes a travel. We rip it out and whip it up the court, attempting our first fast-break opportunity. Michele takes it down the left lane and kicks to Chasi. Chas shot fakes, dribbles right, and puts us on the board first with a sweet five-foot swish.

Now we set up in "cheetah," and I get a tip but not quite turnover on the second pass. Our coaches constantly remind us tips cause tension. The point of a press isn't to get the steal every time. The point is to create a pressure atmosphere and cause the opponent to think and second-guess just a little bit each possession. The Mustangs get it down to their paint, but it's bobbled and picked up by Michele. She outlets to Maci who hits me on a long skip pass. I fake right, drive left baseline, and kiss it off the glass to put us up 4-0.

Whiteside scores on an inbound on the other end, then we go a few possessions without scoring. In the next couple minutes Michele puts in an offensive board, Maci goes three for four at the free throw line, I make one for two from the stripe. MacDonald drives one in for them. This puts us up 10-4 with three and a half minutes left in the first quarter. Alright, good start.

We continue with pressure defense and cause a few turnovers. Then we can't quite capitalize and remain stuck at ten. Jordan keeps at it, and right around the two-minute mark I look up to find that we are suddenly down by one, 10-11. We get to the line a couple more times only to miss. Chas hits another jumper on a skip pass from

Maci, but the Mustangs end with another offensive putback at the last second to end the quarter with us down, 12–15.

Kayla throws me a towel, and I chug some water as we huddle together to reset.

Coach starts in. "Okay, not a bad start, even though we are down. It's only three points, and now that we are through the first quarter and got those tournament jitters shaken out, we will settle in and be fine. We are doing a good job getting to the line, but then we have to make our free throws. Keep up the good defense. When they get a shot up, though, we *have* to have that first rebound. Their putbacks are where they are hurting us. Chip away. Just chip away."

The inbound is ours, and we get it in up top to face the zone. Heidi bounces one in with a smooth jump hook, then we cause an immediate turnover going the other way. Down one. We throw our half-court trap at them this time, and I come up with a steal on a bobbled ball after Maci and Michele set a tight trap. The next possession is almost identical to the last, this time putting Maci at the line, who goes one for two.

MacDonald scores again on the other end, though, and Michele picks up her third foul. After another trip down the court, Heidi decides Michele needs some company on the bench and picks up her third as well. Instead of staying patient like I should, I decide to dribble straight into the paint and hand the ball to the Mustangs. Sigh.

The score is stuck 17–15. We just can't get anything going. Harbaugh hits two free throws to tie it with 4:26 to go, and I completely brick the first in a bonus opportunity. Why can't we make a free throw? They are free! Kaitlynn bricks another pair. We drop to a 2–3 zone, something we rarely do. It unfortunately backfires as Brusett cashes in on a three-pointer. Then I dribble down the court, pick up the ball, and dribble some more. What?! I have absolutely no recollection of the last time I double dribbled. Seventh grade, perhaps?

If I weren't out here on the court, I would be covering my eyes right about now. I glance at the bench to see Coach Schlepp doing just that as we chuck the ball out-of-bounds, and then give up another two points on yet another offensive putback. The last two minutes cannot go by fast enough. Then I miss another flipping free throw. I know positive body language is important, but I find it impossible to control my head falling back, giving me a good look at the ceiling.

Katy finally puts one in for us, but we decide to give the Mustangs the last opportunity to score before halftime by putting Brusett on the line. She misses the first, makes the next, giving them a five-point advantage, 22–27. Eager for a chance to refocus and reset, we sprint to our locker room. I make a conscious effort to shove away the nagging thought reminding me this scenario is thus far mimicking our last two appearances at this particular tournament on this particular day.

"We have got to pick up our game!" Coach starts when we seat ourselves. "We are not being smart with our shots or passes. Slow it down. Pass around. Step it up and have some fun. There is a lot of time left. Be patient on offense and concentrate on keeping a hand in their face and *box out.*"

All heads nod at this statement, as we are being outrebounded and have a free throw percentage sitting at a dismal 32%, only 6–19. Ew. That really is terrible.

"Come out strong in the third quarter. We can do this. Don't let what has happened in the past dictate the future." This last statement hangs in the air.

Wordlessly we huddle.

Second half, second chance. Third time we get to play in the opener of this tournament. Third time's a charm. The ball is in our court. For some reason all kinds of clichés run through my mind as I run toward the bench. Win one for the Gipper. Whoever he is. Let's just suck it up and get it done.

* * *

I wake early the next morning in the hotel room, feeling like I never really got to sleep. All I could think about was last night's game. Plays kept waking me up, begging me to replay them. Michele opening the second half with a power move to the hole. Whiteside answering back with an offensive putback on the other end. Chasi pulling up for a smooth seven-foot jumper. Maci forcing the turnover into my hands then racing down the right lane to receive my long crosscourt bounce pass. Jordan out-rebounding us by nine. Forcing twenty-one turnovers while committing only thirteen ourselves. My brain is a sports reel, and it is on replay.

Since I am awake, I might as well partake in the delicious continental breakfast. Eating is always a good idea. I grope around in the dark and manage to gather my sweats and hoodie. I pull my outerwear on quietly so as not to wake Maci and Heidi, tuck a key in my pocket, then tiptoe out the door. When I reach the breakfast nook near the lobby, I find my coaches deep in conversation, poring over what I can only assume to be stats, while picking at plates of eggs and toast.

I approach their table and greet them. "Good morning, superiors."

"Good morning, Jamie," Coach VanDyke replies.

"Did ya get any sleep, JG?" Coach Schlepp asks.

"Not much." I shrug. "Apparently my brain is too revved up to let me sleep."

"I hear that," agrees Coach Schlepp.

"Could I see that paper for a minute, please?"

Coach Schlepp reaches for the folded-over newspaper next to his plate and hands me the sports page. I scan the headlines and start.

By Fritz Neighbor of the Gazette Staff

BELGRADE- Top-ranked Chester found its hands full again on a Thursday at the State C girls' basketball tournament, but this time came through with a solid second half—and a win, 61-47 over a solid Jordan squad.

The Coyotes, now 24-0, were in danger of losing in the first round at State for the third time in four years. But Michele VanDyke and Jamie Graham combined for 20 second-half points to help Chester erase a 27-22 deficit at intermission.

VanDyke, Graham, and Co. put together the kind of second half you'd expect from a team with a perfect record. But the first half? Call it Coyote Ugly.

"But let's not, Fritz, because it is *ky-oat*, not *ky-oat-ee*," I murmur as I continue to read.

VanDyke and center Heidi Cicon each picked up their third fouls early in the second quarter. Jordan, getting three-pointers from Chantel Harbaugh and Tierani Brusett, outscored the Coyotes 12-5 from there, and Chester fans were starting to worry if history was repeating itself.

"So was I," said VanDyke, who rallied to finish with 13 points and 11 boards. But we've had a lot of experience. We knew this was a game we needed to win, and we knew we had to come out strong in the second half. Which we did."

Maci Tempel hit a baseline jumper, then a layup off her own steal during an 8-0 run as Chester surged ahead 30-29 at 6:00 of the third quarter. Jordan forged ties at 34 and 36, on a three from Brusett and a low-post basket from Dixie Person. But Chasi Buffington (two free throws), Graham (three-point play), and Cicon (low-post basket) combined on a 7-0 Chester run to close the quarter with a 43-36 lead.

By then, Jordan had troubles of its own: center Katie Whiteside was on the bench with four fouls. In the fourth, the Coyotes steadily pulled away.

"We had to pass it more and be patient," said VanDyke, who had eight points in the third frame. "Then we got a lot better open looks. We kept our poise."

It was needed, to give Chester the shot at a title it missed in 1998 and 2000.

The Coyotes will face Brockton, which held off stubborn Twin Bridges 77-68 in a foul-plagued nightcap, at 8 p.m. tonight.

I look back up at my coaches. "Nice to read about a Thursday win for a change."

"Yep." Coach Schlepp nods. "We finally figured out how to treat our thankfully-not-chronic Case of the Thursdays."

His comment makes me smile, as usual, and I walk over to the wonderful breakfast buffet.

Chapter 33

November 30, 2001, senior year, State Class C Tournament, Belgrade, Montana

Well that was a lovely nap. According to the hotel clock radio, it is 10:49 a.m. We are to meet at the hotel restaurant for second breakfast.

"Hey, C," I say as I gently jostle Heidi, who is sleeping beside me. "Time for food."

She mumbles something about boxing out and rolls over. I sit up, dangle my feet over the bed, then stand up and try Maci Lea on the other bed. "Mace. Mace. Time to get up."

Maci inhales through her nose and rolls over to the right. I walk over to the giant window and pull open the blinds. Sunlight streams over my sleepyhead teammates, and I finally see the whites of some eyes. "We gotta be downstairs in ten minutes," I announce. "Then only nine hours until we tipoff for the state semifinal."

This statement inspires some smiles and movement.

"Let's eat," Maci says, enthusiastically, as she gets up and grabs her pullover (or is it a cardigan)?

Our coaches and most of our team are already seated at tables in the corner of the empty restaurant near the lobby of the Quality Inn. The three of us from room 203 scooch into a booth and Heidi hands out menus. I open mine out of habit and fake read it, because I already know I will be ordering a ham and cheese omelette with chocolate milk, thank you very much. There is lots of giggling during our meal, and even though most of us took naps for the last hour or two, it is clear no one slept much last night. We are delirious and delighted. Everyone is just so . . . happy. I can feel it, and I love it.

* * *

Pregame Extreme Dance Party (EDP), singing into bottle microphones

Pregame EDP: Michele and me

Braid hair, check. Put on girly clothes, check. Pack duffel, check. It is quarter past three and time for our traditional pregame Extreme Dance Party. Today's EDP will take place in Michele, Chasi, and Kaitlynn's room. Heidi, Maci, and I make the short journey to room 205 where Michele has just pressed play. Britney Spears sings about an allegedly "lucky" girl who in fact weeps in the evenings, and we dance our butts off on the two queen beds, water bottles for microphones. Alice Cooper comes on next, followed by Survivor. After "Summer of '69" I have a fair number of sweat beads gathering at my temples.

It is time to board the bus.

Al drives us to Perkins in Bozeman, just a ways down the road.[86] I am thankful I ate well this morning, because my stomach is not responding well to the bacon cheeseburger and vanilla milkshake staring at me. There isn't as much of the usual talking during this meal. Coach Schlepp takes care of the bill, double checking to make

---

[86]Bozeman has many chain and fast-food restaurants that Belgrade does not. The Belgrade Special Events Center was built in 1996 with tournaments specifically in mind (Kimmel, 2013).

sure we all stayed under the school's ten-dollar limit, and we board the bus over to the hotel where our pep band is staying.

We walk through the lobby and into a conference room where almost one hundred fans wait to greet us. Our cheerleaders lead everyone in the school song to the tune of the "Washington and Lee Swing," and there is a catch in my throat as I look around the room.

Coach VanDyke gives a touching speech that I can't quite compute due to the fact that I am concentrating very hard on not blubbering like a baby. The pep assembly closes with our dads spelling out C-H-E-S-T-E-R C-O-Y-O-T-E-S, one dad per letter (three dads had to hustle over and do a second letter).[87]

We exit the conference room while our parents, pep band members, and various other town members cheer, "We are proud of you, yeah, we are proud of you, hey, hey, hey!" at the top of their lungs.

Dad as the "S" in "C-O-Y-O-T-E-S," a team cheer the dads led for a pep rally at the hotel in Belgrade

Their energy follows us, and I wipe away a few last tears. As we trek across the parking lot I read "Chester Coyotes" branded in the same black letters on the same yellow bus I rode almost a decade ago. I smile and note just how connected I feel to all those who have proudly sported the Chester Coyote Columbia blue and gold. My posture improves at this thought, and I eagerly board the beast.

* * *

I overhear Coach VanDyke talking to Jim Sargent representing KSEN radio outside our locker room. *"When you think of*

---

[87]Seven of us practiced together most of the year, but Kaitlynn was always there helping with clock or stats and joined practices after being cleared a couple weeks before senior night. Then, for tournaments, we added sophomores Alisha Fossen and Courtney Fraser and freshman Jillien Johnson in order to go through five-on-five scenarios during practice.

208

Brockton, all you hear about is Kayla Lambert all year long. When you talk about the Chester Coyotes, you hear many numbers. If we play smart, the numbers will beat Kayla Lambert."

The confidence in Coach's voice in turn gives me confidence, and I gather with my girls for one last huddle before heading out to the floor. The cheers coming from the stands are deafening as we assume our positions at the northwest corner of the gymnasium. We wait not-so-patiently as the last minutes tick down for the first semifinal game of the night with the Manhattan Christian Eagles versus the Harlowton Engineers. Both these teams are tough, ridiculously athletic, and love to get up and down the court. The Engineers end up pulling out a tight one, with free throws down the stretch, to win by three and advance to Saturday night. We plan on meeting them there, but first things first.

* * *

The 5,500-seat Events Center is packed to capacity as starting lineups are announced. Maci, Chasi, Heidi, Michele, and I take turns shaking hands with Loretta Brown, Jana Nygard, Brandie Dionne, Sekoya Bighorn, and Kayla Lambert. A large chunk of the crowd roars as the tip unfortunately lands first in Nygard's hands. It has been a while since we didn't control the first tip, so this is a little weird. She delivers it to Lambert who turns with a dribble and is surprised by Chasi and Maci both waiting for her. Mace almost grabs a steal, but Lambert manages to get it down to Bighorn on the left wing. Bighorn drives left and makes a crosscourt pass to Nygard who banks in an easy two on the right block because I am caught gawking at the ball.

Shake it off. Our ball. Maci and I set up in the backcourt as we study the 2-2-1 press waiting for us. Maci takes a couple dribbles, hits me on a quick parallel pass, and I zip it immediately to Michele in the middle. (Because everyone knows in order to break the press, ya gotta get it to the middle, of course.)

Michele dribbles across the timeline and sees Chasi cutting down to the right block. A hard bounce pass that we could've gotten away with against another opponent is intercepted by Brown. She finds Lambert as quickly as possible. I get my hands on it, but Lambert dives straight at me, and we roll down to the floor. I keep a low dribble with my right hand as she reaches for the ball but instead grabs my left arm. The whistle stops this fun little wrestling match, and the call ends up being a jump ball. Not sure if that's the call I would've made, but I am not the one making the big bucks.

Our ball on the sideline. Maci takes it out, and we run the same sideline play we've been running the past four years called . . . "sideline." May not be original, but things don't have to be original to be effective. Heidi and Michele set up on the block while Chasi and I hang out a couple feet past half-court, just in case Maci needs us. Heidi cuts low across the block and rubs shoulders with Michele out to the deep corner. Maci heaves it to Heidi, and she shoots a high one toward Michele who has Dionne sealed. Michele attempts to get it back to Heidi but Lambert helps from behind and thwarts that plan.

Lambert outlets the ball up to Nygard, then across to Dionne who bricks a left-handed floater from the paint. I pull down the rebound like a beast. (Actually, the ball falls directly into my hands like manna from heaven, but I chin it like a beast.) Excited for an opportunity to fast break, I hurl it to Michele, then Michele keeps it moving up to Maci, waiting in her favorite spot at the short corner. Maci's shot is a rare miss. This turns out to be in our favor as Michele pulls down the "O" board and gets to the line for the first time tonight. Her first free throw goes in and out, and the next one is just flat-out short. It looks like Maci has the board, but Dionne pulls it away from her and slings it over to, surprise, Lambert.

Chasi and Maci are waiting hungrily. Coach Schlepp has us in a triangle-and-two again tonight. However, this time there is a twist. Instead of two people being face-guarded, Mace and Chas are both solely focusing on Lambert, leaving Heidi, Michele, and me to zone the remaining four players. We understand this means there will be a risk of leaving other players wide-open, but we are committed to giving it a shot.

Maci gets a hand on the ball as Lambert dribbles determinedly down the court. This causes the ball to bounce off Lambert's leg, forcing her to trip and belly flop. The referee from the opposite side of the court calls a block on Chasi to even out the team fouls so far, 1–1. Nygard inbounds from the sideline to Bighorn, and I get caught by a screen set by Dionne. This opens up the paint where Bighorn finds Nygard, and she tosses another one in to put them up 0–4 with 6:53 on the clock.

Coach pulls us in for a time-out where we take a breath and reflect quickly on what the pregame plan was, and the fact that we need to remain flexible now that we are putting theory to practice.

"Okay, we see they are pressing us in that 2–2–1. When we cross half-court, we do not need to force it. I know we are used to fast breaks, but tonight we need to adjust and work it around. They are quick and scrappy, and we can't rely on what 'usually' works. This is the state semifinal. You deserve to be here. Let's play like it."

"Together," I prompt. "One, two, three—"

"Together!"

We hustle out to our spots and set up "sideline" yet again. This time I take it out and lob it to Michele in the middle of the paint. She misses a turn-around jumper, but Heidi gets great position for the rebound and forces the first foul on Lambert. We inbound on "Purdue," which gets Heidi to the line. Her first free throw finally puts us on the board, and the second one dings off the back of the rim into the hands of Chasi. Chas shot fakes and flips it to Michele in the paint who makes an impossible shot from the right elbow. Maci and Chasi swarm Lambert immediately, and Chas picks up a steal then capitalizes with a left-handed putback that gives us our first lead at 5–4.

Unfortunately the Warriors quickly transition and Nygard puts in an eighteen-footer to take the lead right back. We break their press on a few quick passes and find ourselves lining up again with Heidi at the stripe. Heidi ties us 6–6, then gives us another one point lead. Nygard chucks one up from twenty-one feet to steal that lead right back. We quickly transition again, and Brockton picks up their fifth team foul while failing to trap Michele at the east corner.

Phew. I am a bit winded, if I am honest. This may be a long night.

The Warriors break our press and Michele picks up a second questionable foul on what looked like a clean box out to me; the protests from our crowd behind me tell me they agree. Nygard makes the short jumper and gets to the line. When she misses, Lambert picks up the board and gets great position for an unfortunate and-one. Lambert swishes her free throw, and we find ourselves down 7–14 with 4:45 left in the first. Maci brings it up across half-court, hits

211

me at the left elbow, and I reverse it to Heidi, where the ball is unfortunately taken again by the green team.

Back and forth, back and forth. Nygard hits yet another three. Score is 7–17. Down ten. Not ideal. There is a crazy fray on our end which ends with me at the stripe. I make my first two free throws with just under four minutes to go to put us back within single digits. I notice all nine players around me are tightly holding their shorts and seem thankful for this brief break. Not only do I make the free throws, but the scoreboard shows Lambert penalized with two fouls.

Nygard swishes her third flipping three right on the next trip down. Are you kidding me right now?! I miss on the other end, up and down, up and down. Then Nygard scores yet again on an offensive putback after an attempt from Dionne. Down twelve with 2:07 left in the first. Twelve points?!

We regroup with a time-out and decide to continue to stick with our triangle-and-two defense. For only a few seconds, though. After two passes I grab my left wrist with my right hand. This signals my teammates to reconfigure into our 1-3-1 half-court trap which results in an instant Warrior turnover. Maci puts one up from twenty, miss and rebounded by Savannah, miss, then rebounded by Heidi. Miss. Heidi gets to the line, though, and makes one of two.

The rest of the quarter is just as bonkers, with three turnovers by Brockton and a player-control foul called against Maci. Down 11–22 with forty seconds to go. Four of us follow Lambert around, and she misses a leapin' leaner. Fast break for us, and I capitalize with a layup courtesy Heidi's ball-screen. Maci grabs one more steal with eleven seconds to go, misses a three-point attempt, but it is pulled down by Heidi. Come on, C! Three seconds to go. Heidi is short on her first try. Two seconds. She sticks with it grabs her own rebound then . . . and-one! Atta baby!

We head in for a much-needed quarter break, after all that crazy sprinting, and thanks to Heidi are now down only 16–22.

"Great job," Coach starts, as we chug from our green Gatorade bottles and swipe at the sweat in vain.

She continues, "Alright, we did exactly what we planned to do, but Nygard got hot so we had to adjust. Basketball is a game of adjustments. Great job transitioning into our half-court trap. They are struggling with that trap, and now we are forcing some turnovers.

212

Look for the fast break and when you go up, go up hard. Look to draw the foul and get to the line. If it isn't there, pull it back out and *be patient.* Let's start in man-to-man. Everyone play honest and Maci, you faceguard Lambert at all times. Chasi, Jamie, if there is an opportunity for a trap, trap. Hands up, box out, and be strong with that ball. The momentum shifted our way, and we cut our deficit in half that last minute. That's a good reminder that a lot can happen in a short period of time in this game. Keep at it. Keep chipping away."

Chip away. I think I've heard that a time or two, or seventy billion times, over the years. It is proving to be good advice. The second quarter is a crazy track meet. Heidi scores early, then Nygard answers back, then Chasi subs in again and hits a huge three on her likely broken foot.[88] Katy comes in and immediately scores on a beautiful turn-around jumper. I hit a couple free throws, Brown makes a putback for the Warriors, then Michele scores from the elbow.

We turn around expectantly on defense, fire in our eyes. Just as they cross half I tip it from behind to Kaitlynn, who gets it right back to me. I dribble twice and hit Maci ahead on the right lane. She dribbles once, twice, and catches Lambert off guard, the whistle stopping action to record Lambert's third foul with 5:13 left in the half. Maci's off-balance twisty bank shot manages to fall, and I would really, really, really like the referee to please count that. The ref signs to the bookkeeper to record it as a blocking foul on the floor, despite my encouragement with multiple and-one hand pumps for him to count it.

Five minutes left in the half; Montana's all-time leading scorer watching from the bench with three fouls. Excellent.

Instead of capitalizing on this bit of good luck, however, we instead give up a rebound to Nygard followed by a long bomb to Dionne waiting on the other end for an easy two. Would we call that cherry picking? It doesn't really matter what we call it because we were taught way back in junior high that you don't let anyone behind you on the fast break, for crying out loud! Knotted at 30–30.

Take a breath. Reset.

---

[88] Chasi injured her foot during Divisionals. The doctor was thinking it was a little break, but it turned out to be a nasty sprain.

I bring it up the right side and fire it over to Maci on the right wing. Shot fake, back to me. I turn the corner and reverse to Chasi who instantly finds Kaitlynn cutting baseline after working the high-low with Michele. Katy makes an amazing catch and drops one in off the backboard.

Lambert is back in and hits an impossible fade away jump shot from the right baseline. So much for keeping her benched.

Up the right side again to Chasi, back to me, and I cast a lob from twenty-five feet down to Katy who promptly pours in another bucket. One would never know she has only been playing with us for a few weeks.

I let Nygard take it all the way to the deep corner on the left dribble (because Dad always says to first of all force girls left, then they may just keep going and dribble right out-of-bounds), and she continues to go left on the baseline. Katy steps in just behind me and gets rocked on the drive, forcing Nygard to step out-of-bounds. My heart stutters a second as I watch Kaitlynn sit a second and struggle to stand.

"You okay, babe?" I ask as Michele pulls Katy up.

"Never better," she answers as she rubs her tailbone then jogs off down the court.

With 2:55 left in this ridiculously long half, we take our biggest lead of the night, 40–34. We catch our breath at the free throw line, with Lambert then Savannah each draining two. I almost pick it from Bighorn, but she instead hits a baseline 12-footer. Up, down, up, down. Lambert assists Chastity Black Dog, and now it's 42–40. We work it around but lose it underneath. They run the weave and, drat! Lambert sinks a deep three. Luckily my big blond bestie tosses in yet another offensive putback on the other end.

With a minute to go I walk it up and call for "Utah." "Utah" fails miserably, and we find ourselves at the free throw line again, this time with Nygard shooting. Miss. Make. 29.9 seconds left in the half. Maci and I play catch for a few seconds just across half-court. With eleven seconds to go I toss it to Savannah on the left wing, then cut down and rub shoulders with Heidi waiting on the block. I make a pass to Savannah on the left wing again, and her last-second attempt misses.

We turn and race toward our locker room with a score Warriors 44, Coyotes 44.

214

* * *

Brockton opens the second half with possession, and we tip it and quickly force a jump ball, taking it after only five seconds tick off the clock. Maci picks up her third foul, though it looked an awful lot like a player-control foul on Lambert to me. Maci and Chasi now both have three fouls, which obviously isn't ideal.

With 5:17 left in the third, Coach VanDyke is talking to Chasi near the bench, and I make the mistake of chucking it up to Chasi's back. Somehow a technical foul is called? What now??[89] Down 46-51.

I hear Sarge on the radio. *"Buffington just gets hammered right in front of us, but they call her for a double dribble."* I decide it's best not to stop and tell him I completely agree, and instead I run to our bench as Coach beckons us in with a time-out.[90]

At 4:51 Chasi stands strong with her right foot rubbing the black baseline and gets knocked down by Lambert receiving the inbound. Coach Schlepp is momentarily beside himself as it looks like the ref near us may call this a blocking foul. The referee on the other side charges across the court and keeps us in suspense, not revealing his decision of an offensive charge until he has all eyes on him.

Yeah, baby!

That is Lambert's fourth foul.

Now 3:15 left in the quarter, down 47-53.

At 2:09 I tip it to Michele who hits me right back and find myself wide-open. As I somehow manage to miss the open layup I swear I can hear my poor father's groan over the din of the crowd. Sorry about that, Dad. No time to dwell.

Down 56-61 with thirty seconds to go in this third quarter, and I take a break on the bench for the first time tonight.

Chasi goes 1-2 from the free throw line and Katy grabs the miss and gets her own one-and-one opportunity with yet another foul called. Kaitlynn also goes one for two from the stripe, Nygard misses

---

[89] From what anyone could figure, the technical foul was called on Coach VanDyke for touching a player during action.

[90] Jim Sargent announced all our games at State for KSEN, choosing radio over reffing that weekend. I do believe he announced that call as a foul on Chasi as an unbiased ref; it is merely coincidence that he happens to be Chasi's godfather.

a fast-break layup, then Maci misses one on the other end, but Kaitlynn follows and finishes the quarter with a putback at the buzzer! I jump off the bench to give Katy the mighty butt slap she deserves and to check back in for the fourth quarter, down 60–61.

Eight minutes left.

The entire starting five for Brockton has four fouls to start the fourth.

On the next possession, Loretta Brown picks up foul number five after Heidi fights for two offensive rebounds after I brick a jump shot from eight feet. Heidi follows the unfortunate pattern that seems to be trending for us and makes one of two of her free throws.

Lambert takes it all the way to the other end of the court and puts in a nice little floater. It's as if she simply inbounded that ball to herself, before she took it the full length to score.

Dionne picks up her fifth with 5:53 to go, and I break the pattern and make both free throws.

At 4:45 I am called for my fourth blasted foul as Lambert jukes and jives with three of us trying to contain her. Flip. Well at least I am in good company. She makes one and luckily misses only her second free throw of the night.

Four minutes left and Michele makes a pick then takes it from California to Connecticut (heard that on the radio once, too) to put us up, 72–70. However, Lambert pulls it out and chucks it down to a wide-open Nygard on the other end who ties it right back up. I feel like the coaches have mentioned to us once or twice the importance of not getting beat back like that.

With 3:28 on the clock, Michele pulls the tipped-and-bobbled ball down and lands on her knees for what I'm thinking must be a jump ball. Wait a sec. I know that sign. He did not just call Michele for her fifth foul on that oh-so-obvious clean strip!

Are you kidding me?!

Deep breaths, Jamie. Michele handles herself much better than I imagine I would have and jogs with her head up to the bench. The entirety of Brockton's team and bench follow to tell her good game (but we all know what they're really thinking, don't we).

Now 3:19 left and tied at 74 apiece—the eighth time the game has been tied.

Morning Star Foote fouls with 2:41, putting Savannah to the line.

I check in after sitting for a lot longer than I usually have to sit. We are up 78–75, thanks to Chasi hitting that pull-up jumper a couple possessions back. Then we are called for yet another foul after Savannah tries to switch a screen but gets caught behind. Nygard hits two free throws to put them within one.

I walk it up and play catch with Maci for a few seconds, then it goes down to Katy at the short corner. Maci inbounds it to me, and Chasi and I assume the stall position as the two-minute warning comes across the PA system. I make the rookie mistake of picking up my dribble at the top of the key and attempt a crosscourt pass to Maci that is picked off.

My fault, Mace!

We manage to hold them off, Katy pulls down the defensive board and is fouled by Black Dog.

Kaitlynn has been clutch tonight, despite the whole just-recovering-from-open-back-surgery thing, and hits one free throw for her twelfth point. Well let's try something new defensively this time and . . . foul. Again. Nygard makes them both to tie it up at 79.

I get it across half to Maci with 1:06 to play, and she calls a time-out, per bench instructions.

Coach has to shout in order to be heard, even though we are crowded tightly around her on the bench. "Here we are! Tie game, semifinal night at the state tournament. This is exactly where we want to be. Jamie, you inbound to Maci, and then you all take your time! We are in the driver's seat. Work it around until we get a high percentage shot. Don't force anything. Make the extra pass and look to get to the free throw line. Lambert has four fouls. Go at her!"

Lots of nodding and bottom slapping ensues.

"Pick up man-to-man defensively. Box out and chin it on those boards! Know who you have! Stay poised! We got this!"

" 'Win' on three!" Chasi demands. "One, two, three—"

"WIN!"

I stand at the sideline for a bit, while Brockton finishes talking strategy in their huddle. I take a quick look at our crowd and catch James Booth's eye. He is standing on the bottom bleacher just behind the official scorer's bench, cheering his head off. I grin and turn back to my team. I can't believe he is here. We gotta pull through.

217

Chapter 34

*December 1, 2001, senior year, State Class C Tournament,
Belgrade, MT*

5:00 a.m: Crunch, crunch, crunch. What is that? Crunch, crunch.

"C! What in the heck are you doing?!" Maci's voice breaks through the dark.

A lamp switches on above Maci on the next bed, and the light reveals the source of the crunching noise. Heidi sits on our wooden square hotel table hunched over and trying to chew her granola cereal as quietly as possible. I can't stop giggling at our sweet blonde friend as I roll over and force my eyes to close while Maci laughs, sighs, and clicks the light back off.

6:12 a.m.: I open my bleary eyes and peer around the dim hotel room. My brain, like last night, will not stop. My roommates seem to be sleeping again. I roll from one side to the other but cannot get comfortable, so I pull on my sweats and pad down to the breakfast area. I am greeted with an identical scene to yesterday morning, coaches poring over papers and deep in intense conversation.

I approach their table and greet them. "Good morning, superiors."

"Good morning, Jamie," Coach VanDyke replies.

"Get any sleep, JG?" Coach Schlepp asks.

"Not much." I shrug, as that déjà vu feeling kicks in.

"Could I see that paper for a minute, please?"

Coach Schlepp reaches for the folded-over newspaper next to his plate and hands me the sports page. I scan the headlines and start.

```
By Fritz Neighbor
Of the Gazette Staff
```

BELGRADE- The marquee matchup turned into the Jamie Graham show Friday—

Aw, Fritz. Go on.

—and Chester outlasted Brockton 87-81 in the semifinals of the State C girls' basketball tournament. Graham, a senior guard, scored her team's final eight points to help Chester stay unbeaten (25-0) and make its first-ever title game appearance. The Coyotes will take on 24-2 Harlowton, which won an equally hard-fought semifinal game 61-58 over Manhattan Christian.

Brockton's Lady Warriors sprinted out of the gates to a 22-10 lead, then saw Chester reel them in with some withering pressure. In a game that featured 53 turnovers and countless lead changes, it wasn't decided until after Chester star Michele VanDyke went to the bench with her fifth foul.

Enter Graham. She hit back-to-back drives to put Chester up 81-79 then 83-81 with under 45 seconds left, and came up big again when Brockton star Kayla Lambert tried a leaning, contested bank shot that rimmed out. Graham grabbed the board, was fouled by Lambert—it was the fifth foul on Montana's all-time leading scorer—and made both free throws for an 85-81 lead with 18 seconds left.

That basically sealed it.

"We've been waiting our whole lives for this," said Graham, a four-year starter who saw Chester lose in the first round in two previous State tournaments.

"We've never had to rely on one person. That's the beauty of this team. It hurt to have Michele

on the bench, but somebody else always steps up."
Graham smiled. "I made my free throws for a change
(10 out of 10)."

Lambert scored 37 points, despite constant
pressure from Chester's Maci Tempel. At one point,
the Coyotes had two defenders guarding Lambert,
leaving Brockton with a 4-on-3 in its frontcourt.
That's when Jana Nygard snared an offensive
rebound and scored for that 22-10 advantage.

By the 5:00 mark of the second quarter, though,
Chester had switched to a full-court man-to-man.
"You get a double-digit lead, and you tend to be
leery," said Brockton coach Bernard Lambert. "The
players tend to let up. Then when they throw
something new at you defensively, you can't
panic."

Still, the score was tied at 44 at halftime,
with Nygard and Lambert each scoring 14 points.
Chester countered with Graham and Heidi Cicon, the
latter scoring 15 of her team-high 23 points before
intermission.

The game went back and forth the rest of the
way, with Lambert dropping a beautiful behind-the-
back bounce pass to reserve Chastity Black Dog for
a layup and a 65-62 lead with 6:31 to go. Chester
went back in front after a follow by Cicon—one of
Chester's 26 offensive rebounds—and then two free
throws from Graham. The lead changed hands four
more times, then was tied at 79 (after two Bighorn
free throws) and 81 (Black Dog follow shot).

"There were just little things," said coach
Lambert. "We didn't capitalize on a few
possessions. If we had, it might've turned out
different. It's disappointing in the sense that
you play a quality team that close throughout the
game—and again, it comes down to the little
things."

In the end, Graham gave Chester the edge. When
asked what she was thinking while shooting those
free throws in the last minute Graham said, "Well
James Booth was in the crowd tonight, and I was

actually thinking about when his team won State in 1992. Mark Cramer hit two free throws to win in overtime."

Sounds like these ladies are ready for a chance at their own title.

"We've waited four years for this," she said. "Actually, 12 years. Forever, it seems."

It's here now for the Chester Coyotes.

I hand the paper back to Coach Schlepp. "I guess that game was as crazy as it seemed."

"Crazier"—Coach Schlepp's eyes and mouth are wide as he shakes his head, as if in disbelief—"but here we are."

"Finally," he adds with a slightly sassy smile.

"Finally!" Coach VanDyke pipes up in agreement.

I grin, nod, then turn my attention to the buffet.

7:00 a.m.: The lock clicks when I swipe my magic magnetic key card below the door handle. I slowly push open the squeaky hotel room door in case my teammates are still sleeping. The room is dark, and I hear no chatter, so I take this opportunity to lie back down, snuggle in next to Maci, and try to get a little more rest.

We are *finally* here. I close my eyes and let my mind replay the excitement of last night. It was so awesome. Our whole crowd mauled us afterward, and it took forever to get to the showers. James Booth gave me a big hug and was telling me what to do in the championship game. Chris Mattson picked me up and gave me a great big bear hug. Mr. Gordon almost crushed me. Dad was so happy, and I think very relieved. He gave me like seventy-eight forehead kisses. All our dads were so cute and emotional and gave us so many hugs. Rudy of course was giggly and Gary was trying to hold back too many tears. The dads all look so cute in their beards. They haven't shaved since the first game of the season and promised not to unless we lost, so Russ and Mark just look even more rugged and "mountain-manny" than usual.[91] I hugged all the little kids from our crowd and I think

---

[91]Rudy Cicon is Heidi's dad, Gary is Chasi's dad, Russ is Maci and Mari's dad, and Mark is Kaitlynn's dad.

221

the entire pep band, including Miss Goodheart and Pastor Pete.[92] The boys in our class were so sweet, and they all came down and gave us hugs. That same feeling of happiness trickles through my whole body all over again.

We finally made it back to the hotel after what seemed like hours, then had a quick team meeting as well as food and super-delicious ice cream cake to celebrate Michele's birthday (a couple days early). Food never tasted so good. Then we sat around in the hallway for a while with the cheerleaders and parents and random townsfolk. Our cheerleaders decorated top to bottom with good luck signs, streamers, posters with our pictures on it. It was so fun!

Kaitlynn came and grabbed me at some point because *Home Alone* was on TV, which was so perfect because we always have to watch *Home Alone* when it first snows before Christmas. We had to be in our rooms by midnight, but Heidi, Maci, and I didn't finally get quiet until close to one o'clock in the morning. I had a hard time sleeping because I could not stop thinking about the Brockton game, and about tonight. But I better try to get a little more shuteye.

10:53 a.m.: "It's time to go down for brunch," Heidi announces.

I glance over at the clock radio and take a second to get my bearings. Ahhhh, yes!! It is the morning before our state championship basketball game! I wade through the pile of clothes and pull out my sweats and hoodie. How did our room get this messy this fast?

12:30 p.m.: "Disney or CMT?" Chasi asks.

"Let's change it up and go Disney for a while," I reply and hear no objections.

Half of our team is piled here in Chasi, Katy, and Michele's room and the other half are over in the underclassmen's room since it is much tidier than ours.

"Ready to braid my hair, J?" Maci crawls over to the end of the bed I'm on and gets situated as I grab the comb, hair spray, and tiny rubber bands. Michele finds a spot in front of Heidi, who grabs a brush and more spray, and we begin our special pregame traditions for the last time.

---

[92]Pastor Pete was the pastor of the Lutheran church in Chester and played trombone in the pep band. He later performed my wedding ceremony on April 22, 2006.

3:00 p.m.: Extreme Dance Party time! This time we take plenty of pictures as we sing along to "Girls Just Wanna Have Fun," "Eye of the Tiger," "Ain't Too Proud to Beg," etc.

The final rousing Extreme Dance Party

3:30 p.m.: Our group is looking pretty snazzy, I must say, congregated in the lobby. Due to this once-in-a-lifetime occasion, we are all sporting dresses and fancy shoes. The dresses are partly covered by our bulky winter coats, and we each tote a gym bag over one shoulder and a garment bag protecting our precious Coyote uniforms over the other.

"There's Al!" Amanda announces, pointing to the diesel pulling up to the lobby entrance. We file silently yet excitedly onto the bus.

7:30 p.m.: "Here we are, ladies." Coach has our rapt attention for her final pregame speech. "The Engineers match up very well with us. Heidi, Michele, Katy, and Amanda—you will be taking care of the Jones twins in the paint. They are athletic and very strong. You must put a butt on them after every shot and be strong with that ball. They are also capable of blocking shots, so remember to shot fake."

Our four bigs nod as she moves on to guard play.

"Maci, Chasi, Jamie, and Savannah—Halsey, Miller, and Galahan are their starting guards, and they are fast and ferocious defensively. They will go all out to try to make steals, though, so use that to your advantage. When they match up with full-court pressure, make one move and go. You must shot and pass fake. Switch on screens and get a hand in their face. The Jones twins are the only two who average in double digits, but make sure to get a hand in those shooters' faces.

223

Danielle Dick comes in off the bench and will shoot the three. Just play them honest and we should be fine."

The four of us nod our acknowledgement.

"Defensively Coach Schlepp has us starting out in our usual— 'cheetah' after a make, full-court man after a miss. Watch for the signal to change into 'five' or our half-court trap."

More nodding.

"Just relax. Enjoy yourselves. You are in a place you have never been before. We have been working on a lot of things for many years, and let's just let it show. We came through last night and are right where we want to be. Let's just have some fun and get it done."

Huddled and waiting to run out to "The Final Countdown" before the state championship game against Harlowton, December 1, 2001

* * *

I proudly, yet nervously, stand next to my teammates out on the volleyball line across from the Harlowton Engineers, who mirror us on the opposite end. The announcer calls out our managers, reserves, starters, coaches; we raise our arms together to huddle, listen to a few reminders from Coach at the bench, bawl, "Together!" and take the court.

224

Starting lineups versus Harlowton, December 1, 2001

I shake hands with Halsey lined up across from me at center court and proceed to wipe the bottom of my shoes several times and test my AND1 light-blue-and-white sneakers with my toe. Yep, the floor sweepers are legit, and I still love that lacquer scent.

The starting lineups I have daydreamed about so many times blur quickly by, but I stop a second to take a quick sweep of the crowd. The sea of blue and gold is cheering and clapping, voices gathered into one excited roar. I feel a catch in my throat looking out at hundreds and hundreds of Chester fans.

Wow.

I blink to refocus and join our final pregame huddle. In attempt to be heard over the crowd, Coach shouts, "Here we are! We made it. This is what you have all been waiting for. So go out there and show everyone that you are champions!"

Heart pounding, energy surging, I join my voice with my team— "Coyotes!"–then run out for the opening tip.

This is it. There is no place I would rather be. Please, God, be with us as we compete tonight. I make my rounds one last time and connect with my four teammates. Then I toe the middle circle, bend my knees, let out a deep exhale, fix my stare on that spiraling Spalding . . . and here we go.

Michele directs the tip over to Maci lined up on her left, and Maci brings it across the timeline. Harlo matches up in a tight man, and I V-cut and receive a pass from Maci high on the right wing. I

225

toss it into Michele on the right elbow and relocate while Maci screens away for Chasi. We remember our reminders to be patient, pass it around, get touches inside, and do that in a basic motion offense. Harlo is quick, though, and Ashley Jones comes up with a pick on an attempt from Chasi to Michele cutting across the key.

I chase Ashley down and get into position to force her to either put it up contended or look to pass. Her knee barely misses my nose as she skies up, but her attempt is hard and Michele rips that sucker down just as it clears the rim.

And we're off.

Michele kicks the ball up to Maci who pulls back on the right wing and hits Michele on the trail. Michele pump fakes left, takes a long step and one dribble right and puts us on the board first, 2-0.

We apply our "cheetah" press and Michele tips Miller's pass back to Ashley, but I can't quite get my hands on it. Chas gets called for an off-ball foul while preventing Halsey from cutting across her face—things may be a little physical tonight. Halsey takes it out on the side and gets it in to Amy Jones who is short from fifteen. I box and grab the rebound, then a foul is called on Galahan. We still don't score, Harlo barrels back, Heidi picks it, out to Maci who chucks it down the court, and Michele is fouled. On the inbound, Heidi is fouled on a short attempt.

Whew. Take a few breaths. Six minutes left in the first quarter. I am pretty sure we have already run the equivalent of an endurance run.

Heidi goes one for two from the line, putting us up 3-0, then the Engineers get on the board with a short jumper from Amy Jones. I miss a drive to the hole, they sprint back down and also miss a layup, then the outlet goes to Chasi the other way. I know these girls have won state track the last three years, and I can't help but wonder if they are confused as to what kind of contest we are competing in tonight.

Heidi scores on a trail pass from Michele, Maci picks Miller's pocket and is hammered. Michele is called on a questionable travel, then Miller pops a deep three on the left wing, despite my hand in her face, tying it at five with 4:39 to go. Up, down, up, down, then Miller hits another three off a break, this time from the right side.

Chasi gets it down to Heidi on the block, but she is stopped by a Jones wall, then one twin finds the other working the high-low option.

The game continues at this incredibly fast pace, and we miss while Miller puts in a layup to put us down 5–12. Michele scores twice, but Harlo answers back both times, and then Miller sinks her third from downtown to lift Harlo up 9–19 with 1:10 to go. This first quarter is crazy, and our poor coaches are forced to call a second time-out already.

Amanda picks up an assist as Kaitlynn keeps her pattern up from last night and sinks a turnaround jumper on the right block. Danielle Dick hits a jumper, and then I miss yet another layup on the other end. Then Amanda fights for the board, and we get the ball under the basket with nine seconds to go in the quarter. Maci catches at the deep corner, looks and looks for someone to pass to, decides to take it baseline herself and . . . scores with a second to spare!

Down 13–21 end of one.

This is obviously not ideal, but we started down in this tournament's first two games, and things ended up working out for us. Besides, when the boys won in '92, they were down by fourteen in the fourth quarter. If they can do it, we can do it. I jog back to the bench and anticipate Coach reminding us to be patient with it offensively and keep an eye on Miller (to be clear, it was not noted and could not have been anticipated in the scouting report that she would be shooting out of her mind tonight).

"Alright!" Coach shouts so as to be heard above the crowd's roar. "We have got to be patient with the ball offensively until we have the high percentage shot. Make that extra pass! And keep an eye on Miller; she obviously has the hot hand tonight."

Heads bob with understanding, and I pat myself on the back for knowing, as usual, just what Coach will say. Now to put that good advice to practice. Chip away.

The second quarter starts at a slightly slower pace, and Heidi closes the gap a bit at 7:19 with a jumper in the key. We run several more up and backs, and Heidi then banks in the next bucket of the game at 5:37. Freeser has subbed in for Harlo and answers back with a bank on the left block. Freeser sneaks around under Katy and comes up with a steal. I anticipate her dribble and all but steal it back. Unfortunately I can't keep my footing and acquire a souvenir on my thigh as it meets with the black rubber mat wrapped around the court's perimeter. Savannah hands me a sweat rag as she subs in for me, and I make sure she knows who she is guarding.

I am greeted by my teammates and managers on the bench with high fives, and Michele pats my thigh as I take a seat beside her. "Hey, Jamers."

"Hey, Chelers," I reply. "Fancy meeting you here."

"What do ya say we get back in there and try a little something different?" she proposes.

"Sounds good to me," I answer back. "What did you have in mind?"

"I am thinking we should try to get ahead so we can win this thing," she finishes.

"I like the way you think, babe," I agree, as we watch Chasi assist Katy at 4:36 in yet another turnaround jumper to put us within four.

I, along with the rest of our bench and crowd, jump to my feet and cheer. "Atta baby, Kaitlynn Rae! Let's go, ladies!"

Amy Jones scores on the other end, Maci's attempt from fifteen falls short, then Chasi picks up her second foul, team fifth, with 4:01 left in the half. I sub in for Maci at 3:36 then drive in, jump stop, spin, and put up a left-handed jumper. The ball is clearly tipped, but the referee apparently thinks I just chucked the thing out-of-bounds randomly and gives them possession. If only we had instant replay access.

Katy and Heidi make a stop down low on the other end, but I notice Heidi keeling over just after the whistle. "You okay, C?" I bend down so we are face to face and rub her sweaty back.

"I'm okay," she replies, clearly lying and looking like she's about to hurl.

Katy subs right back in (after Michele just subbed in for her) to give Heidi a break. We turn it over on the inbound, Halsey misses on a drive, then Maci passes to Michele. Chele makes a power move to the hole inching us a little closer, 21–25, with 2:53 left in the half.

Miller brings it back up, Maci gets a hand on her crossover, and Chas is fouled as she dives for the loose ball to put us in bonus. It looks like we will again shoot a fair number of free throws tonight.

Not sure if we will have an opportunity to shoot quite as many as last night, but time will tell.[93]

Chasi swishes both to finally put us back within two, 23–25. Unfortunately we are also fouling, and Michele is called for her third. Amy Jones puts in her eighth point of the night to extend their lead to four yet again. Michele doesn't back down, takes it to the rack on the other end, and is hammered. She puts in both free throws and heads to the bench for a breather (and more importantly, so she doesn't pick up a fourth foul before half) with 1:59 left, trailing 25–27.

Harlo is super patient, taking close to forty seconds off the clock and finishing with another flipping three-pointer for Miller! We again had a hand right in her face, for crying out loud! I make one move to get past Halsey and flick it to Chasi on the left wing. The ball is taken away after Chasi's attempt to lob it inside to Katy. Then Chasi is called for her third foul as Amy goes to the line with 1:07 remaining.[94]

Amy Jones makes both her free throws, and then I get to the line with just under a minute left in the half, down 25–32. Halsey catches my finger on the foul, and I must say, this right middle finger hurts like a son of a bleep. After going 10–10 from the charity stripe last night, I break my streak, hitting the back of the iron on my first chance at the bonus. Ahh! Don't miss a free throw in the state championship game, Jamie![95]

Shake it off. Next play.

Maci almost picks it as Harlo crosses half-court, but Miller tosses it in toward Amy Jones, who is working for position down low. Amanda steps around and grabs the steal. That's my girl! She quickly gets rid of it, but the ball bounces off Savannah's back. This is a circus. Kaitlynn is luckily right there to pick the bobbled ball up, and

---

[93]We had forty-nine free throw attempts against Brockton. Though we shot almost 10% below our 70% goal, we still made thirty free throws, which is a ton.

[94]For how sick Heidi was that night, Amy Jones was just as sick, having been diagnosed and put on antibiotics for strep throat only a couple days before.

[95]Mom took me to the doctor Monday morning, and I really did break my right middle finger, deflecting a pass just before half. After shooting a dismal 9–19 from the line (47%) that night, I still managed to pull out the best free throw percentage for the team on the year, just under 80% (62–78). Prior to the state championship game, I was shooting 53–59 (just under 90%).

I take Kaitlynn's handoff. I follow Savannah and Katy up the court and note how they create a bit of a natural double screen for me. Hmm, what to do? I know Coach doesn't love when I pull up without any passing, but it would be nice to redeem myself. So I pull up without any passing and know it is in as soon as I release. Down 28–32.

Maci picks Miller's pocket as soon as she crosses half-court, is caught with a retaliative reach by Miller, and makes her first free throw. Miller receives the outlet pass after Maci's miss on her second attempt, and I can see she is not planning on stopping. I establish position at the block. Hands up, not budging because I got here first, dang it, and Miller is called for her third foul on a player-control call. We get the ball quickly down the court, and I shoot up another three-point attempt. It bounces deep off the rim just as the first-half buzzer sends us into the locker room, down 29–32.

I struggle to follow everything the coaches tell us at halftime: something about state championship game, once in a lifetime opportunity, leave it all on the court, been waiting for this our whole lives, et cetera et cetera. All I can seem to think about is how crazy this feels.

We have prepared and planned and practiced for this for years, yet it certainly does not seem to be going as planned. We know all the plays, we have done all the drills, but maybe no drill could have prepared us exactly for *this*. Now we are in a place where we have never been before. Now we have to be brave and trust ourselves, trust each other. Now we need to dig in, grab one (as Dad would say), and get it done.

* * *

The game continues to be bonkers. We finally take a lead 33–32 at 6:49 after Michele opens the third quarter with a drive, then I make two free throws. One Jones answers back at 6:12, and the other Jones scores at 5:39. Harlo up 33–36. We run "Connecticut," and Maci drives baseline and puts in a sweet scoop shot at 5:19. Amy Jones scores again at the block, we go a possession without scoring, then Danielle Dick pops a three. Oh, for Pete's sake!

Heidi hits Michele on some high-low action to put it at 37–41, then Chasi is called for her fourth foul with 4:05 left in the third. We do not score again, then Heidi picks up her first foul on Amy, who does score again. Thirty seconds tick off the clock, and I pick it from Galahan then score coast-to-coast. Now down 39–43.

Next, Amy goes in for a layup and—thank goodness—misses; I pick myself up off the ground after attempting to take a charge, manage to pull down the board and *give* her foul number one. Amy Jones quickly picks up foul number two on the other end when Heidi puts in an offensive rebound, makes one free throw, then Maci makes a steal and takes it all the way in for a layup. Now 2:23 left in the quarter—so much great effort, yet still down, 42–43.

At 2:05 Maci makes yet another steal, and I almost break the backboard on a high miss. For the love. Thankfully my girl Heidi follows and redeems me. Up one!

But not for long.

Coach Schlepp assumes a Mike Piazza stance and signals for us to drop into a plain old 2–3 zone. Now Galahan sinks a long three! That's gotta be like their seventh three of the game! Down again.

Michele takes over the last minute of the third quarter and scores six unanswered points. We half-run half-skip back to the bench with our biggest lead of the game, 50–46.

"Atta way!" Coach greets us excitedly. "Just keep taking it to the hole, and be ready to shoot some free throws. They will likely continue with that full-court man-to-man. Maci, Jamie, you are doing a great job making one move and going. We know they are aggressive, so make sure you all meet your passes."

"Get a butt on them every time!" Coach Schlepp adds, his intense eyes shining. "Be strong!"

Coach VanDyke nods in agreement then smiles up at our expectant faces. "Fourth quarter of the state championship game. This is what we have been waiting for. Let's finish."

" 'Finish' on three!" Maci cues us in. "One, two, three—"

"FINISH!"

Harlo has possession, and we again drop into our 2–3 with a goal of limiting their opportunities from the paint. We do limit their opportunities from the paint on this first possession, but Miller sinks her fifth flippin' three of the night! Drat the luck.

The next minute sees a lot of action, not a lot of scoring, and key fouls on the Jones twins: Ashley now has four and Amy three. Amy's

231

third also puts us into a bonus situation with 6:54 remaining in regulation. Maci misses the front end, Heidi grabs a rebound, misses, Michele jumps out of the gym to grab it but somehow lands directly on her tailbone. Ouch. Savannah grabs a third offensive board and . . . and-one! Yes! Pump fakes all around.

Savannah sinks her free throw. Up 53–49 with just under seven minutes to go. Now let's just keep this more-than-one-possession cushion here for a minute, shall we?

With 6:48 left in the fourth, the Engineers work it around the perimeter. The twins were having a heyday under the basket last quarter, so our coaches have us in a zone. This is working to keep opportunities out of their paint. Their three guards, however, absolutely have the green light on the perimeter and . . . they hit another three. Sigh. Danielle Dick pops a long ball at the top of the key to put them within one, 53–52. You have got to be flipping kidding me. Just when we get up four, they answer with a three. Michele drives but misses down on our end. Heidi grabs the board but is tied up for a jump. Maci hits me on the inbound, and I hit her as she steps in the short corner. Nothing there. Mace dribbles back up and tosses it again to me. There is Michele, flashing. Must get ball to Michele. Drat! Amy Jones sneaks around and intercepts my feeble attempt. I should have thrown it high!

Time to turn and sprint, again. Jones takes a couple dribbles before getting it up to Miller. Okay, hands up in our 2–3 again. Easy now. Miller hits Halsey, back to Miller for another long bomb?! Miss. Sidestepped that one. Let's score.

Alright, my girls are filling the lanes and there's Savannah. I bounce it down to her breaking toward the right lane, but the angle is a little questionable. The ball is bobbled. Shoot! And by "shoot" I mean should I have? Too late to debate now.

Amy Jones picks up the steal and hits Dick, to Miller, to Galahan, back to Miller on the right wing and . . . what is happening?! Swish. Even with a hand right in her face, Miller drains number six from behind the arc. It is as if she were unconscious. Down 53–55 on a wild 6–0 run from the white-hot Engineers with 5:21 on the clock.

I stop to catch my breath and notice something I do not usually feel during games. It feels strange, so I take another deep breath to be sure. Yep. I am exhausted. Perhaps this feeling can be blamed on last night's brutal two-hour battle with Brockton. Or the fact that I have barely had a wink of sleep all weekend. Or that I have not been able to eat but a few fries of all three pregame meals for the nerves. Can't dwell. No excuses.

Gotta suck it up.

Time out. "Alright," Coach starts, "we are okay. Take a deep breath and relax. They are feeling it. We are going to stick with the 2-3 for now. I know they are hitting, but the three is still a lower-percentage shot than having a Jones with the ball at the block. Keep those hands up, keep talking. Keep putting a hand in the shooter's face. Make a great box out and be strong with that ball when you pull down a rebound! They are aggressive, and they will foul. Just get it in on this inbound and work it around in high-low. Take care of the ball."

"Coyotes on three"—I put my fist in the center of the huddle and the rest of the hands quickly pile on.

"Coyotes!"

I inbound it to Savannah. She takes a couple dribbles and makes a too-high pass to Heidi. Another turnover. We quickly transition yet again. Miller dribbles right-handed up the left side, stops at the left wing and hits Amy at the free throw line. She pulls up and is short. I tear down another board. Why not become a fantastic rebounder the last game of my high school career?

I pump it out to Michele. She dribbles left, crosses right and is fouled. Excellent. Now both Jones twins have four fouls. Chele misses her first. Chasi subs back in for Savannah. Chele misses her second, but Heidi is there for the board. She is hammered and goes to the line. Heidi has been all over those off-side rebounds. Stud.

Heidi prepares herself at the line while Coach Schlepp instructs me to change our defense up to man-to-man. Yes, sir. I instruct my girls to know who they are guarding as they fill their spots at the hash marks. I watch Heidi make both free throws. The scoreboard clicks to 55-55, and the clock ticks down under five minutes. Not even five minutes to go in our state championship game?? Too surreal to process at the moment.

Miller directs traffic to Halsey. Halsey loses her dribble and tosses it down to a twin on the right block. Turnaround jumper is short. Heidi pulls down another board and outlets to Maci. Maci dribbles hard to the opposite elbow and pulls up for two . . . swish! Up two. We all run a few more sprints—because, well, why not—until Harlo calls a time-out with 3:40 remaining.

I struggle to hear Coach during this time-out, as she is drowned out by the standing, screaming, stomping crowd. I have been in enough of these huddles that I get the gist, though.

Back out to the floor. Harlo's ball on the sideline. Good D now. Play straight up. We are sticking in man-to-man. That's what we love best. We got this. Watch her stomach. "Deny! Help! Deny! Ball! Deny! Help!"

I catch Galahan launching up a three from the deep corner and . . .

You. Have. Got. To. Be. Kidding. Me.

Down 57–58 with 3:12 on the clock.

Heidi inbounds to Maci. She crosses the timeline and bounces it to Michele at the high post. Down to Heidi, back to Michele, over to Maci for an attempt at the elbow. Short. Halsey, the best 800-meter runner in the state, bolts with the board but overshoots the pass to Galahan on the fast break. I grab the stray bullet and dribble up the left-hand side.

Two dribbles with my left, cross to my right, back to left, right. Miller is waiting for me at the block. Just like I have practiced hundreds of times in an empty gym, I dribble at her right, spin a 360, and put up a wildly contested left-handed shot. Somehow I manage to stay on my feet. There was some contact somewhere, but no foul, and I say a quick prayer of thanks as I watch the ball nearly reach the ceiling before falling through the net. As I turn and hustle back, I can't help but smile when I see Coach Schlepp shaking his head and burying it in his hands. Hey, after all those threes they've hit, a little luck is due our way.

Up 59–58 and 2:28 to go.

Heidi fouls, then Ashley scores in the key on an inbound play to put them back up a point. I walk it up a few dribbles, then throw it long to Maci on the left-hand side. She crosses half and hits Michele at the free throw line. Four defenders collapse, but Michele jukes, jives, and nails it. Now we go up one again. They work it around up top, eventually dump it to Ashley, then she spins and scores.

We have got to put some distance between us on the scoreboard! Down one again. Only 1:30 to go. Time is running out.

Another quick transition and Chas gets the long outlet pass from Maci. Chasi is still clearly favoring her left ankle as she does a little skip-hop. The ball is short, but the foul called sends Amy Jones out of the game with her fifth. That is huge. Chasi takes her time at the line, but she is short on her first. She makes the second one to knot it up at 62.

Miller crosses half and hits Halsey, who drives baseline and collides with Chasi near the sideline. I feel like that call could have gone either way, as Chas seemed to have good position while switching that screen. Chasi's fourth. Dang it.

Halsey inbounds way across the court to Ashley on the far elbow. She pump fakes, dribbles once to the left, and banks it in with a right-handed power layup. I breathe, jog with my dribble, and try to process the situation as I steal a glance at the giant cubed scoreboard hovering resolutely overhead. Down 62–64 with just 1:05 to go.

I dribble hard left, then swing to Maci opposite me. She goes down to Savannah on the right wing, back to Maci, back to Savannah. Sav fires it down to Michele on the block, who fights for position, and the whistle shrieks. Ashley is out now with her fifth, too. Okay, we got this. Fifty-three seconds. Michele takes her first shot behind the charity stripe and tallies her twenty-first point. Her second attempt rolls around but falls in the hands of Harlo. They cross half and call a thirty-second time-out.

Chasi is the first to greet us and brings everyone together for the huddle. "We got this, ladies. We got this!" she confidently asserts, and gives butt slaps all around.

"Match up here on this inbounds," Coach instructs. "Faceguard and make it tough for them to pass it in. If they do get the ball in, Maci and Jamie, you two jump out on a trap immediately. Let's surprise them and force a turnover. Then cut hard, set good screens, and take it to the hole! The Jones twins are out, so we have the size advantage. If you find yourself stuck, call a time-out. Let's win!"

" 'Lady Coyotes' on three! One, two, three!" I lead.

"Lady Coyotes!"

We follow the plan and trap Miller immediately on the inbound. She tosses it toward Galahan, but Michele comes out of nowhere with the steal. It takes her four dribbles to get to our hoop, but Miller is right on her heels. Michele lands like a ton of bricks directly on her right hip. She struggles to stand back up. No foul called, but Coach calls a time-out with 40.6 seconds left. Michele limps slowly to the bench. Down 63–64.

"You okay, Michele?" mother asks daughter.

"Yep, I'm fine," Michele responds, though her wince would suggest otherwise.

"Great job executing that trap and steal out there," Coach praises. "Michele, you take it out underneath, and we run 'four.' Then everyone play great defense and make another stop."

She pauses and glances up at the scoreboard. "In forty seconds, we will be state champions."

Well that sounds easy enough. We hustle out to our positions—Michele to inbound, and Maci, Savannah, Heidi, and I spread out around the perimeter. I know that determined look on Michele's face. Glad I am not the one guarding her. Michele tosses it into Maci at the deep corner and steps decisively to the low right block to post up her defender. The ball barely touches Maci's hands before snapping right back to Michele who is immediately fouled on a reach. Michele kneels down at the free throw line for a second to gather herself. I run over and rub her back. "You can do this, Chelers. Great job."

I pull her up then run over to Coach Schlepp to discuss strategy. He puts his arm around my shoulders, slimy sweat and all. As we watch Michele can her first free throw, he instructs me to signal to pick up full court defensively. Michele covers her face with her hands—an outward sign of the relief we all feel to at least be tied—and turns around for a deep exhale. The next shot is off to the right, and Harlo controls the rebound. The score is now tied at 64.

Galahan pushes the ball up the court, crossing over as Savannah forces her to zig and then zag. Galahan hits Dick, and Maci is there with intense pressure. Dick passes back to Galahan, who tries to find a seam, then she shoots it back over to Dick who is stuffed by Michele. The ball bounces out-of-bounds, and Harlo sets up in a box with twenty seconds to go. Halsey receives the ball from the ref, and she finds Robertson rolling open after a down-screen. Halsey steps in and screens for Miller, but Maci is a step ahead, and Miller is forced to pass to Dick on the top of the key. She pump fakes and gets a shot up and . . . misses!

Whistle.

I watch in slow motion as the referee points accusingly to Michele. Blocking foul. I look to the clock—12.7 seconds—and run through the situation in my head. They have two free throw attempts. If she misses both, we can grab the rebound with plenty of time to get down, score, and win. If she makes the first one and misses the next, same scenario. If she makes both, well . . . I hustle over to check in at our bench, just to make sure we are on the same page. My coaches huddle close and instruct me to get the ball—make or miss—immediately across half-court as quickly as possible, and call a time-out.

Noted.

We take a quick time-out after Dick's first swished free throw, in an attempt to ice her. She refuses to be iced, however, and puts her team up 64–66. Michele rips the ball out of the net and promptly delivers it to me. I bust my butt toward our bench and cross half-court with a left-handed dribble. I jump stop and urgently signal for a time-out. Gotta stop the clock.

Our huddle stays standing but leans in as close as possible in order to get a good look at the final play Coach has drawn up on her trusty whiteboard. She shouts our last-second instructions, "Run 'sideline'! But this time Jamie, you start on the opposite block with Michele down low. That means Heidi and Savannah, you two will be up at half-court. Maci, inbound it to Jamie as she rubs off Michele's shoulder on that cross screen."

We all nod to show that we understand our roles.

"Then Michele"—Coach pauses as she locks eyes with her daughter in a look that somehow holds love, faith, and pride all mixed together—"you seal. When Jamie passes it in, take it hard to the hole. You can do this!"

She continues to the rest of us, "Everyone pick up your man after the ball goes in and *don't foul!*"

Heads nod vigorously.

Coach finishes, "Let's win!"

"Win!" we echo with conviction.

I hustle down to the right block and hear our crowd chanting, "Yes! We do! We believe in you!"

When Maci is given the ball, I walk Halsey up to the right elbow to set up the screen, then bolt diagonally across the key and rub shoulders with Michele, who is standing stationary on the left block. My shoulder pulls her around into position for the seal, and Maci thrusts it to me from the sideline to the deep, left corner. Without hesitation I pop it right into my Chelers. Michele takes a power dribble on her drop step and goes up. The ball goes hard off the glass.

Five seconds to go.

Michele snatches it right back and goes up again. Her second attempt is hard, too.

Three seconds to go.

Michele sticks with it, skies over the throng, and secures the rebound at the peak of her jump. Okay, Chelers, there's no more time to pad your stats. We gotta do this now. She lands, jumps, shoots . . .

A whistle shrieks while the ball floats through the air. The scene again switches to slow motion. My eyes, and the other eight thousandish eyes surrounding me, are fixed on the spiraling sphere. I am 90 percent sure a foul has been called against Harlo, but the most important thing in this instant is where that ball lands. Off the backboard and . . .

IN!

I shout "Yeeeeees!!!" at the top of my lungs, and my cry joins those of the hundreds of frenzied Chester fans—and thousands who are just enjoying a good, and admittedly insane, game—behind me.

Savannah slaps the floor and flies back up, holding her hand in a tight fist. Heidi appears to be doing a plyometrics drill on her tiptoes. Maci and I fist pump simultaneously then join Savannah and Heidi to maul Michele. I turn to the bench for instruction, but only see Columbia-blue towels being whipped around furiously. Coach Schlepp side-jumps back and forth, as if he is doing a defensive slide drill. Chasi pummels Coach VanDyke with a bear hug, and Kaitlynn springs up and latches on to Amanda, like an infant koala bear clinging to her mother.

After I spring around the floor past half-court and back, charged with adrenaline, I snap back into point-guard mode. I catch Maci by the elbows, staring her straight in the face. "Pick up man-to-man! No fouls! No fouls!"

Maci instantly joins me in reminding Heidi, Savannah, and Michele. Then we turn to check and confirm with the bench. Coach Schlepp looks like a sumo wrestler preparing for a match. His hands gesture madly, imploring us *not to foul, for the love!*

Harlo calls for a time-out. Our coaches again remind us to pick up man and play straight up. Coach VanDyke says, "When Michele puts it in, just contain them until the clock runs out. Hands up but hands off! In 2.1 seconds, we will be state champions!!"

Well that sure has a nice ring to it. Is this really finally going to happen?

We run out confidently to assume our free throw positions. We line up for what seems like forever before the Engineers join us. I walk back and forth from half-court to my teammates, reminding them and myself, "We got this, ladies! Let's go! We got this!"

Suddenly I stop and look out over our crowd, because Dad always reminds me to "take the time to take it all in."

I feel that lump rise up in my throat again. Richie whips around her trusty yellow "flag," and I smile. I continue to scan the bleachers. For a second it feels like I am watching the 1992 boys' championship game on VHS yet again, searching for familiar faces in the crowd. Everyone clapping and shouting encouragement. So excited. So immersed in the moment. So many of the same people, but jeans not quite as whitewashed and hairstyles not quite as big. This time it is us, though. It is our time. We are the ones at the free throw line with only seconds left at our very own state championship game.

Finally, all the players settle in to their spots. The referee on the sideline holds up his index finger, indicating hopefully the last shot of the game. All eyes are fixed on the ball as the other referee bounces it to Michele. She dribbles once, gathers, and shoots . . .

It bounces long. The Engineers grab the board, but the buzzer announces the end of regulation before they can think about attempting a shot.

Overtime.

Four extra minutes. Score 0–0. Both Jones twins have fouled out. We should dominate the boards. We just need to be patient, get it inside, and play intense defense. Oh, and not let them drill anymore flipping three-pointers on us.

The ball goes into our possession immediately. Thirty seconds tick off the clock as we miss several opportunities to score: Maci gets her own rebound on an elbow attempt, then the ball is knocked out; I inbound to Heidi, to Michele, she misses; I miss two attempts off offensive rebounds. Then there is a jump ball that goes to Harlo.

Halsey inbounds to Miller, who jogs it up. Miller hits Halsey at the top of the key. I give her an arm's length, and she dribbles hard right toward the hole. Michele helps before she gets to baseline and Halsey fumbles it out of bounds. Another chance. I walk it up and call "Baylor." I lob it deep to Michele who has to chase it down. She dribbles out and hits Maci, who is stopped on the drive. The ball is tipped and grabbed by Galahan. Maci sprints back between their fast break and strips a layup attempt at the other side. The clock is paused at 2:59.

Harlo takes the ball out of bounds. I cheat middle as I guard the inbounder. We force the throw out to Freeser a few feet past the arc. Michele sags while Maci and I do all in our power to prevent Miller from touching the precious rock. Freeser swings to Galahan who puts up a quick three. Wide right. Savannah grabs the board and gets it to Maci.

Let's set it up again. Heidi and Michele set up in a high-low. We work it around patiently. After a few passes around the perimeter, Maci bounces it in to Heidi on the right block. Her shot is long. We take four more attempts off misses and offensive boards but end up fouling at 2:29. Dangit! There is a lid on our rim!

We jog to the other end to watch Miller thankfully miss the front end of a one-and-one. First time she's missed all night, I swear. But we miss the defensive rebound! Ah! Robertson gets the board and tosses it out to Miller, to Galahan, to Dick who pulls up for three . . .

Miss. Thank goodness.

We spread it out down on the other end. From the bench our coaches signal for us to run "fist." Heidi sets up at the high post, Michele and Savannah drop to the deep corners, and I parallel Maci.

Maci holds up a fist then hits Heidi. Maci cuts across Michele. I follow, receive the chest pass, take a quick dribble and remember to "kiss it off the glass," like Dad always says, instead of slamming it off.

Boom! We finally score! Up 68–66 with 1:58 left in this extra half-quarter.

Defensively we are man-to-man, and we guards do a lot of switching on top. Maci anticipates an attempted handoff and grabs yet another steal. She goes coast to coast and . . . miss but fouled! I squat down to tie my shoe with 1:30 to go. (The tying my shoe thing is a farce, I just need a quick second to kneel.) Come on, Mace. First free throw is hard. Ahh! I can't imagine what our team free throw percentage is tonight! Or this weekend for that matter. Can't dwell. Next shot. Swish! Attababy, Maci Lea! Up three with 1:30 to go.

Now just play smart, make a stop, and the game is finally ours.

Maci forces Miller to take an off-balance baseline jumper, I get another rebound (this must be a record for me) and Miller fouls. I take a second to look over at our crowd and encourage them to stand up. I want to go hug them all but feel that would be inappropriate at this point. Richie promptly whips around her trusty yellow "flag."

Okay, free throw line with 1:15 on the clock in overtime at my very own state championship game. Couldn't think of any place I would rather be. Dribble, dribble, dribble. Spin. Breathe. Follow through. Son of a bleep! Next shot. Same routine. Make.

One more stop, and it is over.

Help, deny, ball, deny, help. Just like the good old shell drill we have done so many thousands of times over the years. Alright, Galahan misses on a turnaround jumper attempt. But somehow we miss the rebound! Out to Miller for three . . .

She cannot miss! That is her seventh on the night!

We still have the one-point lead with fifty seconds left. I walk it up and play a little catch with Maci. Their guards are quick, but Dick fouls at twenty-eight seconds. I find myself at the line yet again. First shot, good. Coach Schlepp lets everyone in the gym know we would like a timeout. Coach VanDyke reminds us it is probably not a good idea to let Miller get the ball at the arc anymore. Noted. We head back out to line up at the stripe once again.

How did I miss that?!

Boarded by them. Remember how we are supposed to be dominating all the boards now? I watch Galahan dribble hard up the left side of the court. Savannah almost has the steal, four players crash to the floor, but Dick comes out with it. Savannah tips it again. This time she is called for the foul.

The scoreboard blazes 11.5 in bright red, us up 71–69.

Unlike us, Harlo is actually making the majority of their free throws tonight, and Galahan is clutch, tying the contest. Coach MacCart immediately calls a timeout. We hustle to huddle to take in our instructions. Coach draws up a play and I note how steady her hand is. I visualize the play in my head as I trot down the full length of the court to receive the inbound pass from Maci. I turn to face the Engineers ready to pick up just in front of half-court. I just went through the play in my mind, but for some reason I decide to chuck a long bomb down to an only-kind-of-open Savannah at the left wing. The ball sails right through her fingers and out of bounds. What was that, Jamie?!

That was bad. My stomach feels fine, though. No gut-punch feeling or formidable churning. I take this as a good sign. I turn and give a small apology shrug to Coach Schlepp then pick up on D.

Five seconds left.

The Engineers hastily pump the ball up the court. Inbound to Halsey. Halsey to Galahan, Galahan to Halsey. Halsey chucks one up from the top of the key, but the buzzer declares her attempt too late, and it springs off the rim anyway.

Double overtime.

My heartbeat matches Colt's cadence on the drums as our faithful pep band plays their encouragement in the form of "Sweet Child o' Mine."

"Okay!" Coach gathers us all for something like the eighty-eighth huddle of the night. "Everybody take a deep breath." Her hands are out in front of her, each finger stretched as if she is trying to fit them into tight winter gloves. This time I notice they are shaking a bit. "Heads up. We got this. Let's spread out in a four-out with Heidi running the paint. Catch it with confidence. Jump stop, elbows out, chin it. Make smart passes, control the ball, and look to score. You can all score. If you are open, shoot! Then crash the boards. Defensively we cannot foul. Stay low and turn them. No more long bombs!" Coach catches my eye as she makes this final reminder, and I swear I see her eyes twinkle as a flicker of a smile flashes across her face.

"Let's do this, ladies!" I urge. "WIN on three! One, two, three—"

"—WIN!"

I toe the outside of the familiar circle yet again and briefly wonder what the record is for overtimes in a state championship game. Michele tips it over to Maci for the third time tonight. Maci sets us up and finds Heidi at the high post. Heidi kicks back out to Michele on the right wing, Michele to Savannah at the top of the key, reverse to me, down to Michele who takes it up . . . fouled. That's my girl, Chelers. Makes her first free throw but misses the next. This turns out to be to our advantage though, because Heidi sneaks around behind Dick for a beautiful putback plus the foul! That's also my girl, C!

Man I love these girls.

I check the clock. Still 3:37 left, but now we have a chance at a four-point lead if Heidi can just . . . not quite. But Michele soars onto the scene and has a chance to put one in. Miss. Heidi gets her millionth offensive board and flicks it out to Maci at the point. Maci takes a dribble into the paint. She is double-teamed, tosses a left-handed pass to me, I dribble twice and, foul on Miller! That's it! She is outta here. No more threes for her tonight, for the love! Miller sits with 23 out of her team's 71 points.

I clench my jaw and give the orange orb a satisfied slap. Now I just need to put the nail in the coffin.

Jamie Marie!! Stop missing free throws! The second one snaps through the bottom of the net to put us up 75–71 with 3:25 remaining. Let's make a flipping stop and then take some time off this never-ending clock! Halsey sprints down the court, gets it to Freeser on the block. She banks one in. I cannot imagine how my poor father is handling all this.

Big breath, shoulders back, chin up. I walk the ball up on a left-handed dribble. When I cross half-court I shoot it to Maci waiting on the other side. She cuts to the opposite wing after a pass over to Michele. I cut, too, as Savannah gets it up top. Repeat. Maci drives in on the right side, stops, and streaks the ball across the paint to Savannah. She sets, shoots, and scores! Attababy, Savannah!

Dick misses short on the other end, and I muscle another rebound. Apparently I am suddenly now a beast as far as rebounding goes. Michele and Heidi get a few attempts inside. It looks like they are padding their stats. Maci gets a hand on the seemingly slippery ball and pops it to me. I squeeze that sucker, squat, and stick my elbows out for good measure. The coaches are urging me to take it back out and reset. What my coaches are saying makes sense, but I cannot help myself from driving when Galahan and Halsey jump out at me. Two other Engineers are waiting for me. I feel several hands on my arms, and fling the ball toward the hoop. Let's say that was a pass to Heidi, who goes up and is fouled by Galahan. It is Galahan's fifth, too. They are dropping like flies.

With 2:13 still left in the second overtime, we are up 77–73, and my big blonde bestie steps up to the line. It's good! Second shot, even prettier than the first. Coach Schlepp sends us back, no press. The third two-minute warning is announced over the loudspeaker with us up 79–73. This is the first time we have led by more than four the entire night. This has to be the tipping point, right?

The Engineers penetrate in, kick out, penetrate in again. The ball is bobbled to Dick, and she pulls up for a two. So much for being up by more than four. Maci and I keep the ball up top, then Halsey fouls me with 1:32 remaining. And. I. Miss. Both. Argh! I glance up in the bleachers just under our basket. My poor father looks as if he may have a heart attack. He is sprawled out across the middle bleacher. He rolls his head up to the ceiling, eyes closed. Hang in there, Papa.

On the other end I come up with a steal off a tip from Maci. I keep my dribble just past half-court and Halsey reaches and fouls. Now let's make a couple for a change. Cripes! Maybe I should try with my left hand, or perhaps I should give it a shot with my eyes closed, for crying out loud. Can't imagine that going any worse than these last tries. Finally I put one in.

Dick throws up an airball that sails out of bounds. Maci inbounds it again to me. I gather, dribble past Halsey, then Halsey fouls out. With 50.3 seconds to go in this second overtime, all five of their starters are out. The crowd has been a steady rumble all night, but now I hear something a little different.

What is that? Oh, jeez.

"Jamie! Jamie!" becomes the clear cry. So our entire crowd is chanting my name. This should be pretty exciting, but I know what it is. It is a pity chant, due to my unbelievably poor free throw shooting. I will be blaming all of this on Michele later. If she would have just made that dang free throw, it would have saved me from all these embarrassing misses.[96]

The chanting is sweet, but it does not do the trick. Sigh. We run down to defend again with forty-five seconds still to go, up 80–75. The Engineers frantically pass it around, miss twice, and we get the rebound. Hmm, now if I were a coach in this game, who would I tell my girls to foul at this point? Yep, let's foul Graham.

I connect again with our crowd and signal my excitement with my hands in the air. The mass of blue and gold stands as I jog to the line. They launch to their feet. They may be a little sore tomorrow what with all the squats they have done tonight. The crowd chants my name as I at least finish with two swishes, making it 83–75.

Oh, man. This actually is it. Ten seconds.

Nine, eight, seven, six, five, four, three, two, one . . .

Harlo throws up an inconsequential three. It bricks long. Maci pulls down the last rebound of our team's career and is not going to let go of that ball. Maybe ever. This time the buzzer blare is music to my ears, though difficult to hear over the reaction of the crowd. Up until this point, the crowd roar has held a consistent tone and volume. There is now a new pitch and decibel: higher, louder, final.

I hold up a fist and slide-hop toward our bench. I spin, slide-hop, spin and slide-hop again. Kaitlynn meets me just past half-court for the winning embrace we have practiced oh-so-many times. She gives me another spin for good measure. Then we squeeze and squeeze and turn in circles and must look like lovers enjoying their first dance together as a married couple. Heidi is pummeled by Jillien and Courtney who have sprung off the bench, hoarse from cheering all

---

[96]I still love to tease Michele about this because obviously if she wouldn't have tied us with that last incredible shot, we wouldn't have had even one extra chance to win, let alone the several we were given in the overtime periods. Harlo's free throw percentage on the night was 75% (6–8). Our percentage was only 51% (26–51). This was clearly to our advantage, though, as we made more than three times the number of free throws they attempted. We made 77 of 141 free throw attempts on the weekend; that is *a lot* of free throws!

Celebrating as state champions moments after the final buzzer sounded

weekend. Savannah and Michele wrap arms around each other, elated and exhausted. Chasi walks towards her teammates and holds her hands on her head as tears of relief release. Amanda lifts up Maci, and the ball, then lifts them up once more with a mighty squeeze. Our coaches cling tightly together for several moments. Their embrace displays respect, love, joy, and an understanding that maybe only those who journey through a shared experience together can fully feel. I try to lock in to exactly how I am feeling right here, right now.

To be honest, I am tired. Maybe this is the feeling referred to in that quote: *Leave it all on the court.*

Our team hugs every Chester fan in the entire arena. I receive lots of hugs and handshakes and high fives from people I have never seen before. Maybe this is what it feels like to be famous. These poor fans are getting a good slathering of drippy Jamie sweat. No one seems to mind.

Tears stream freely down my face as I hug and hug and hug. I hug my teammates and my coaches. I hope my clutches communicate how much I love each of them. My family makes its way down to the court. My little cousins latch on. My cute grandmas

246

Mom and Dad hugging me, all
with tears in our eyes

and grandpa give a squeeze. Then my aunts and uncles. A picture is taken with me and each family member. I turn and face my parents.

I burrow my head in my dad's chest and cry and cry. Dad's strong arms hold me close. He kisses the top of my head and a tear drops on my forehead. Mom rubs my back and sheds her own tears. How can I thank these two for all they have done for me? I attempt and fail to form words, so I just keep hugging them.

A voice over the loudspeaker announces that it is trophy time.

The announcer acknowledges the thousands of fans who have shown up all three nights. He notes it has been a record attendance weekend at a Montana state basketball tournament, girls or boys. Certificates are handed out to five teams. The bronze trophy goes to the Manhattan Christian Eagles. The silver goes to the Harlowton Engineers. Then the sweet, sweet, shiny golden trophy is brought out, just for us. We send Kaitlynn over to receive the award. She shakes hands appreciatively then thrusts the heavy wooden memento into the air, physical evidence that our ultimate goal has finally been reached. I can already picture the trophy propped proudly in the display case behind the glass in the entrance of our high school gym.

We huddle together again, one last time. The trophy gleams in the center of our huddle, index fingers pointing proudly around it. Our parents proceed with taking a billion more pictures, this time including the cut-down nets and exquisite trophy, for proof.

I smile for each lens. I smile and smile.

Chasi and me   Maci and me   Heidi, me, and Kaitlynn

Michele and me with our famous
(perhaps infamous to some?)
"We're number one" pose

Amanda, me, and the net
elated and exhausted

Seniors flexing with our trophy with Coach VanDyke

Grandma Joyce Graham, me, Heidi Cicon, Pearl Cicon

Dad, Mom, and me with the trophy

James Booth (from the 1992 Coyote state championship team) and me posing in the hotel hallway after beating Harlo, December 1, 2001

* * *

The air is permeated with the smell of chlorine. I tread in the deep end of our hotel pool in my street clothes. As I take in this idyllic scene I still cannot stop grinning. What a night. It took what seemed like years to get to the locker room after the photo shoots.

On the bus ride back to the hotel we died laughing when we got as far as, "*I've paid my dues. Time after time,*" but had no clue what came next because we had skipped that song so many times while running sprints in practice. We were at least able to nail the chorus of, "*We are the champions . . . of the world!*"

After our feeble attempt to sing along with Queen, Coach VanDyke shared with us that in all these four years of high school basketball we lost only six games. Not only that, but tonight was our one hundredth win. Wow. It is pretty incredible how that worked out. Jim Sargent asserted on the radio that no one could have written a better book. (Well, I probably could have, but I get what he was saying.)

Throwing Coach VanDyke and Coach Schlepp in the pool at the hotel

We scarfed down a ton of pizza, and then we grabbed Coach VanDyke and tossed her in the pool. She put up a good fight and managed to pull me in, too. As I paddle by her now, I see our dads looking out on us with their arms folded across their chests. I can't be sure what they are saying, but I feel their approval and pride as they nod and smile, donning those bushy beards and goatees. Our moms are smiling and giggling and clicking pictures and mostly making sure we all have everything we need, as usual.

I hope I remember this feeling forever.

Splash!

I laugh as Coach Schlepp is tossed into the pool by several of his players and a few of our pep band crew members. The laughter of my teammates rings out and stretches my grin somehow even wider across my face.

251

Whoa, I swear I hear Annie's infectious giggle somehow echoing among their laughter. How can that be?

I close my eyes and let the water hold me gently as I float on my back. A feeling of indescribable peace washes over me.

I think about all the people who are a part of this but who are not here tonight. I think of my brother and how I always wanted to do the things he did.[97] I think about all the Coyote athletes I cheered for when I was a kid. I think about all the teammates I have had over the years. It is amazing how many people I have had relationships with because of this game, how many people have shaped and impacted me.

I think about Carly[98] and Annie. My mind flashes back to that first senior night when I watched Carly and Annie embrace in the locker room. Now I understand how that hug was about so much more than basketball. That hug symbolizes why we play. It is what makes all those seven-minute drills and endurance runs and sprained ankles and broken fingers worth it. It is what picks you up at those times when you are not sure if you can give any more. It is what allows you to take that next step forward. It is trust and joy and friendship and forgiveness and love.

And I think about Brent. My heart does that weird flutter-flip thing as I rest my left elbow over the edge of the pool. When will that reaction stop? With my right hand I instinctively reach for the chain tucked beneath my T-shirt and pull out the key that is pressed against my chest. I gently rub the inscription with my thumb. I close my eyes and pull in a slow breath through my nose. A tear trickles down my cheek as I breathe out. But I smile.

It is all about the relationships, isn't it?

Last year at Jeff's graduation the valedictorian, Hannah, shared a proverb: *It takes a village to raise a child.* I caught the basic gist of that statement then, but its meaning settles deep within me tonight. When I was in third grade, I decided I wanted to win a state championship for our town; I wanted to do something special for the people of Chester. I look around tonight, though, and think about all the

---

[97]Jeff had an out-of-state tournament with his college team, the Northern Lights, and I called him to give him all the weekend's details Sunday when we got home.

[98]Carly was at a tournament playing for Carroll College that weekend.

people I am forever connected to, cared for, loved by, and wonder. I wonder if it is the other way around. Have I had it backwards all this time? Maybe it is not what I have given my town. Instead, maybe it is what the kind, supportive, loving people of this town have given me.

At an assembly on Monday morning following State we
were presented with our long-awaited banner

2001 Chester Lady Coyotes, State Class C Champions

Flexing one more time at graduation, May 19, 2002
Kayla Matkin, Deborah Brown, Maci Tempel, Heidi Cicon, Chasi
Buffington, Michele VanDyke, Kaitlynn Engstrom, Jamie Graham,
Emily Tranberg, Tina Johns, Megann Shepherd

Notes on People

Alisch, Kristen: A manager my senior year.

Anderson, Jason: A classmate of my brother's and one of his best friends.

Anttila, Hannele: A foreign exchange student from Sweden who graduated with us. She always thought we were crazy for eating "bird seed" (sunflower seeds).

Barrows, Brian: Superintendent my junior year.

Behem, Gloria: Miss Behem. Our school librarian.

Belt Lady Huskies (2000): Rachel Durocher #32, Kourtney Volk #52, Molly Sweeney #4, Justine Larson #10, Jodie Reishus #12, Heather Elam #40, Laura Keaster #14, Trista Garza #20, Nichole Widhalm #24, Hallie McCafferty #50, Cassie Gondeiro #30, Megan Wichman #34, manager Amy Bumgarner, cheerleaders Skye Coughlan, Barbara Bessette, Stacie Paer, assistant coach Bruce Keaster, head coach Aaron Huether

Belt Lady Huskies (2001): Molly Sweeney #4, Justine Larson #10, Heather Elam # 40, Laura Keaster #14, Trista Garza #20, Nichole Widhalm #24, Hallie McCafferty #50, Cassie Gondiero #30, Megan Wichman #34, Anna Burnham #44, Lexi Coughlan #42, Kelsey Bumgarner #54, Carley Raska #12, Kelly Wall #52, Nikki Wall #32, cheerleaders Barbara Bessette, Skye Coughlan, Kandi Reishus, Brandi Roubinek, Sarah Schell, Rhiannon Vigen, head coach Bruce Keaster

Big Sandy Lady Pioneers (1998): Katherine Bitz, Kristy Upham, Sasha Ritter, Celeste Darlington, Eryn Darlington, Amy Silvan, Jillian Johnsrud, Darice Grass, Jessica Curl, Amanda Pokorny, Tiffany Jamieson, coach Roy Lackner

Big Sandy Lady Pioneers (2000): Katherine Bitz, Haley Grubb, Ashley Goodian, Linda Givens, Sheena Darlington, Lindsey Danreuther, Eryn Darlington, Amy Silvan, Kristy Upham, Celeste Darlington, manager Michelle Larish, head coach Roy Lackner

Box Elder Lady Bears (1998): Kristie Pullin, LeAnn Montes, Aimee Montes, Sommer Rosette, Melody Descharm,

Rosemary Burns, Dorrina Ojeda, Ramona Gardipee, Tessie Lamere, Garliee Henderson, Pricilla (PJ) Friede, Josie Rosette, Tina Belcourt, managers Sarah Parisian and Pricilla Koop, assistant coach Chad Sunchild, head coach Marlee Sunchild

Box Elder Lady Bears (2000): Rosemary Crebs #20, Kristie Pullin #14, Josie Rosette #34, Sara Big Knife #10, Tami Infante #22, Nicole Mitchell #32, Chassidy Parisian #40, Tasheena Duran #42, Brandy Lawrence #52, Amanda Windy Boy #30, managers Danae Infante and Cassidy Pullin, assistant coach Luke Henry, head coach Shiloh Schwab

Box Elder Lady Bears (2001): Kristie Pullin #14, Lindsey Harris #32, Josie Rosette #34, Ray-lyn Shambo #40, Sara Big Knife #12, Tami Infante #22, Chassidy Parisian #42, Tasheena Duran #44, Brandy Lawrence #52, Amanda Windy Boy #10, Ann Favel #4, Gerri Eagleman #20, Rebecca Eagleman #24, Codi Raining Bird #30, managers Cassidy Pullin and Candace Morsette, assistant coach Luke Henry, head coach Shiloh Schwab-Hannum

Brockton Lady Warriors (2000): Kayla Lambert, Kari Dillon, Morning Star Foote, Loretta Brown, Sekoya Bighorn, Mastewin Walking Eagle, Jana Nygard, Timothea Red Eagle, Lori Bear Cub, Wilma Yellow Hammer, Edith Youpee, Jamelle Kennedy, Amanda Black Dog, Chastity Black Dog, Robin Perry, assistant coach Chuck Weinberger, head coach Bernard Lambert

Brockton Lady Warriors (2001): Morning Star Foote #3, Kayla Lambert #4, Loretta Brown #10, Caitlin Dillon #12, Sekoya Bighorn #14, Mastewin Walking Eagle #15, Jana Nygard #21, Marlyss Lone Bear #22, Wilma Yellow Hammer #30, Miranda Scott #31, Brandie Dionne #32, Chastity Black Dog #50, manager Olivia Lone Bear, assistant coaches Gary Fisher and Loren Boadle, head coach Bernard Lambert

Brown, Debbie: She was a year younger in school, but she graduated a year earlier with us. Debbie played basketball with us my junior year, but her shoulder kept popping out of socket, so she did not get to play my senior year. She is also one of Hugh Brown's (my mom's boss) ten kids.

Brown, Hannah: A year older than me and one of my brother's classmates. She was one of my mom's boss, Hugh Brown's, ten kids.

Brown, Hugh: Served as the county attorney in Chester for thirty-two years. My mom worked for him for nearly thirty-six years, and he recently retired in January of 2020. He and his wife Marilyn had ten kids who graduated from Chester.

Buckentin, Becky: Grew up in and played for Denton. Her mother, Roxann, played basketball for my dad from 1979-1981 when he coached in Denton.

Buffington, Gary: Chasi's dad. We could always pick out Gary's encouraging voice while on the court.

Buffington, Gay: Chasi's sweet mom.

Buker, Richard S. Jr, MD: An incredible man who served as a doctor to the Chester community, and all of Liberty County and beyond, for forty-eight and a half years! Larry Halverson, MD—the brother-in-law of Mr. Kulpas ("Coach K.")—has written a biography about him entitled, *Windblown: The Remarkable Life of Richard S. Buker Jr., MD, A Family Doctor.* The book's website is at https://www.publishingconceptsllc.com/product/windblown/.

Centerville Lady Miners (1998): Jessica Workman, Erica Pribyl, Jessie Yuhas, Fanci Lyman, Tifany Lyman, Kristen Lorang, Hannah Cowgill, Amanda Weil, Rena Medvec, Stefanie Jones, Heidi Erdman, Nicole Bolton, Trista Oriet, coaches Mike Botsford and Art Kruger

Chelmo, Jeff PA: Moved to Chester when I was in high school and lived just behind the alley from our house. Another doctor, Anna Earl, lived right next door to us, so I always felt very safe and lucky if worrying if there would be any medical emergencies.

Chester Coyotes Boys' Basketball (1991 state class C champions): Cody Thorson #10, James Booth #12, Hubbel Rockman #14, Tim Meldrum# 22, Cory Laird #23, Mark Cramer #24, Jerry Moos #30, Steve Webb #32, Mike Hilton #34, Tom Dahinden #40, Brad Kammerzell #42, Jay Marble #44, Darrell Carlstad #50, Aaron Rocks, managers Jeremy Hawks, Christi Henderson, Amy Streit, cheerleaders Kathy Englund, Angie

Fritz, Julie Hilton, Sonja Claxton, coaches Mike McLean and Jim Graham

Chester Coyotes Boys' Basketball (1992 state class C champions): James Booth #11, Hubbel Rockman #15, Darrell Carlstad #21, Tim Meldrum #23, Mark Cramer #25, Jerry Moos #31, Cody Thorson #33, Mike Hilton #35, Jeff Harrison #41, Lucas Kammerzell #43, Cory Laird #45, Brock Gummer #50, Josh Brown #51, manager Jeremy Hawks, cheerleaders Angie Fritz, Lana Steven, Kathy Englund, Erin Albee, Monica Ottman, assistant coach Jim Graham, head coach Mike McLean

Chester Coyotes Football (1998 state class C champions): Chris Ray #60, Jared Christenot #12, Ryan Gagnon #18, Matt Hill #89, Casey FitzSimmons #30, Brian Schlepp #17, Zeb Engstrom #88, Jeff Graham #22, Jeff Cicon #80, Camon Hunnewell #75, Adam Ghekiere #77, Brent Riggin #42, Jason Anderson #35, Colt Diemert #38, Bill Novak, #55, Logan Lybeck #64, Phillip Jeffrey "PJ" #70, Joe Wolery #65, Geoff Osterman #74, Levi Johnson #82, Lance Evans #25, Scott Riggin #50, Sean Wienert #26, Brad Oraw #40, manager Dru Lyders, cheerleaders Kendra Matkin, Amanda Kolstad, and Krista McConnell, head coach Bill Schlepp, assistant coaches Jim Graham and Dan Wooley

Chester Coyotes Volleyball (1992 state class C champions): Jamie Nordstrom, Bobbie Grammar, Kim Stone, Jolene Standiford, Tessa Sheldon, Mindy Mattson, Angie Morkrid, Kalena Kealoha, Mandi Jacobson, Angela Stone, Colleen Harwood, Darci Anderson, Kim Fossen, Rikki Evans, manager Jason Stack, assistant coach Steve Hamel, head coach Don Van Dessel

Chester Coyotes Wrestling (1974 state class B-C champions): Colin Lybeck, Kelly Adams, Roger Seidlitz, Barry Turner, Jim Dolezal, Lon Schaub, Buster Brown, Butch Jeppesen, Bobby Thompson, Brad Turner; cheerleaders Darcy Nelson, Nita Fenger, Jackie Jensen, Kaye Glee; managers Dana Boyer and John Seidlitz; coaches Gerald Kulpas and Steve Wood

Chester Coyotes Wrestling (1975 state class B-C champions): Colin Lybeck, Mark Lakey, Brad Turner, Bobby Thompson, Nathan Lakey, Roger Seidlitz, Dale Wickum, Butch Jeppesen, Neil

Leltch, Mark Seidlitz, Jody Smith, Kelly Adams, Chad Lybeck, Bruce Clark (Brent's dad), Mick Seidlitz, Dale Soper, Jerry Blair, Jimmy Cushing; assistant coach Rudy Skonord, head coach Steve Wood

Chester Lady Coyotes (1998): Maci Tempel #10, Jamie Graham #12, Heidi Cicon #20, Trisha Hilton #22, Megan Mattson #24, Lisa Wickum #30, Annie Diemert #32, Devan Lalum #34, Carly VanDyke #40, Michele VanDyke #42, Chasi Buffington #44, Carlane Jensen #50, managers Stacee Walstad and Kayla Matkin, cheerleaders Amanda Kolstad, Krista McConnell, Kendra Matkin, assistant coach Willie Schlepp, head coach Linda VanDyke

Chester Lady Coyotes JV (1998): Mystel McKinley #13, Candy Hawks #15, Emily Tranberg #21, Mari Tempel #23, Kari Hawks #25, Kali Nelson #31, Kaitlynn Engstrom #33, Andrea Novak #34, Heidi FitzSimmons #35, Cassie Johnston #41, Megann Shepherd #45

Chester Lady Coyotes (1999): Maci Tempel #10, Megan Mattson #24, Trisha Hilton #22, Jamie Graham #12, Chasi Buffington #32, Emily Tranberg #21, Heidi Cicon #20, Michele VanDyke #42, Kaitlynn Engstrom #40, Devan Lalum #34, Carlane Jensen #50, managers Kayla Matkin, Stacee Walstad, & Marissa Stokes, assistant coach Willie Schlepp, head coach Linda VanDyke

Chester Lady Coyotes (2000): Maci Tempel #10, Deborah Brown #11, Jamie Graham #12, Emily Tranberg #21, Savannah Fisher #22, Amanda Schlepp #23, Heidi Cicon #24, Mari Tempel #31, Chasi Buffington #32, Kaitlynn Engstrom #40, Michele VanDyke #42, Carlane Jensen #50, managers Kayla Matkin, Meaghen Kraft, and Marissa Stokes, cheerleaders Kari Hawks, Kali Nelson, Heidi FitzSimmons, and Jamie Sparks, assistant coach Willie Schlepp, head coach Linda VanDyke

Chester Lady Coyotes (2001 state class C champions): Maci Tempel #10, Jamie Graham #12, Savannah Fisher #22, Amanda Schlepp #23, Heidi Cicon #24, Chasi Buffington #32, Kaitlynn Engstrom #40, Michele VanDyke #42, reserves Jillien Johnson, Courtney Fraser, Alisha Fossen

Chester Lady Coyotes JV (2001): Renata Munfrada, Heidi Overlie, Heidi Swanson, Shawny Norick, Courtney Fraser, Desiree Johnson, Sierra Munfrada, Jillien Johnson, Alisha Fossen

Cicon, Gail: Mrs. Cicon. Heidi's mom and was our elementary music teacher.

Cicon, Jeff: Classmate and friend of mine since preschool. Heidi Cicon's cousin.

Cicon, Rudy: Heidi's dad and always referred to himself as my "other dad."

Clark, Brent: My on-again, off-again boyfriend in high school.

Clark, Bruce and Mary: Brent, Matthew, and Mitchells' parents.

Clark, Matthew and Mitchell: Brent's younger twin brothers.

Cushing, Ardith "Tinky": Longtime Chester community member.

Dafoe, Marjorie: Classmate who played sports with us in junior high, and then focused on her horses and shop classes in high school.

Decker, Chris: Classmate and friend of mine since preschool.

Denton Lady Trojans (1998): Lorinda Lucas #34, Shannon Danzer #20, Kelley Edwards #44, Katie Edwards#12, Katie Hatlelid #30, Cami Poser #50, Tiffany Wickens #42, Jennifer Conard #24, Crystal Gremaux #14, Becky Buckentin #10, Danielle Music #32, and Stacy Gilkey #40, assistant coach Jodi Morgan, head coach Glen Todd

Diemert, Colt: Classmate and friend of mine. Colt and I briefly "dated" in seventh grade, and he also dated Chasi and Michele at certain points throughout junior high and high school. He is the youngest of Annie's brothers.

Diemert, Ed and Marcia: Annie Diemert's parents.

Diemert, Kacey: One of our three cheerleaders my senior year.

Duprey, Alycia: My husband Jeremy's sister.

Duprey, Naomi: My husband Jeremy's sister.

Edwards, Sara, Kelley, and Katie: Sisters that grew up in Denton, MT, where my family lived when I was born.

Engstrom, Zeb: A year older than me. One of my brother's classmates.

Erickson, Pete "Pastor Pete": Pastor at the Lutheran church in Chester when I was in junior high and high school. He and his wife Tonja and three girls, Emma, Lara, and Siri lived in Chester from 1998-2007.

FitzSimmons, Casey: Senior when I was a freshman.

FitzSimmons, Heidi: A year older than me. One of my brother's classmates.

Frederickson, Colt: A classmate and friend of mine since kindergarten and the drummer for pep band my junior and senior year.

Frederickson, Courtney: Sister of my classmate Colt Frederickson. She died in a car accident on March 7, 1996.

Gagnon, Cory: Classmate and friend of mine since preschool.

Gardiner Lady Bruins (1998): Amber Anderson #10, Emily Kujawa #12, Sadie Hoe #14, Roylynn Wiedenmeyer #20, Stephanie Cole #22, Kati O'Neil #24, Jessica Burgard #30, Mandy Demaree #32, Melanie Holland #34, Dora Brake #40, Molly Buss #42, Stephanie Goss #44, Naisha McNulty alternate, managers Aimee Gallaher, Celine Ford, stats Glenn Hinton, assistant coach Patty Kremer, head coach Jenny Shriver

Gliko, Reece: Montana all-time leading scorer 1990-1993.

Goodheart, Wendy: Her first job teaching band and choir was in Chester my junior year. She conducted the pep band and was one of my favorites.

Gordon, Dustin: Mr. Gordon. My high school math teacher, taught math and coached basketball in Chester for seven years. Moved to Fairfield in where he taught, is now principal, and has been girls' head BB coach for fourteen years.

Gordon, Joni: Mrs. Gordon. Our high school history teacher, and Coach Dustin Gordon's wife.

Graham, Jeff: My big brother, one grade ahead in school.

Graham, Jim: My dad.

Graham, Joyce: Grandma Joyce. My dad's mom.

Graham, Karen: My mom.

Graham, Kathy (Ullman): My dad's younger sister.

Green, Al: Our faithful bus driver—come rain, snow, or shine.

Guardipee, Tara and Tamara: Standouts for the Heart Butte Lady Warriors.

Hamel, Steve and Richie: Some of my parents' best friends. I babysat their boys, William and Michael several summers and lots of times in between. Steve was our assistant volleyball coach, alongside head coach Don Van Dessel. He was head volleyball coach in 1984-85 and assistant volleyball coach from 1990-1992, 1994-2002. Steve was also Richie's lucky husband, and he is still one of my parents' best friends. Richie was the one who flew the yellow sports bra like a flag. She passed away of pancreatic cancer in 2009. Just after her diagnosis, the town rallied around Richie's dream to build Chester a new pool, one big enough so Chester could host swim team meets. Richie was the first to jump in the pool at its grand opening in the summer of 2008.

Hamel, William and Michael: I babysat these two boys for years and years, starting when Michael was a newborn and William was two. Sons of Steve and Richie Hamel.

Hanson, Amy Beth: Grew up in Chester, maiden name Chvilicek; her dad was superintendent for many years.

Hanson, Glenda: Mrs. Hanson was my first and third grade teacher.

Harlowton Lady Engineers (2000): Amy Jones, Ashley Jones, Breanna Garner, Erin Jones, Jamee Galahan, Kelsey Miller, Cody Halsey, Ashley Jones, Danielle Dick, Sharrie Scally, Tonya Mager, Shelia Dalgarno, Kristi Thompson, Krystal Robertson, Joni Freeser, managers Allyssa Miller, Ellen Valle, stats Terry Freeser, assistant coach Rob Galahan, head coach John MacCart

Harlowton Lady Engineers (2001): Kaliegh Brook #10, Jamee Galahn #12, Kelsey Miller #14, Cody Halsey #20, Ashley Jones #22, Danielle Dick #24, Kristi Thompson #30, Amy Jones #32, Sharrie Scally #34, Joni Freeser #40, Krystal Robertson #42, managers Staci Pederson and Alyssa Miller, stats Terry Freeser, assistant coach Rob Galahan, head coach John MacCart

Harrison Lady Wildcats (2000): Lacey Edmindson, Jill Brooke, Jenna Lehman, Sam Singleton, Billi Suhr, Marissa Rosselott, Letty Powell, Randee Gunn, Michelle Dykman, Julie Wagner, Ruth Cobain, Erica Maichel, Sadie Ypma, Chelsea Ehlers, managers Joe Husar and Erik Jorgensen, assistant coach LeAnne DeFrance, head coach Lisa Cooper

Hawks, Kari: A year older than me and good friends with Brent. One of our cheerleaders.

Heimbigner, Harry: Worked for Liberty County and still lives there today. His son is, "Mr. H.," mentioned in Preseason section.

Heimbigner, Neil: "Mr. H." Taught fourth, fifth, and sixth grade social studies from 1990-1998. His parents, Harry and Shirley, live in Chester and support high school athletics to this day.

Henderson, Brian: I went on to play at Rocky Mountain College in Billings, MT for Coach "Hendo." College basketball was a completely different experience for me. Not necessarily good different or bad different—just different. I loved Coach Henderson, as well as his assistants—Coach Chris Mouat, Coach JD Gustin, and Coach Rich Hash—and am grateful for my opportunities and experiences at RMC.

Herron, Clay: My neighbor and best friend for a while back in preschool.

Highwood Mountaineers (1992): Kris Knudson #10, Casey McGowen #12, Lee Larson #20, Reece Gliko #22, Conn Forder #24, Matt Heggem #30, Jess Grossman #32, Dustin Bergstrom #40, Peter Graham #42, Jason Hankins #44, manager Danny Lamotte, cheerleaders Robyn Bramlette, Emilie Graham, Monica Heggem, Kelly Knudson, Kandy Kolste, Jamie Shepherd, and Kerry Zanto, assistant coaches Mike Nelson and Richy Powell, head coach Doug Vanderpan

Highwood Lady Mountaineers (2001): Josey Jordan #3, Tamariel Townsend #11, Jessalyn Bahnmiller #23, Kristen Johnson #25, Katrina Hartman #21, Kirsten Schipf #31, Justine Edwards # 33, Brenna Birkeland #00, Megan Grove #13, Nicole Zitzka #15, Jenna Jordan #41, Chelsea Sperl #45, managers Jean Britzius and Whitney Baum, assistant coach Laurie Baum, head coach Dave Bahnmiller

Hitchcock, Laura: A talented three-sport athlete from Brady.

Hoff, Rusty: High school science teacher my senior year.

Houle, Trista: Classmate and friend of mine.

Hull, Dolan: Senior when I was a freshman.

Hunnewell, Camon: Senior when I was a freshman.

Hutchins, Robin: Band director at Chester in 1998–99.

Jeffrey, Phillip "PJ": Classmate and friend of mine.

Jensen, Carlane: A year older than me and one of my brother's classmates. Teammate for three years.

Jensen, Julane: Carlane Jensen's mom. She was always taking pictures, always positive, and my favorite thing she yelled from the crowd was during free throws, "Picture it going in, Carlane!"

Johns, Tina: One of our three cheerleaders my senior year.

Johnson, Jeremiah: He was my first kiss when we briefly dated in junior high and is also Heidi Cicon's cousin. Today he is married to Kayla Matkin, who was our manager.

Johnson, Johanna: A year older than me. One of my brother's classmates.

Johnson, Tony: He was two years older than me, went to school in Joplin-Inverness (JI), and killed in a car accident on May 29, 1999. I dated his younger brother Jeremiah in eighth grade. Jeremiah is now married to Kayla Matkin.

Johnson, Wade: Classmate and friend of mine.

Jones, Amy and Ashley: Twins from Harlowton that were the same age as me. They were both extremely athletic and excelled in basketball, volleyball, and track. They both competed in track and field in college at Montana State University. I was lucky enough to teach for a year with Amy in Big Timber, MT.

Jordan Lady Mustangs (2001): Callie Weeding #12, Tierani Brusett #14, Chantel Harbaugh #20, Tristan MacDonald #22, Erica Nelson #30, Tarra MacDonald #32, Shauna Awbery #34, Cortani Brusett #40, Katie Whiteside #42, Dixie Pierson #44, manager Richard Murnion, assistant coach Carline Cole-Beverage, head coach Brad Breidenbach

Kealoha, Danielle: Three years older than me and one of Annie's best friends.

Keith, Curtis: Classmate and friend of mine and my first "boyfriend" in grade school.

Kimball, Peggy: Longtime community member. She and her husband, Bill, owned Liberty Drug for years.

Kleinsasser, Eric: Senior when I was a freshman.

Kulpas, Gerry: "Coach K." Taught high school social studies and coached at various levels in Chester for twenty-six years.

Lakey, Mark and Christi: Some of my parents' best friends who farm west of Chester.

LaSorte, Joe: My parents' longtime neighbor across the alley.

Mangold, Brian: Classmate and friend of mine.

Matkin, Gail: Kayla's mom.

Matkin, Kayla: Classmate who played sports with us in junior high and was our basketball manager throughout high school.

Mattson, Bob and Dave: The Mattson farm, about seventeen miles north of Chester, was homesteaded in 1910 by Andrew and Minnie Mattson. One of their sons, Allen, farmed until 1976. Their sons Bob and Dave farmed until 2015, when Dave passed. The farm is currently run by one of Bob's sons, Jeff.

Mattson, Carol, "Mama Carol": Bob Mattson's wife, mother of Kevin, Jeff, and Chris, all CHS graduates.

Mattson, Chris: Graduated in 1996. Cousin of my teammate Megan Mattson. One of the oat-picking crew!

McKinley, Mystel: Classmate and teammate through junior high. Mystel moved to eastern Montana after our freshman year.

McKinley, Ryah: A year older than me. One of my brother's classmates.

McLean, Mike: Coach McLean. Taught and coached in Chester from 1982-1993; coached at CMR high school in Great Falls from 1993-2004; taught at CMR from 1993-2015; currently men's assistant coach at University of Providence in Great Falls, MT.

Miller, Jared: Two years older than me and from Kremlin-Gilford. He was on the State KG championship when they beat our boys in 1999. He dated Katy for a couple years in high school.

Moore, Jon: Mr. Moore. Taught and coached in Chester from 1996-1999.

Murphy, Elaine: Miss Murphy. Taught second grade in Chester for many, many years.

Nelson, Kali: A year older than me. One of my brother's classmates.

Novak, Andrea: A year older than me. One of my brother's classmates.

Novak, Mike and Margaret: Owned and operated Mike's IGA (later renamed Mike's Thriftway) for thirty-five years. Their son, Bill, played on the state championship football team in 1998, and their daughter Andrea was the salutatorian in my brother's class and played basketball with me my freshman and sophomore years.

Oraw, Steve: Longtime CHS announcer.

Osterman, Geoff: Classmate and friend of mine.

Owens, Kylene: Classmate and friend of mine.

Perdue, Jerry, Donna, and Brent: Jerry was a janitor at CHS and Donna was a lunch lady. Their son Brent was a year younger than me. They all three died in a car accident on August 21, 1995 and are survived by sons Brandon and Brian.

Plevna Lady Cougars (1998): Stephanie Buerkle #14, Maranda Sieler #15, Lindsay Klos #30, Stephanie Stickney #32, Brandi Gray #33, Brea MacKay #34, Lavonne Nemitz #35, Leanne Klos #40, Katy Sparks #42, Gena Meier #45, Toni O'Connor #52, Melissa Meier #54, Lacey O'Connor #55, managers Tim Mangold, Chris Ehrich, Kristy Fuchs, Jasi Johnson, and Dirk O'Connor, assistant coach Jim McDaniel, head coach Jay Schumaker

Rasmussen, Renee: Mrs. Rasmussen. Taught English, drama, and journalism in Chester for fifteen years—1991-2006—and is currently superintendent at Bainville Public Schools in Bainville, MT.

Raunig, Don: Purchased and ran the Chester Motors Ford dealership in 1970 until he and his wife Betty moved to Billings in 2010.

Riggin, Scott: Two years older than me. He dated Katy for a few years. He won State wrestling two years.

Rooley, Bob: Our fourth, fifth, and sixth grade science teacher and high school government teacher.

Sargent, Sue: Fourth grade teacher in Chester and wife of Jim Sargent. Taught in Chester from 1981-2010.

Schlepp, Amanda and Brian: Our neighbors when we were kids; their dad Bill was principal and high school football coach; mom Stacy worked with my mom and babysat Jeff and me. Brian was one of my brother's best friends.

Schlepp, Kellie: Coach Willie Schlepp's wife and cheerleader coach in Chester while I was in high school. Kellie and Willie taught and coached in Chester from 1999-2004.

Schmitz, Megan (Graham): Wife of my brother and mama to my nieces, Cadence and Ellison and nephews, Jace and Jimmer.

Shepherd, Megann: Classmate and friend of mine.

Sparks, Jamie: One of our three cheerleaders my senior year.

St. John, Kevin: Mr. St. John. Chester high school history teacher and boys' basketball coach from 1993-1999.

Stanford Lady Wolves (2000): Jacklynn Oliver #52, Josie Youderian #22, Allison Smith #33, Jennifer Ridgeway #21, Joni Samson #44, P.J. Crosmer #42, Chelsea Dingley #24, Callie Hagen #30, Kara Kochivar #20, Britni Hammer #34, Leah Smith #40, Shannel Oliver #50, Danny Raprager #32, managers Farah Valenzuela and Klint Dingley, assistant coach Doree Gackle, head coach Scott Wildung

Stokes, Marissa: A year younger than me and one of our managers. Marissa, Savannah, and I were all in Amanda's wedding.

Stuart, Jake and Joey: The Stuart brothers were decorated student-athletes from Kremlin-Gilford high school. Jake and I both ended up playing together for the Rocky Mountain College Battlin' Bears and you couldn't find a more humble all-star.

Stubbs, Adam: A junior when I was a senior. He was good friends with lots of people in our class, hung out with us often, and was hilarious.

Sveum, Mike: A student from Sunburst. Mike and I were friends all through high school, and he had hinted that he wanted to date a few different times. We went to the Chester prom together in 2001, and then went to his prom in Sunburst together in 2002. We dated casually for a few months at the end of my senior year during track season.

Tempel, Judy "Mama Jude": Maci and Mari's awesome mom.

Thompson, Chance: Classmate and friend of mine.

Tranberg, Emily: Classmate and teammate.

Tranberg, John: Emily Tranberg's brother, three years younger than me.

Turner, Debbie: Cook at CHS when I was in high school. She made the best food and often spoiled me with special treats! Her daughter Jamie was one of our cheerleaders.

Valier Lady Panthers (1998): Niche Wellman, Hayley Powers, Kendra Offerdahl, Tawna VandenBos, Mindy Kuka, Amber VandenBos, Nicole Crawford, Krystal Kuka, Nina Wilson, Colleen Brophy, Autumn Mierswinski, managers Blair

Durham, Renae Kovatch, Teresa Henke, head coach Barry Rowlison, assistant coach Stacey O'Neal

Van Dessel, Don: Head volleyball in Chester from 1988-2002. He coached the team that won Chester's only volleyball state championship in 1992.

VandeSandt, Curtis: A year older than me. One of my brother's classmates.

VanDyke, Isaac: The third of the five VanDyke children. Three years younger than me. He was in our wedding, and I played the keyboard at his wedding while my husband performed the ceremony.

VanDyke, Jessica: The youngest of the five VanDyke children. She played for her mom, Linda, who coached at Chester for four more years, from 2006-2010, when Jessica got to high school. Jessica graduated from high school in 2011, then played college basketball one year at Carroll College and three years at Central Washington, where her sister Carly was one of her coaches.

VanDyke, Kim: Mr. VanDyke. Husband to Linda "Coach" VanDyke, dad to Carly, Michele, Travis (two years younger than me), Isaac (three years younger than me), and Jessica (eight years younger).

VanDyke, Linda "Coach": Coach VanDyke coached girls' basketball at Chester High School for a total of nine years: my freshmen through senior year plus one more year after that (1998-2002), then again from November 2006-March 2010.

Violett, Mitch: Two years younger than me and became a very close friend my senior year.

Walstad, Stacee: Was a manager my freshman and sophomore years. We referred to her as "Mama Stacee" as she always kept us organized and in line.

Weinert, Sean: A year older than me. One of my brother's classmates.

White Sulphur Springs Lady Hornets (1998): Rachel Griffith #10, Vanessa Forsman #12, Erin Case #14, Dana Moe #20, Lisa Locke #22, Carrie Gebhardt #24, Laci Clayton #32, Betsy Gebhardt #34, Solveig Berg #40, Sammi Alltucker #42, Susie Knight #44, Saide Pierce #52, Elizabeth (Liz) Sulser #54, managers Kyle Cunningham, Chelsea Toavs, video Eva Hoyt, assistant coach Janie Barfuss, head coach Terry Bakken

Wicks, John: A junior when I was a senior. He hung out with our class often as well, and really is one of the funniest people I have ever known.

Wickum, Magen: Passed away of cancer on August 25, 1997, just before she would have started her senior year of high school.

Winifred Lady Red Raiders (2000): Sheila Donsbach #30, Jessica Knox #15, Cari Seilstad #45, Carmen Ehlert #33, Candee Meckling #25, Shantel Warneke #11, Kinder Willson #35, Jena Heggem #40, Theresa Molden #10, Laura Stulc #20, Davin Udelhoven #22, Donita Maberry #41, Alyssia Roberts #43, Lindsey Schmitt #31, managers Robin Boyce, Kari Econom and Kelsey Willson, cheerleaders Shalisa Maberry, Heidi Shammel, Rachel Udelhoven, Amber Udelhoven, and Adrianne Udelhoven, assistant coach Laura Gilskey, head coach Marietta Boyce

Wolery, Joe: A year older than me. One of my brother's classmates.

Wolfe, Doug: A junior when I was a freshman and older brother of my classmate Matt.

Wolfe, Matt: Classmate and friend of mine. He dated Heidi for several years in high school and into college. He is now married to Kayla Matkin's cousin, Sarah, and he still makes me laugh as much as he did in high school.

Woods, Katherine and Preston: Classmates and friends of mine.

Soundtrack

Songs are listed in the order in which they appear in the book.

"The Final Countdown" by Europe
"Brick" by Ben Folds Five
"Bitter Sweet Symphony" by The Verve
"I Want It That Way" by the Backstreet Boys
"Tubthumping" by Chumbawamba
"Semi-Charmed Life" by Third Eye Blind
"Washington and Lee Swing"
"When I See You Smile" by Bad English
"Follow Me" by Uncle Kracker
"I'm Like a Bird" by Nelly Furtado
"Runaway" by Del Shannon
"Sugar Shack" by Jimmy Gilmer and The Fireballs
"Wannabe" by the Spice Girls
"What's My Age Again?" by Blink-182
"Smile" by Lonestar
"I Think We're Alone Now" by Tiffany
"Girls Just Wanna Have Fun" by Cyndi Lauper
"Every Rose Has Its Thorn" by Poison
"Please Remember" by LeAnn Rimes
"Who I Am" by Jessica Andrews
"It's My Life" by Bon Jovi
"She's in Love with the Boy" by Trisha Yearwood
"We Are the Champions" by Queen
Did I Shave My Legs for This? by Deana Carter (album)
Yourself or Someone Like You by Matchbox 20 (album)
"I Was Born the Day You Kissed Me" by Rascal Flatts
"Ain't Too Proud to Beg" by the Temptations
"Right Kind of Wrong" by LeAnn Rimes
"Can't Touch This" by MC Hammer
"Come On Over Baby" by Christina Aguilera
"The Power" by Snap
"The Devil Went Down to Georgia" by The Charlie Daniels Band
"These Days" by Rascal Flatts
"Lucky" by Britney Spears
"Summer of '69" by Bryan Adams

References

All trips, bozeman, mt. Belgrade. (2019) Retrieved May 16, 2019 from https://www.bozemannet.com/belgrade_montana/.

5 things you might not know about st. patrick's day. Great Falls Tribune. (March 14, 2018). Retrieved April 11, 2019 from https://www.greatfallstribune.com/story/entertainment/2018/03/14/st-patricks-day-parade/424922002/.

9/11 timeline. History. (2019). Retrieved April 24, 2019 from https://www.history.com/topics/21st-century/9-11-timeline.

Brady, montana. Retrieved January 18, 2020 from https://en.wikipedia.org/wiki/Brady,_Montana.

Bridger year by year results. Max Preps. Retrieved March 19, 2019 from http://www.maxpreps.com/local/team/records/year_by_year_results.aspx?gendersport=girls,volleyball&schoolid=835af415-9e05-46d7-964c-7e209b46c2aa.

Centerville public schools. (2019). Retrieved February 21, 2019 from https://www.centerville.k12.mt.us/domain/102.

Central montana: box elder. (2019). Retrieved April 10, 2019 from http://centralmontana.com/communities/boxelder.htm.

Central montana: brady. (2019). Retrieved March 19, 2019 from https://centralmontana.com/communities/Brady.htm.

Central montana: highwood (2019). Retrieved April 30, 2019 from https://centralmontana.com/communities/Highwood.htm.

Central montana: stanford. (2019). Retrieved April 5, 2019 from https://centralmontana.com/communities/stanford.htm.

(The) city/county of butte, silver bow. (2019) Retrieved April 11, 2019 from https://co.silverbow.mt.us/481/History-Culture.

City of Havre. (2019). Retrieved August 19, 2019 from https://www.ci.havre.mt.us/.

Cnn breaking news: terrorist attacks on the united states. Cnn.com/transcripts. (2003). Retrieved April 24, 2019 from http://www.cnn.com/TRANSCRIPTS/0109/11/bn.01.html.

(The) collision of athletics and consolidation. AASA. Graves, Bill. (2019). Retrieved April 30, 2019 from http://www.aasa.org/SchoolAdministratorArticle.aspx?id=13226

Dakota matrix minerals. (2019). Retrieved April 11, 2019 from https://www.dakotamatrix.com/content/butte-mineral-specimens.

Dutton, brady schools to merge. (January 10, 2005). *Billings Gazette.* Retrieved August 30, 2019 from https://billingsgazette.com/news/state-and-regional/montana/dutton-brady-schools-to-merge/article_fa0e483c-68bf-51fe-9532-ab8a30a4f4f2.html.

Elks hoop shot. (2019). Retrieved March 22, 2019 from www.elks.org/hoopshoot.

Find your center in the middle of montana. (2019). Retrieved August 19, 2019 from http://www.enjoylewistown.com/.

Fort benton: the birthplace of montana. (2013). Retrieved April 24, 2019 from http://www.fortbenton.com/.

Garfield county museum. (2019). Retrieved May 8, 2019 from https://www.visitmt.com/listings/general/dinosaur-museum/garfield-county-museum.html.

Gardiner, mt. (2019). Retrieved March 13, 2019 from
https://www.visitgardinermt.com/.

Great Falls Tribune. Montes sisters. (2019). Retrieved April 10,
2019 from
https://www.greatfallstribune.com/story/sports/2018/12/13/sister
s-leann-aimee-montes-lead-box-elder-goat-girls-basketball-
list/2305493002/.

Great Falls Tribune. Sunday conversation. (May 17, 2018).
Retrieved February 26, 2019 from
https://www.greatfallstribune.com/story/sports/2018/05/17/sund
ay-conversation-roy-lackners-big-sandy-coaching-career-had-
many-highlights/621675002/.

Harold News. *Three locals inducted into montana hall of fame.*
(January 19, 2017). Retrieved April 12, 2019 from
http://www.wolfpointherald.com/index.php/wp-sports/5997-
three-locals-inducted-into-mihof.

Harrison public school. (2019). Retrieved April 11, 2019 from
https://sites.google.com/a/harrison.k12.mt.us/hhswildcats/.

Heart butte. (2019). Retrieved February 20, 2019 from
https://www.visitmt.com/places-to-go/cities-and-towns/heart-
butte.html.

Higgins, Grady. *From fairfield to the wnba: jill barta humbled by
support, pro hoops opportunity.* (April 13, 2018). Retrieved
May 2, 2019 from
https://www.greatfallstribune.com/story/sports/2018/04/13/fairfi
eld-wnba-jill-barta-humbled-support-pro-hoops-
opportunity/516666002/.

History of montana hi-line. (2018). Retrieved February 18, 2018
from http://www.bigskyfishing.com/Montana-Info/Hi-
Line/history-hi-line.shtm.

History of plevna, montana. (October 12, 2018). Retrieved March 7, 2019 from https://www.falloncountyextra.com/2018/10/12/history-of-plevna-montana/.

(The) history of valier, montana. (n.d.) Retrieved February 13, 2019 from http://www.valier.org/history.html.

(The) last best plates. (May 19, 2015). Donaldson, Lynn. Retrieved April 4, 2019 from http://thelastbestplates.com/2015/05/19/circle-montana-great-place-around/.

Mansch, Scott. *GOAT girls' basketball: a look at tradition-rich fairfield.* (December 17, 2018). Retrieved May 2, 2019 from https://www.greatfallstribune.com/story/sports/2018/12/17/goat-girls-basketball-look-tradition-rich-fairfield-eagles/2343658002/.

Montana, circle. (2019). Retrieved April 4, 2019 from https://www.visitmt.com/places-to-go/cities-and-towns/circle.html.

Kimmel, Slim. *Montana gym rankings: no. 3, belgrade.* (July 24, 2013). Retrieved May 16, 2019 from https://billingsgazette.com/sports/high-school/blogs/gazprepsports/basketball/montana-gym-rankings-no---belgrade/article_1278492c-39e5-549c-a5f3-478cbeb0d538.html.

Montana high school association. All-time records for all mhsa sports. (2019). Retrieved May 1, 2019 from https://www.mhsa.org/page/show/2279568-records.

Puckett, J. (2010). *The Dream: The Story of the 1978 and 1979 Peerless Panthers.* Amherst, NH: Aubade Publishing.

Ravalli Republic. *Rocky erickson's top 10 montana high school basketball records of all time.* (January 16, 2019). Retrieved April 12, 2019 from https://ravallirepublic.com/sports/high-school/basketball/article_d1f775a9-1d27-5fef-91bc-9193be008839.html.

Roberts, montana. (2019) Retrieved August 19, 2019 from https://en.wikipedia.org/wiki/Roberts,_Montana.

Shelby montana facts. (2019). Retrieved February 14, 2019 from http://shelbymtchamber.org/shelby-mt-facts/ https://billingsgazette.com/sports/highschool/blogs/gazprepsports/basketball/montana-gym-rankings-no---shelby/article_f794fa0a-2ab4-5ac4-add9-dfd549880a1a.html.

Spa hot springs. (2019). Retrieved March 14, 2019 from https://www.spahotsprings.com/our-history.html.

(The) struggles of small towns facing school consolidations. (February 16, 2001). Retrieved January 19, 2020 from https://www.abcfoxmontana.com/featured/student-of-the-week/the-struggles-of-small-towns-facing-school-consolidations/article_d7a282b8-0d40-5c56-b2c9-2aec32724de8.html.

Sunburst, montana. (2018). Retrieved April 30, 2019 from http://www.sunburstmt.org/.

Sweet grass hills backcountry drive. (2019). Retrieved August 18, 2019 from https://www.bigskyfishing.com/scenic-drives/sweetgrass-hills.php.

White wolf. (2019). Retrieved April 5, 2019 from https://www.russellcountry.com/white-wolf-stanford-montana.html.

Winifred, montana. (n.d.). Retrieved April 30, 2019 from http://www.winifredmontana.com/.

Index